A journey quite different

A journey quite different

Collected walks ❁ Lincoln Allison

MANCHESTER UNIVERSITY PRESS

Published by Manchester University Press
Oxford Road, Manchester M13 9PL, UK

British Library cataloguing in publication data
Allison, Lincoln
A journey quite different: collected walks.
1. Walking—Great Britain
I. Title
796.5'1'0924 GV99.44.G7

ISBN 0 7190 2282 7 *hardback*

Distributed exclusively in the USA and Canada
by St. Martin's Press, New York

Library of Congress cataloging in publication data
applied for

Typeset in Janson
by Koinonia Limited, Manchester

Printed in Great Britain
by Billings & Sons Limited, Worcester

Contents

Acknowledgements — *page vii*

Introduction *The footsore philosopher* — 1

1 In darkest London — *11*
2 A day out in Liverpool — *17*
3 Strolling across Sussex — *23*
4 Pottering in the Five Towns — *28*
5 In the deep Fens — *34*
6 The road to Bristol — *41*
7 Aberdeen in winter — *46*
8 Down the Rhondda — *53*
9 On a damp day in Dublin — *59*
10 Cowes that cannot be milked — *64*
11 A long walk to the chip shop — *70*
12 A day in the forest — *75*
13 The not-so-Black Country — *81*
14 The great white northern mystery tour — *87*
15 Starting at the end — *93*
16 Lancs. of the setting sun — *99*
17 In search of Surrey — *105*
18 What Manchester does today — *110*
19 To Hull and back — *116*
20 There are, of course, daffodils — *122*
21 Up the creek — *128*
22 *Costa Inglese* — *134*
23 Dear auld Glasgie toun — *140*
24 Dwy Dref Cymraig — *146*
25 Shredded Wheat country — *152*
26 Scott-ish walk — *159*
27 Walking home — *166*
28 On the levels — *173*
29 Rockingham game pie — *177*
30 The rambler's heartland — *180*
31 The small world of Jersey — *183*
32 Area of outstanding natural controversy — *187*
33 On the blossom trail — *191*
34 Fat land — *195*
35 The last train from Skegness — *198*
36 Return to London — *202*

Acknowledgements

Numbers one to twenty-seven of these essays first appeared in *New Society* and numbers twenty-eight to thirty-five first appeared in *The Countryman*. I am grateful to *New Society* and to its current editor, David Lipsey, for permission to reprint. I am equally grateful to *The Countryman* and its editor, Christopher Hall, for permission and encouragement.

An even greater debt, however, is due to Paul Barker, editor of *New Society* from 1968 to 1986. These essays owe a great deal to his advice and support and it is quite simply true to say that this book would not have come into existence without his stimulating talents as an editor. But as an editor he is not, of course, responsible for any of the gross errors or even grosser opinions which I may have perpetrated on my travels.

Most of the titles of the essays are the same titles which I originally chose. But in some cases an editorial suggestion produced a title which I considered to do the job better, so I am also grateful to a number of editors, assistant editors and sub-editors for these.

Lincoln Allison
October 1986

Introduction ***The Footsore Philosopher***

This book was written by the side of the road. Its existence came about in the following way: in the late seventies my principal academic work, both as a teacher and as a researcher, was in what my course title grandly described as the 'Political Aspects of Environmental Planning'. One of my weaknesses in dealing with this subject, I considered, was that I didn't *know* big cities. I had visited most of them and I knew a fair amount about them in a dry, statistical sort of way, but I had never lived in one and I had the frustrating feeling that I didn't really know what they were like. My personal circumstances were not such that I could remedy this by changing my life altogether. Nor were my tastes, for that matter. But I did resolve on a partial remedy; I would walk across London. That, I hoped, would give me some sort of 'feel' for the place, for its size, variety and problems.

I wrote a short account of my walk. It was entirely preoccupied with 'planning'. I was interested in understanding the factors which had made the city, distinguishing between those which were so long-established or irredeemable that they were to be considered as God-given or fateful, and those which could be attributed to modern policies, and from which lessons could be learned. Never averse to earning a couple of bob, particularly from something I rather fancy doing anyway, I submitted the essay to Paul Barker, then editor of *New Society*.

The essay was a hotch-potch of impressions and theoretical comments; of the two, he preferred the impressions so I rewrote the essay, cutting out all the theory, and it was published. A number of people expressed a liking for it and I arranged with Paul Barker to do a series of walks. The idea was to visit a variety of places in Britain, preferably those which were unfamiliar to me. I interpreted this to mean that I should try and walk across something with a recognisable unity, such as a conurbation, forest or national park. I had a destination, but no specific intentions as to what I should write about. I should merely offer the reader the maximum of variety and honesty about what I saw and heard over an easy-paced walk of about twenty miles.

The second walk, across Liverpool, was eventful. I was shocked by Liverpool. The extent of the city's decline was not widely realised in 1980 and 'Toxteth' was, to me, a dimly-remembered area name to be compared with 'Croxteth'. The shock came through the writing and provoked somebody (presumably Liverpudlian and a student) to daub the outside wall of my room at the University of Warwick with slogans in red paint such as 'NOBODY KNOCKS SCOTTY ROAD AND LIVES'. The feeling of having moved somebody was a rare and heady one. Subsquent walks took me away from the urban preoccupations of the first two into something like a fair sample of the British landscape. Eventually, after twenty-six of these walks, we decided that they had run a reasonable natural course and concluded with something which was, in some respects, the opposite of the original conception, a walk through the area in which I had grown up.

This was not the end of the story, however. At a seminar in Birmingham on the problems of the countryside I was lucky enough to meet Christopher Hall, editor of *The Countryman*, and I arranged with him to continue my career as a professional walker, though to do it quarterly and at shorter length to suit his magazine. The result has been a series of rural walks whose underlying preoccupation is with the condition of the countryside. Finally, to complete the collection, I returned to London to retrace, more or less, my steps of seven and a half years earlier.

Put together, these essays constitute a verbal portrait of Britain. As a portrait, with many rivals, it is best advertised by what it is not.

It is not, of course, the kind of glossy romantic account of life in Britain which can be found in large numbers in bookshops and the travel sections of libraries. This mass market often caters for a pastoral fantasy which has become part of a collective escapism; the origins of the genre go right back to the beginning of industrialisation. I have no particularly strong desire to debunk this fantasy. For one thing, it has been lived out; it has affected our design and nurture of the land to the extent that the appearance of many English villages could scarcely be improved by a painter of romantic landscapes, however prosaic and modern the life within them is. It is simply that my emphases were different: on entering a village I was often more interested in the graffiti on the bus shelter than in Dick Turpin's alleged stay at the local pub.

But nor are these essays a contribution to the 'decline of Britain' industry. Urban decay, unemployment, punks and riots exist, as do thatched cottages and village fêtes. But thatched cottages and urban riots also have it in common that myths are built on them, as if they were the only reality. In the case of riots it is the critical intellectual's myth of a wicked, tortured empire approaching its apocalypse. In a different corner of the bookshop from that which contains the piles of books with thatched cottages on the cover is to be found a pile whose cover pictures depict angry and derelict urban scenes. The books have titles such as *The Break-up of Britain* and *Britain in Torment*.

Despite being written for two magazines, this is not journalism. Journalists produce 'news'; this is concerned with the fashionable, the important and the symbolic. Therefore it is about disaster, crises, portents and acts of violence. Journalists always get their story. If they are sent out to do a story on urban poverty they will pass a thousand prosperous houses and as many people going about their business to fnd a derelict building. They have been known to organise riots. Journalism is about self-fulfilling prophecy. This book is a work of anti-journalism. In July 1981, when rioting was discovered and any self-respecting journalist was combing the cities for trouble, I was in the Isle of Wight, sitting on a sheep-cropped down, watching a joyful group of men and women in their early twenties picnicking and playing leap-frog.

I almost invariably took photographs on my journeys. These have occasionally been used as photographs, but more often as the basis for artist's sketches. In neither form do they appear here. Comparing them with my prose, I am inclined to conclude that the camera always lies; it freezes a split second from a particular angle. An infinite number of possible photographs are rejected for every one which is taken. Certainly, my photographs constitute a much less interesting and honest record than what I wrote. You can say that a five-mile stretch of country is boring, but it is difficult to use a photograph to illustrate this. It is difficult to use pictures to illustrate any complexity. So my photographs tended to be 'classic' shots of semi-derelict alleys, thatched cottages and street-wise urchins.

Thus I am making my pitch to be considered as a 'travel-writer' rather than a producer of pictures or journalism or romantic sentimentality or one-dimensional analyses of decline. Most serious 'travel writing' is based on long journeys which have a natural story of their own. Will he get there? What will happen to him? But they also have certain disadvantages. A genuine journey must follow a single, practical line: this can be both unreal and limiting. It is tempting to break the rule in any case; thus we find Paul Theroux in *A Kingdom by the Sea*, in what is supposed to be a journey round the coasts of Britain, turning up in Wigan (which is not by the sea) because he has a point he wants to make about Orwell.

The traveller on the long journey normally has certain preoccupations, even obsessions, which justify his huge investment; he is unlikely to act from that most detached of motives, mild curiosity. A particularly bad contemporary example is Richard West's *An English Journey* in which the determination to report that 'nobody works in England any more' and 'we have transformed an industrial country into an industrial museum' pre-empts any ability to look at things afresh.

It is, anyway, difficult to be fresh on a long journey, one which takes weeks or months. The natural rhythm of such journeys involves increasing homesickness and declining sensitivity to one's surroundings. I once made a journey of seven thousand miles, taking three months, across north and central America: the last places I visited were in Eastern Canada and New England, and I can hardly remember them. Paul Theroux reached Aberdeen tired and stale. He was overcharged and not treated as the important chap that he really is. He turned his verbal venom on the city and reported it as a soulless, over-priced hell-hole. I found a very different Aberdeen.

I live in the centre of England, which means that, in the real conditions of the late twentieth century, I am no more than three hours from home anywhere in my own country. This is an age when a day out can take you hundreds or even thousands of miles; it seems silly to pretend that we still live in a time in which some sort of grand tour remains the appropriate way of seeing things.

Although this book is a collection of small journeys there is a sense in which they constitute one big journey. The overt reason for my first walk across London was a curiosity connected with the 'Political Aspects of Environmental Planning'. But I can see now, in the way that one sometimes can see later, that there was another, less conscious, but potentially stronger, motive. I had just returned from a period living in America. I had decided, never having thought about the matter before, that, although I wanted to go everywhere as a visitor, I wanted my home to be in England. 'What do they know of England, that only England know?' was the rhetorical question which Rudyard Kipling posed. Living in America and deciding to live in England made me more curious than perhaps most people are about what England is like. I wanted to explore every corner of my land.

When it comes to territory, almost everybody has a mental map of what is theirs. Such maps are generally hazy: they have frontiers, but also vague borderlands and disputed regions. The territory with which people identify is likely to shift, at least on the margins. A Scot may feel more or less British at different times depending on a variety of public and private circumstances; this is true, in a subtly different way, for an Englishman.

These shades of identification and their shifting nature have many different aspects. Coming over the tops and looking down on Burnley I felt a stronger sense of belonging than I did anywhere else described on the book, though I have never slept a night in the town. I wasn't even born in Lancashire and my twenty years' exile from the place render my affection somewhat patronising and sentimental. I felt a weaker, but still real, affiliation to Manchester, but quite alien in Liverpool. On the other hand, I felt that Land's End and the Cornish coast belonged to me as much as to any Cornishman. In London I felt, and always will feel, utterly provincial. In Easterhouse I felt completely foreign, but as I got closer to the heart of Glasgow and saw reassuringly familiar sights like universities and cricket pitches, I was more at home. Dublin seemed initially less of an alien territory, but an Englishman in Dublin is bound to feel half-foreign, that he is in a city which is both English and anti-English. The Irish reciprocate this ambiguity. From having a Minister of Culture (Desmond Guinness in 1961) who wanted to tear down every Geogian building in Dublin because he saw them as symbols of English oppression they now, rightly, treasure Georgian houses as part of their heritage.

Mental maps may be unstable, complex and ill-defined but there is no real doubt that Jersey, Aberdeen and, in some sense, Dublin, are part of 'my' country in ways that Bruges or Boulogne are not, for all their physical proximity, and Ontario is not, however close its links of history and sentiment. This book is confined to home territory, albeit in its broadest interpretation. If I were writing my own blurb (which everybody has to, these days) I could truthfully claim to have written about places from San Francisco to Samarkand and from the Sahara to the Jotunheimen Mountains of Norway where the Hall of the Mountain King is said to be hidden. These 'away' pieces are overwhelmingly outnumbered by the 'home' ones, though; the latter come a lot cheaper. But an artistic justification was often added to this accountant's reason; I was presented with the argument that my writing was more original and less travel-writerish the more homely and ordinary the scene I was describing. Thus a book on walking around the British Isles: low on expenses, high on artistic commitment.

It is an immense privilege to be paid to walk, freely and with no other purpose than to see what there is. Most people will know the couplet by W. H. Davies, the 'supertramp':

> What is life, if, full of care
> We have no time to stand and stare?

But, almost invariably, they never *do* stand and stare. Most people live lives whch are ninety-nine per cent purposeful and only one per cent observant. They drive cars, catch buses and hurry about their business, taking their beliefs about what is happening from each other (whether personally or through other media) rather than from the direct use of their senses. Thus people believe many completely false propositions about their own country. They believe it is mostly 'built-up', whereas less than ten per cent of it is urban land, even on a very broad definition. Or they believe that 'pollution' is getting worse and worse whereas, in most respects, the situation is far better than it was a generation ago. Or they believe that most people now live in high-rise accommodation (only three per cent of the population live above the second floor). They believe that the countryside has been turned into a great arable prairie. (There are actually many countervailing tendencies to industrial agriculture, and many landowners, including huge ones like the Forestry Commission, the National Trust and the Duchy of Cornwall, which are very concerned with the quality of the landscape.) Most people are the epistemological victims of 'news'.

Perhaps the most tangible consequence of the privilege is having been to the kind of places where I had never been before and where most people never go. Britain remains a wonderful place to walk, with immense rights of access to land (for example, there are rights of way over eighty-two per cent of private farms) and a great variety of style and atmosphere available within a day's walk.

People realise this only in a limited way. They do go out a lot to the cliffs, mountains and moors, the better known pastoral countryside and the 'nice' towns. But they ignore the forests, the industrial cities and towns, the older residential areas and many other kinds of place. My own most particular discovery during these walks has been of the wetlands and flatlands. As a northerner, I instinctively identify with hills and mountains, but in the course of professional walking I have come to respond strongly to the flatlands and wetlands, to the Fens, the Essex marshes, Sedgemoor and the Wentlloog Levels (which lie between Newport and Cardiff). I think that preserving the atmosphere of these places is one of the most important objectives for conservation. Another little-regarded, but fascinating landscape, is that of the new towns, memorials to the twentieth century ideal of the self-sufficient, communal town. These vary from the optimistic gentility of the Letchworth and Welwyn garden cities, to the planned welfare ideal of Stevenage and Hemel Hempstead, to the pragmatic capitalism of Milton Keynes.

As a philosopher (of sorts) I was under no illusions about the objectivity of my accounts of places. Objectivity can only occur when there is a formalised and agreed (and therefore unique) language of description. Physics and geometry approach obectivity. Real descriptions, by real authors, using natural languages, involve an infinite number of evaluative choices between perceptions and the words which 'fit' them. This whole book is subjective; it is about the relationship between 'I' and the land.

But I would claim a kind of truth. I have walked: the most intimate and committed form of travel. I have reported my reactions to things without shame. I have not cheated on method. I was certainly tempted at times. For example, I was told that painted on a wall in the Central Necropolis of Glasgow, surely one of the world's most elaborate collections of tombs, was the question 'WHO SAYS YOU CAN'T TAKE IT

WITH YOU?' But I couldn't find the line myself and so was unable to repeat it. In collecting these pieces together I have, similarly, resisted any temptations to introduce hindsight or greater accuracy. Still in Glasgow, a correspondent informed me that I couldn't possibly have heard the metro passing underneath Glasgow Green, because it doesn't go under Glasgow Green. All I can say is, I did hear it on a piece of grass which is pretty adjacent to Glasgow Green.

As a matter of contingency, this book is about Thatcher's Britain. My first walk across London was at the end of May 1979, the month in which Margaret Thatcher became Prime Minister. (I can date it from a vivid memory of sitting exhausted in south London and watching coaches full of Nottingham Forest supporters pass by on their way to the European Cup Final in Munich.) Thus these walks began with the Thatcher regime and have taken place entirely during its period of office. It would be odd if someone who earned his living teaching politics did not have some sort of theory connecting what he saw with the politics of the age. For what it is worth, here follows the one full capitulation to the temptations of theory which you will find in this book.

In the late nineteenth century, the dynamic and unstable urban society which industrialisation had created in Britin was stabilised and enriched by the invention of a wide range of institutions, which together constituted the world's first predominantly urban society. These institutions were political, social and cultural: the County Borough system of urban government, the local bobby, the Football League, the Labour Party, the Free Library, and a hundred others. This society was in many respects very successful; it improved the quality and security of its people's lives and inspired their loyalty and, later, nostalgia to an extent that would have pleased Disraeli and dismayed Marx. Many of these institutions may never formally die, though they have already changed their nature and become less important.

Nostalgia may confer a certain stability on this way of life, but in reality it always carried forces for rapid change: aspirations for space, wealth and social status, people determined to 'get on' or resolved that their children would live differently from them. Even as it was being stabilised this society was decaying. There is no paradox here because 'society' is, after all, only a way of talking about the network of relationships which exist between millions of people. The beginnings of this decay were noted before the Second World War (by the Orwell of *Coming up for Air* rather than the Orwell of *The Road to Wigan Pier*, for instance). The process was delayed by the war but has accelerated since.

Mrs Thatcher's significance cannot be couched in terms of any clear ideology. Pundits like to associate her with dramatic ideals and beliefs, but these often turn out to be mere words or phrases. 'Monetarism' is no more than a rather limited belief in the relationship between inflation and the money supply: a belief as vague as it is limited because it is difficult to decide what constitutes 'money' in modern conditions. Mrs Thatcher has little more than a passing interest in 'Victorian values', which were complex and contradictory in any case.

What is special about Mrs Thatcher's government is that she has uniquely *not* tried to contain the major forces for change, but has let them happen. Her government has not tried, as its predecessors did, to shore up a sense of social unity by constructing a division of incomes based on a corporatist consensus. It has not attempted to preserve old industries and the 'communities' which developed alongside them. It has allowed the dominant part of the provision of dwellings to be on a market basis, outside the control of public authorities. (On the other hand, political lethargy and democratic power have forced it to maintain many institutions like the green belt system and the National Health Service.)

Much of what I saw could thus be seen as the symbol both of long-term social forces and of the current government's unique acceptance of them. On the one hand, the posthumous silence of whole areas of Liverpool, Colne retreating up its hill, Bradford (like New York) made over to a new people. On the other, the leafy prosperity of so many 'residential' areas, the quiet solidity of grey stone Pennine villages, the productive opulence of lowland farms. But that is enough of the general. . . .

Certain particular moments have remained in my memory with a vivid quality out of all proportion to any significance they seemed to have at the time. A tawny owl floating through a Surrey wood at dusk. The intense smoky stillness of the Wentlloog Levels in very late autumn (or was it very early winter?) The sound of the Thames lapping against the Essex bank punctuated, strangely, by a girl's voice speaking in Russian through the announcement system of the Mikhail Lermontov.

Travelling alone intensifies sensation. The satisfaction of getting to the top of something and looking down. The miserable irritation of discovering that the place is not like the map and that one is, in a manner of speaking, sort of. . . lost. Even in this least intrepid of travel books, the twinge of fear alone on a mountainside in winter or passing four unoccupied youths in a deserted street. The consoling relief of good beer after ten miles in the hot sun: in terms of the classical economists' theories of marginal utility I am inclined to believe that the third pint is generally the best.

It is to describe these moments and sensations that the essays were written; the occasional satisfaction from writing lies in the sense of having picked a combination of words which seems to fit.

1 *In Darkest London*

(May 1979)

I just walked across London. I did it twice really; the first day from Richmond to Blackheath and the second day from Blackheath to Epping Forest.

It was an odd thing to do, certainly if judged by the comments of those friends to whom I announced the intention. It was also a very tiring thing to do. So why do it? The traditional Engish justification of heroic enterprise, 'Because it's there', is a little misleading; 'to see what's there' would capture the spirit better. 'Because he's daft', my wife's explanation, is unfair but there are personal reasons. I had driven through London. I had been a tourist in London. I had visited middle-class friends in London. But these experiences were superficial and, anyway, had only covered a small slice of the cake, from the middle out towards the North-West. They did nothing to resolve my curiosity about what the place is *really* like.

That curiosity has, I suspect, very deep cultural roots. The English have often been accused, eloquently and persuasively, of anti-urbanism, of a failure to accept and adapt to urban life. We have produced characters such as Ebenezer Howard and William Morris, who thought that cities were intolerable places and that, by reform according to Howard and by revolution according to Morris, London would have to be disbanded and dispersed. But what they failed to understand is that the opposite of the repulsion is London's fascination. It represents the centre, the big time, it has all kinds of sophistication and complexity. It has – as a friend of mine once said of the street he lived on in New York – all the bad girls you'd ever hope to meet.

These explain the ability of people to put up with conditions the RSPCA would prohibit for livestock. (Rush-hour on the tube is only the most obvious.) They also explain my own fascination. I have lived the greater part of my life in agreeable places with green fields not very far away. I wanted to know how people put up with the big city and what makes it so attractive and, in a sense, I wanted to get away from theories and jargon, from preconceived notions of 'housing classes' and 'inner-city decay' and 'multiple deprivation' to simply see what places are like, though I realise that a *tabula rasa* mind is neither possible nor desirable. So I set off, equipped with a familiar and comfortable pair of shoes, a little money and an *A to Z*.

From the middle of Richmond I make my way through some suburban villas, divert rather aimlessly into the Deer Park and out again and then cut north across Kew Gardens, marvelling at the 1p admission fee. 'It's yer peppercorn, innit?' says the man who took the money, with that knowledgeble air which Londoners have. The gardens are fantastically beautiful. Then I go along the Mortlake Road and along the Kew Meadow Path, following the river as far as Barnes High Street. I am beginning to wonder if London really exists. There seem to be trees and open country on every horizon and my shoes are muddy from walking along the river. Barnes does nothing to solve the mystery. The High Street has a range of small and personal shops which seem to be more suited to a medium-to-small market town. This is followed by, of all things, a village green complete with pond and a large rather marshy wood called Barnes Common. I am penetrating deeper and deeper into what looks on the map like London.

At Putney Bridge the old church is overshadowed by an office block. I turn away from the river and soon smell the sickly sweet smell of Young's brewery. Pausing for a rest opposite Wandsworth Town Hall, I realise that the last traces of rural deceit have vanished. A couple of old men sit on the bench next to me looking at the traffic while some black lads come out of the nearby college and begin to read pamphlets on youth employment. There is a lot of litter and a lot of noise and I begin to sense the wearing on the nerves which is the most tiring effect of urban walking.

Clapham Common is a boring open space. I watch some Asian boys play football, even though it is the cricket season and I inspect the surfaces available for playing cricket. No wonder the immigrants of South London produce more footballers than cricketers; it's all down to topographical determinism. In Brixton I stop to look at the map and an old black man slaps me on the back and cackles 'Ah'll bet that made ya jump', but he says it in such an incomprehensible accent that I only appreciate the simplicity of the message when it is repeated three times. I go into a rather ill-kempt pub for some refreshment, rather fearing that I will feel out of place. To my relief, exactly half the occupants are white and half black, while the barman has one earring and a T-shirt which pre-dates Scotland's misfortunes in Argentina. An old black man is trying to explain to an old white woman about how to get a rebate on the gas bill. She contradicts him several times and says that she didn't have to take the form in last year. Without knowing anything about it, I am convinced he is right. He is also very patient and when she won't believe him, he relieves his frustration by winking at me in a resigned sort of way.

In the afternoon I make slower progress, pausing to explore some of the old LCC flats, the sort that are four or five storeys high where each flat has a balcony looking into an enclosed space. For the most part they are built of dark brick and look rather grim. But inside I am pleasantly surprised by the friendly, communal atmosphere of some of them, though the atmosphere changes markedly from one block to the next. For instance, the graffitinometer records vastly different scores. Still pondering what makes the difference I reach Blackheath Station, exhausted out of all proportion by the fifteen or so miles walked.

Day two begins, exactly as its predecessor, in an atmosphere of unreality. The Blackheath itself is very spacious and its panorama extends from the apparent rural fringe of Shooters Hill in the east to the city away to the north-west. Then a free trip to the Suffolk Collection and through Greenwich to the river at the Cutty Sark. I had regarded the dotted line in the *A to Z* marked 'footway tunnel' with some suspicion. But it exists all right, a damp, white-tiled tube under the river with a huge lift at either end. When I reach the far side, I find myself in the strangest, the most moving and memorable, place on my journey – the Isle of Dogs.

The initial sensation of the Isle is of an eerie silence. There are no through roads and very few cars. The aeroplanes, which so savagely disrupt the rustic fantasy of south-west London, are nowhere to be heard, so the silence is broken only by the occasional hooting of ships on the river and in the docks. On the eastern edge old terrace houses are interspersed with modern flats, but much of the centre of the south of the Isle is just a wilderness. Sheep, goats, and ponies graze and I walk down a cobbled street surrounded by fifteen-foot sycamore saplings where once there were houses. This wilderness is not completely deserted; it is patrolled by squadrons of small boys on 'chopper' bikes. The boys are all white and remarkably English-looking for Londoners.

The Isle of Dogs is one of those places which, though it is ugly, at least is ugly in its own way and proud of it. The pride is apparent in the cocky, friendly way the kids come up and talk to me. The first group ask me, 'Excuse me, mister, d'yer know if it's true there's a fair at Black'eaf?' and they are followed by a lone youth who, quite wrongly assuming me to be one of nature's mechanics, asks, 'Please mister, why d'yer fink moi boike squeaks? Is it 'cos there ain't any oil?' and we discuss pedal problems for a while. The pride is obvious in the absence of any reference to the more prosperous London football clubs; Millwall FC really does rule, despite its problems. This pride is formally symbolised in the series of murals down the East Ferry Road which depict the struggles of the Isle against its enemies, from the Normans to the Luftwaffe and the GLC. Though I suspect these may have been painted by a sentimental outsider, a suspicion encouraged by some of the embarrassed graffiti which have been appended.

The North of the Isle is less eerie, though it has its on strangeness, largely because of the enormously high brick walls which hide the docks from the road. I buy some chips on the West Ferry Road and endure the irony of being asked the way by a lorry driver whose accent indicates that he comes from some (northern) part not very far distant from mine.

After the Isle, I walk through Poplar, Limehouse, Mile End and Bow. These, I take it, constitute the real East End. They are overwhelmingly and appallingly ugly. The old houses are depressingly derelict, the new flats depressingly huge. Admittedly, it is raining by now. A skinny, black-haired punk with a swastika armband seems, though not typical, symbolic of something. The biggest open space in the area is one gouged out where people used to live by the Greater London Council Parks Department, Landscape Division. Saplings versus vandals and I'm placing no bets. Beyond the Bow High Street, if you follow the Lea upstream, you find one of the most totally industrial zones I have ever seen – a completely mechanical, functional landscape of new roads, pylons, huge warehouses and factories. This is what William Morris called 'the lovely river Lea (where old Izaak Walton used to fish, you know)'. In theory it is due to merge into the Lea Valley Regional Park, though the theory seems hopelessly optimistic.

It is a relief to reach even the bleak expanse of Hackney Marshes, though no sooner do I reach it than I make the worst mistake of the expedition. I fail to cross the river and I am forced to follow it round in a huge crescent, my journey becoming unnecessarily longer with every weary stride. Pausing to rest at the Lea Bridge I gaze rather aimlessly at the power station. I am joined in a barely comprehensible conversation by an Irishman. It turns out that he is demolishing the power station, which looks brand new and was in fact built in 1954, to make way for one which is oil-fired! It is yet another conversation in which two citizens of the world marvel at its mysteries.

My mistake is only rectified by a long flog up the Lea Bridge Road, a classic inter-war ribbon development with cinemas and shops in distinctively Edwardian and twenties styles backed by acres of semis. At last I reach Epping Forest, my ultimate if rather randomly chosen destination. I like the Forest and I am surprised by the extent to which it is a genuine, and very English, forest with a high proportion of old oaks. But I also like those parts where the Forest forms a kind of convoluted coastline with the suburban houses, gardens and cricket fields giving way to thick woods. The last part of my walk is down an avenue of villas leading away from the Forest and it is just the time when the commuters come home carrying evening papers and occasional packages of food or drink. A curious flicker of envy effects me and then passes.

It would be foolish to draw general conclusions from the experience of walking across London, but I would argue that walking is a unique and important way of learning and it did leave me with some clear impressions and images. In the first place, London *looks* like two completely different places. Inner London has those interminable four- and five-storey blocks of flats. The houses were usually built before 1914 and are in poor condition. Outer London is that colossal girdle of villas and semis, lilacs and forsythia, which many foreigners think is the most typically English landscape of all. Often the transition between the two is dramatic; crossing Hackney Marshes from south to north, for instance, or leaving the middle of Lewisham going east.

Both Londons are nicer than I imagined. Inner London has very, very few places which could be called slums by the standards of Paris, New York, Athens and San Francisco – and I have done more than my share of walking in these cities. Most relations between people are more friendly than I expected. Race relations, for instance: I realise that attitudes to race are often schizophrenic, that apparent amity can hide potential hatred. But most of the race relations which you actually see appear remarkably and comparatively amicable. On the big estates, white and black children seem to play together in a random way, as if they didn't notice colour. Probably great racial hatred and large self-segregated groups do exist in London. But, at least, in very large parts of that city people of different races mix together for some of their lives and talk to one another civilly, which is more than can be said for many parts of the world where different races live in close proximity.

If I lost much of my fear of the inner city, I also lost much of my contempt for the far greater reality of Outer London. Certainly, it is 'suburban' if we mean by that a place which is not traditionally urban and definitely not rural. But it is unfair to equate 'suburbia' in this simple descriptive sense with the connotations that the word is often given. 'Suburbia' in its emotive sense means a one-class life, narrow-minded in its social views and boringly bland and repetitive in its physical presence. There exist such suburbs in England and many more of them in America. But most of the Outer London I saw had more charm than these. Age has lent it horticultural, architectural and social variety; time and the English talent for gardening have outdated the intellectual fashion for despising suburbia, so eloquently expressed by Orwell and Waugh in the thirties. London has the pleasantest suburbs in the world.

I was left pondering why the city gets such a bad press from the media and the academics. The answer would be very long, I suspect, and would trace our intellectual history at least into Victorian times. I myself still prefer the small town to the big time. But the real gain of the expedition is that I have more affection for London than I did before I went.

2 *A day out in Liverpool*

(February 1980)

Strange that I should never have been to Liverpool, having been brought up in Lancashire. Even stranger, perhaps, that though I've lived thirty-three years without going to Liverpool, I can wait no longer and we are dashing up the M6 on a wet winter's Saturday morning, trying to avoid that speed at which the car starts shaking, which would otherwise be our optimum speed. South to north is the logical way to do it; I pick an appropriate spot on the *A to Z*. The J-registered, chauffeuse-driven limousine purrs away into the distance and I am on my own.

Already Liverpool has a surprise. I am in Grassendale Park, a spacious quiet world of Georgian mansions which exists between stone gateposts and the river. This could be Leamington or Cheltenham, if it weren't for glimpses of the huge, grey, choppy Mersey at the ends of the roads. The mansions are painted pink, pale green and magnolia. Some of them are in perfect condition, others are in danger of collapse. On the other side of an overgrown and litter-strewn lane, labelled 'Private Road: Do not leave litter' is a more modest place: new private houses with some council flats. It is very pleasant, a lot of grass and the river to look at. There are a few graffiti, though I am surprised by what is written on the garden door of a big old house, 'LFC RULE OK/OR/EFC RULE OK'. This must be a very broad-minded part of town.

I make my way towards Liverpool along the broad promenade overlooking the Mersey. The river is more like the sea, broader than the Mississippi, with small waves lapping up against the wall. There are a few buoys, one tug and the maritime atmosphere is increased by the distant dock cranes, both on this side and as part of the flat, grey, industrial landscape of the Wirral on the other side. The river is thirty feet below and there are life belts on (nearly) every lamppost. The only other inhabitants of the promenade are dog-walkers, mainly those tough-looking middle-aged women who abound in Lancashire and upon whom Thora Hird based her acting career. Nobody is throwing sticks to the dogs, but one man is getting his dog to retrieve a length of plastic pipe. At the end of the promenade are two vans parked within a foot of each other. Both contain a single man reading the *Sun* and both say 'Liverpool City Security Force'. 'Who the hell. . ?' I think to myself. One of three passing boys shares my puzzlement: 'Is dem der police?' he asks. 'Nah, dem's der guards,' his friend replies. One of the guards addresses me: 'Nice day for a walk,' very sarky and scouse. 'I like it,' I reply.

I make a lot of progress up Jericho Lane and Aigburth Road, but it is boring, just parks and a main road. I am attracted by the brightly-coloured terraced houses (and the name) of Tramway Street. It leads into a lively and attractive working-class area of about two dozen streets, the sort of place many people wish that they'd come from. The nice thing about this place is that the streets are so full. Boys play football, milkmen collect money, women stand talking and young men pore over their cars. One of them is demonstrating the windscreen on his Mini: 'It's nor' ordinary glass – it's practically shatterproof, dat.' The houses have the old backyards and alleys, so there are no gardens. Swinging into Dingle Vale, I discover that they do their gardening in a kind of fortified glass city overlooking the river. The railway line runs right through the middle of it. At the top of Dingle Mount, I catch my first glimpse of the Anglican Cathedral and, trying to make some time up, I walk quickly towards the centre of the city, using the cathedral tower as a landmark. It is a long, depressing walk: barrack-like flats, worse than those the GLC put up, a few shabby streets left standing and a lot of damp, muddy grass and heaps of rubble.

I have always liked looking at buildings, but Liverpool's Anglican Cathedral is one of the few buildings which has ever made me laugh out loud. It looks so absurd from where I first see it as a whole: a huge, falsely Gothic, brown-black stone fantasy arising out of a plain of rubble and debris and crumbling Georgian houses. It is like seeing the Doge's Palace where a cricket pavilion should be, or Sydney Opera House next to a semi-detached house. Nothing about the place, inside or out, dispels this feeling of unreality. It seems to be on a different scale from other cathedrals. And of course, it was built by another of those ubiquitous Gilbert Scotts, this time Sir Giles

(1880-1960).

It's a rule that if you see one you have to see them both, so I make my way past the elegant and well-preserved Georgian houses of Rodney Street, now the offices and surgeries of the leading professionals, in search of the Catholic Cathedral. This really is something completely different, a round, concrete thing which, overall, gives a kind of wigwam effect. Questions race through my mind. Is there nothing can be done to stop modern concrete buildings showing the damp? Was it specifically designed to be as different as possible from the one down the road? Is it the biggest circular room in the world? Has it ever been used in a science fiction film? Had Sir Frederick Gibberd just visited Las Vegas before he designed it? Certainly the psychedelic violet light which comes from the windows is more like the 'Wee Kirk o' the Heather Wedding and Funeral Parlour – compare our rates with those at City Hall' than the vernacular stained glass of an English cathedral. But, though I can't resist a little mockery, it is quite impressive; after all, it is a cathedral built for a secular age and on a pared-down budget. It would be interesting to see it full of people.

By the time I leave the cathedral, the sun has come out. I make my way down into the shopping centre. It is as packed as a football ground, more packed than most. There is a lot to be said for this centre; it has a cheerful atmosphere, some varied buildings, though few particularly attractive ones, and broad streets which, traffic removed, have become lively squares. But crowds like these are no good for a walker. I dive off into a narrow street where I think the Cavern is, a shrine to anyone of my generation. Before I find it, I find the other clubs where the younger generation hang out, all black plastic and kinkiness. *Probe* has dozens of them lounging round the door. I have never seen such a concentration of teenage fashion. Three lads pass me, dressed identically in black plastic trousers, white waiters' jackets and swastika T-shirts. Charming.

Round the corner, the Cavern, despite its large neon sign, is closed and rather forlorn. It actually has a shrine above the door, a modern sculpture representing Mother Liverpool and Her Four Famous Sons.

I also discover The Grapes, just by the Cavern. It is filled with a jolly, very mixed, crowd of late lunchtime drinkers. I try my first ever pint of Higson's; if points are out of ten, then it's worth seven. I always enjoy listening to people's conversations in pubs far away from home. (I rarely drink alone where I'm known; they always think you've quarrelled with your wife.) In this case, there is a conversation of such outstanding merit that it cannot be ignored. A totally bald man, with a refined accent, probably in his early thirties, is talking to a rather ordinary-looking man of his own age who is wearing a brown sports jacket and corduroy trousers. The bald man is very slim and muscular: he is wearing white shoes, tight pink jeans, a black T-shirt and pink tinted spectacles. He announces that 'London is so conservative after New York' and his friend, who has a strong Liverpool accent and is fairly drunk, replies 'Yeh, well let's face it, I mean, London and Liverpool weren't ready to cope with your temperament, were they?' They repeat, rather falsely it seems to me, how glad they are to see one another again and then talk about how conservative David Hockney is.

When I emerge from the maze of narrow streets it is to an area as deserted as the previous one was crowded. This is the commercial, 'city', part of Liverpool and everything in it is very clean, very big and imposing. Using the Liver Building, with its strange stone birds, as a target, I make my way down to the Pier Head. Here there is a combined bus and boat station, reminiscent of Venice in many ways, involving a boardwalk from which you can see the Wirral and the river and the boats. The Isle of Man ferry is loading and the much smaller ferry to Birkenhead chugs past it and out across the water. That old song from the sixties comes irresistibly to mind (Gerry and the Pacemakers, wasn't it?) I've heard it said that the most impressive way to enter Britain from abroad is by ship to Liverpool and I can see why the claim was made: it looks every inch a real city from here, like a compact, English version of New York.

Going up towards Everton from the Pier Head I am walking through deserted streets surrounded by factories and warehouses and occasional heaps of rubble. I am well aware that there are no shops here, because I am hungry and have reached the stage when I would buy practically anything edible. But the silence is eerie, frightening. You hardly get silence like this anywhere on earth; certainly, it doesn't exist in the countryside, though it may in a desert or in a pine forest in winter.

The first people I see are three youths standing by a boarded-up chapel which overlooks the great motorway cutting which runs where Scotland Road used to be. One of them is shaking something which rattles: I realise it is an aerosol can of paint. He proceeds to write 'SEX PISTOLS' in about ten seconds flat. Now I have always resolved that if I ever saw anybody actually doing that then I would thump them and this is the first time my resolution has been put to the test. But I haven't got the heart. Not really because I'm scared; although there are three, they're very puny. More because I just don't think they would understand the objection. The main road has been torn up, the building abandoned, the streets are in lumps and there are graffiti everywhere. How do I explain why I object to a kid writing on a wall?

On the other side of the motorway the squalor is worse, if anything. I follow Scotland Road (there is some of it left, here) towards Bootle. I find a shop with hot pies. In the shop they are arguing about the score in the Liverpool game. 'De other lot scored in ninety flippin' seconds,' says an old man, but the baker indicates that it doesn't worry him. I order a steak and kidney pie and a meat and potato pie. Curiously, they are identical, inside and out; both contain a kind of thick gravy. But I think they're delicious; they remind me strongly of the pies I used to eat as a boy. In fact I have something of an aversion to meat in meat pies as it usually resembles reinforced greyhound cartilage. But why are meatless meat pies so common in Lancashire? Has it got something to do with our teeth?

Going up Stanley Road towards Bootle, the townscape degenerates into the most sordid I have ever seen. Urban life cannot get any more raw than this. Nowhere else have I seen men pissing in the street in such a public way. There's a lot of vomit on the streets, most of it apparently special fried rice, though I don't examine it too closely. All the shops are boarded up. This isn't because they are closed; it is because Rule One of life round here is that glass gets broken. Rule Two is that any other surface gets written on, politically for the most part, with the UDA, UVF, SAS, SWP and IRA well represented.

Although this is the biggest concentration of rock-bottom urban circumstances I have seen in England (it has more in common with Brooklyn or Glasgow), it ends fairly abruptly at the Bootle border where there is a large new complex of offices and shops shielding the more respectable parts to the north from the squalor. There is a small park on the right as I enter Bootle. Its iron gates announce with quiet dignity: 'RESENTED BY THE WOMEN OF BOOTLE'.

Walking through Bootle and up into Litherland and Orrell the surroundings are increasingly indistinct and anonymous, twentieth-century factories and semis. My main problem, apart from having to make a lot of ground, is to cross the curious roadless gap which exists on the map between Litherland and Bootle. I go down a snicket and pass a farmhouse, beleaguered among the semis, and cross a patch of thick mud to the footbridge over the Leeds–Liverpool canal. The gap looks as curious in real life as it does on the map – five hundred yards of damp grass down which run the canal and a line of huge pylons. It is full of rubbish and there is no attempt to make it into a park, no trees, no football, no golf. In fact the only people are, like me, crossing it.

But it is enough to make Crosby a completely separate place, where there are no graffiti, no broken windows and nothing for under twenty thousand. I have actually been to Crosby a couple of times to play rugby, but don't remember anything. I ask the only man I see where the road to Hightown is, 'Yes, the countryside is that way,' he says puzzled.

After so much town the country comes as a shock. It is signalled by a forest of rugby posts on the left on a huge flat plain looking over to the sandhills and the coast in the gathering gloom. The village of Little Crosby is cosily familiar; the architecture of the cottages and the stone walls around the gardens remind me of other Lancashire villages, fifty miles away. unfortunately, though, my R/V is in Hightown which is still three miles away and it is practically dark.

The countryside is like Poland or Prussia, with its huge flat fields interspersed with swathes of woodland, except that the road is very English, in that it suddenly veers away at a lunatic right angle across the flat landscape. Walking is no fun at all under these circumstances and, anyway, my toe is hurting. So I stick out a thumb and approximately the eighteenth car stops. A Mini containing three young lads going to Southport for a night out plays Samaritan to the Pharisee Volvos and Sadducee Jags. Sometimes I actually like the younger generation.

Ah well, as they say in Burnley, it's a day out, isn't it?

3 *Strolling across Sussex*

(March 1980)

Amberley, Sussex, where the River Arun flows through a gap in the South Downs, is the starting point of my exploration of the wealthy and mysterious Deep South of England. It gives good access to the downs and is an easy day's walk from Brighton. If you are looking for a rural idyll (which I am, intermittently) then you could do sometimes better, but usually worse, than Amberley. It is sleekly and quietly properous on a misty Saturday morning. Foreign cars stand brightly outside thatched cottages. A woman paints the outside of her house and a young man exercises two collies, one gold and one black.

There is a lot of thatch. One house, called 'The Thatched Cottage', is covered in it. Another, called 'The Thatched House', has none at all. The narrow and winding streets give the impression of a hill village and, indeed, the village does have a sharp drop to the plain of the Arun on the north side, but it is only sixty or seventy feet.

In the village shop I inquire about a map. They have none. I look for something to eat, but nothing particularly attracts me. I buy a packet of Iraqi dates for 28p as I must have something. I have a personal interest in Iraqi dates. An ex-student of mine, who heads the Iraqi Dates Administration (at least he said he did), chose English cellophane for the wrapping from fourteen alternatives because he could not erase the memory of my nobility and wisdom from his mind. Leaving Amberley, there are two discordant notes; the cereal-packet quality of the school's architecture and a sanitary towel lying on the pavement.

In fact, no map is really necessary. A winding lane goes up the down and, to my relief, meets the clearly signposted South Downs Way. The Way is everything I once imagined the Pennine Way to be, an express eight-lane pedoway which is visible to the horizon. There are signs of a distinct lack of sympathy with the Way on the part of local farmers. It is surrounded on both sides by barbed wire and often badly churned up where it has been used for moving and feeding cattle and by tractors. It is, really, the opposite of the Pennine Way. You can't find that half the time and so it is only too easy to leave it voluntarily or involuntarily. The South Downs Way is easy to find, very difficult to leave. A lot of cattle are fed here by the continental method, using metal feeding baskets. One farmer uses the Way itself, with the cows poking their heads through broad blue metal fencing to eat the hay. I pass a whole row of these incurious heads. Only one, called 45A, takes any notice of me.

For most of its course, the Way runs along the very top of the Downs. It is a dramatic, geometrically simple, landscape. North and south, the land slopes roundly away to disappear towards misty, green and empty horizons. It is very unfamiliar landscape to my eyes, which are used to the intimacy and detail of Warwickshire. How can it be such an empty place, close to so many people on the South Coast? The answer, I suppose, is chalk. There is no water on the top of the Downs and, thus, no villages or farmhouses. Just enormous, parabolic fields, some of them meadows, some of them stony and ploughed, with green winter barley poking through the stones. The steeper ridges are unused, dotted with gorse bushes.

I walk several miles through this landscape without seeing anybody. There is little sound except for the constant twittering of larks and the chugging of an aeroplane towing a glider to the North. It sounds like the aeronautical equivalent of my car and I shouldn't like to be in it. The going is sometimes difficult because the mud is quite thick in places. Then, suddenly, a surfaced lane runs right up to the top of the ridge and a fleet of cars disgorges no fewer than nineteen middle-aged walkers in full dress of boots and shooting sticks. As they straggle along the path a lot of 'afternoon, afternoon' takes place. I manage to give about six and receive about seventeen. Thank God they are going in the opposite direction. This is a land best appreciated in solitude.

A little further on I meet a solitary walker who is also going in the opposite direction, a sad-looking young man with a blue woolly hat. (Am I sad-looking? I wonder.) There is a strange paradox when solitary walkers meet. You want to recognise a kindred spirit, but you don't want to disturb each other's solitude. He makes it very clear what the form is with one of the curtest, politest, hellos that the human voice can achieve. At the next junction with a lane a very strange thing is happening. About a dozen men, in camouflage uniforms and forage caps, appear to be rounding up (or moving on) literally, hundreds of bullocks. The only explanation I can think of is that they are clearing the ground for a good old Saturday afternoon battle.

A mile or so later, I meet another solitary walker who is not at all distant. A big, old, bald man hobbles up to me in a state of considerable excitement. 'I've taken the number of that car,' he says, pointing to a maroon car which has appeared on the down a few hundred yards in front of me. 'I shall report him. I 'spec the policeman'll tell me he's too busy. But it's too bad. It really is. They have miles and miles and miles of roads to take their cars on. And then they have to come and invade the bridleway.' I sympathise with him and move on, indulging in a quick fantasy in which three roaring motorbikes come up the down and I pick them off, bang, bang, bang, each with a bullet from my high-velocity rifle, in the left hand side of his black leather jacket. Level with the offending vehicle, DDT 405T, I see it is a middle-aged man and his blonde lady companion (wife?). One of the features of a chalk down, presumably, is that it is all too easy a surface to drive on. I briefly contemplate heaving a rock through his windscreen, but am constrained by whatever it is that keeps most of us out of gaol and move on.

On the other side of the dual carriageway A24, which I cross at a sprint, the Way climbs steeply back to the top of the Downs again. Once on the top, it is the most perfect walking surface I have ever experienced, a chalky cart track which is neither hard nor soft. And, anyway, it is good for the morale to walk along the top of anything. The Way finally merges into an unclassified road and I find myself in a place called Sompting, the first real habitation I have come across in maybe fifteen miles of walking.

The sea! I have been looking forward to the moment when my land-bound heart would leap at the first glimpse of a blue horizon or the first crash of wave on shore. Unfortunately that moment will not come. I walk endlessly through Lancing. Obviously, the sea is somewhere here; there are houses called 'Seagull's Rest' and 'The Ocean Wave'. There is also a rash of scruffy little caravan sites. The architecture is distinctly seaside architecture, strange, cheap-looking bungalows which you don't find inland; 1930s tat. But there is no sign of the sea itself, until, at last, I realise that in following the signs for Brighton I have been walking beside it for some time. The trouble is, on this cliffless part of the coast, it is hidden behind what appear to be a row of mock Tudor boathouses, a fence, a sort of mini-estuary and a sea wall. It makes no sound because it is entirely calm.

The street lights are now coming on and I am very late. In Shoreham I manage to catch a green Southdown double-decker bus equipped with that rare, old-fashioned luxury, a conductress who is able to discuss routes and destinations with passing strangers. It is still light enough to see outside and what I see contradicts my preconceptions of the Sussex coast. It is heavily industrial: factories, warehouses, oil storage depots and a large power station. But Brighton, which seems to begin, in spirit, half-way through Hove, is anything but a disappointment. It is a grand, elegant town. I have not been there since I was ten, and places can often seem utterly different if you haven't been there since you were ten. Anyway, the only thing I can remember is the onion shapes of the domes on the Pavilion.

The enviable quality which Brighton exudes is that of being fashionable. A fashionable place is one to which people go simply because it is the place to go. The 'in crowd', the 'fast set' – all of those phrases we use which suggest that some people are central and others merely peripheral to an interesting social life – the reality seems to be in Brighton. Nor is it just one set of people who come to Brighton. Even now, in the very early spring, some hotels are full and there is every kind of car parked in front of them: Porsches, Rolls, Daimlers, but also some ancient Cortinas and Morris Minor estates. It may be purely subjective, it may be an illusion, but to me the sea front at Brighton has that magical excitement which is possessed by very few places but which is abundant in, for instance, St Mark's Square in Venice and Fifth Avenue in New York. It is a feeling that most people come here at some time in their lives and that there is nobody the possibility of whose presence can be discounted. The excitement lies in the fact that you might just meet the rich, the famous, your long-lost friend or your first lover.

In this respect Brighton is utterly unlike other English resorts; at least, the ones I know. They all have the air of being finished. I'm very fond of dear old Morecambe and of Seaton Carew. But they look like places where nobody goes any more. Of course, some people go to Morecambe, sometimes, but you only have to go there to know what they mean when they say that nobody goes there any more. Brighton is not like that. People go to Brighton. I wander round the Lanes. These are narrow streets, full of restaurants, antique shops, bookshops, chic clothes shops and so on, and they are still well-lit and populated at night, even though most of the shops are shut. I am obsessed by the questions of Brighton's uniqueness, the huge difference between its fate and that of other resorts. All right, it's in a good place and has diverse functions – a resort, a regional centre, a university town. But Morecambe has a university nearby and the M6 should have helped it. In the end, it is just the mystical chemistry of fashion, which regenerates itself.

I repair to a free house for refreshment. King and Barnes Sussex Bitter, pleasant texture but a bit short on flavour. It is very much a young person's pub. There is loud conversation comparing the qualities required to go round the bends at Silverstone with those required by the bends at Brands Hatch, a conversation which may or may not be informed by experience. There are several very pretty girls, dressed and made-up to full advantage. The few (students?) who haven't bothered and who are in corduroy jeans look half alive by comparison.

Walking through Hove and Brighton on Sunday morning does nothing to dispel my impression of it; rather, it is enhanced. Admittedly, these are very favourable circumstances to see a place. It is a warm, sunny morning. The sky is blue and so is the sea; the crocuses are out. A kind of subliminal English rite of spring is going on which consists of strolling, gardening, chatting and being cheerful. That awful Sunday morning feeling which affects most towns is banished.

What really impresses me is the sustained elegance of the architecture. It is not just, like many places, a few nice buildings, and then massive ordinariness, but miles of beautiful Regency buildings, some tatty, but most gleaming in the morning sun. The Palace Pier is being renovated. It is a splendid pier and I feel quite at home there, having seen *Oh What a Lovely War* so many times. It is the height of architectural insanity to put a structure of wood and cast iron in the sea, but I get the impression that they will spend anything to keep the Palace Pier. The news on the West Pier is not so good; a notice at the end if it mentions danger and the receivers. The beach, of course, is not a beach at all, but a collection of stones which rattle when waves recede. A thousandth of the sand in Morecambe Bay would enhance Brighton. That, and fewer Watney's pubs.

The places I would most like to live are those elegant squares which have the sea front as a fourth side. The architectural highlights are the hotels, especially the balconied opulence of The Grand and The Norfolk. And, of course, the inspired lunacy of that Pavilion: it would be very strange and wonderful if you didn't know it existed and simply came across it whilst wandering through the town. Painted on the boards around a building site are the names 'ORWELL – DARWIN – EINSTEIN'. This raises possibilities of a new genre; my offering would be 'HUME – WELLINGTON – McILROY'.

In the afternoon, I make my way eastwards through the strolling crowds to the Marina. This is a brand new yacht city sharing a new sea wall with the Seajet terminal and served by curving flyovers. Most of the yachts are out on such a pleasant afternoon. The white cliffs extend eastwards as far as the eye can see. I am intrigued by the fact that you have to go through a traffic light to get your yacht through the canal which runs between the marina and the harbour. Chaps in yellow wellies are saying things like, 'I was weather bound in here for four days, once.' Well, I can think of worse places.

4 *Pottering in the Five Towns*

(June 1980)

Walking from Meir Heath, north-west towards the Potteries, I am on a classic ribbon of suburban houses along a ridge with a rolling, cluttered countryside beyond. As the ridge descends so does the status of the area; detached houses with a riot of blossom on their well-established trees going down into council houses whose unkempt lawns are ablaze only with dandelions. One council house, though, has a miniature fairyland of gnomes, ponds, mice, windmills and towers.

At the A50 I swing left towards Longton. At first, there is a lot of derelict and unused land and buildings: boarded-up shops, bricked-up houses and small plots of rubbly emptiness. But Longton itself is an industrial landscape of considerable charm. I am first attracted by a group of bottle ovens in dark brown brick and I quicken my pace towards them like a tourist in Greece spotting his first Doric column. Crumbling, as they are, at the end of a cobbled alley, they look older than any Greek pillar. A notice warns that they are protected by guard dogs; the largest building of the complex is now used as a furniture warehouse. Down a cobbled street between two small factories and turning right in the general direction of Stoke, I come across a far more splendid collection of ovens, the Parthenon of the piece. I walk round it, watching how the effect of the whole changes with the different combinations of height and shape as the angle changes. At the front, I find that they are the Gladstone Bottle Ovens. They incorporate a museum, closed today, and have been given a conservation award by the Royal Institute of Chartered Surveyors. Thirty five thousand pounds are needed to preserve them. I hope to God they get them; it seems a piddling sum for the preservation of something so interesting and unusual.

But the charm of this landscape is not just a matter of the curious shapes of the bottle ovens. All through Longton I have the feeling that the town is close to the mistily nostalgic vision of industrial society, a world of clogs clattering on the cobbles, coals burning in the grate, street parties on Jubilee day, and hot buttered crumpets and a mug of tea without pausing to take your muffler off when you come back from the match on a Saturday. I try to analyse what it is about the landscape that suggests these images. The scale is the most general feature. Like the cotton-weaving towns of north Lancashire or the woollen towns of West Yorkshire, Longton has factories which are small and varied: Colclough, Cara, Tuscon, Phoenix, Sanders, James Birks, James Kent. . . there are literally dozens of small factories, mostly still in use, with the occasional new name and premises, like Tootal, rising out of the old landscape. The houses, too, are on a small scale. In Longton, there seems only to be one kind of house: the late Victorian, by-law house, arranged in neat terraces with doors and windows straight on to the pavement. These were built in an ordered age when you needn't give a second thought to putting your best china next to the window which was right on the pavement. But people still do in these peaceful streets, most houses displaying flowers as well as colourful china. An acceptably discordant note comes from the machine-gun game which is going on in the background: 'uh-uh-uh-uh-uh-uh' followed by a hectic chase down the back street. I suddenly realise what else it is that gives the place its intimate atmosphere. It pre-dates planning; there is no zoning, no industrial or residential areas, but a row of houses opposite a factory or a works blending into a row of shops.

Downtown Longton, Market Street and King Street, still has something of the Bennettian charm despite some uncompromisingly functional modern buildings. I contemplate a drink in the Crown and Anchor, largely motivated by a desire to see the advertised ballroom, but decide to make more progress. Fenton lacks the charm of Longton, being small and exposed, on a hill. Large open spaces intrude to the very middle of the town, a reclaimed colliery with its grassy miniature mountain away to the left and a stony parkland, possibly retired clay pits, to the right. At the top of the town are three pubs and a caravan sales yard. I choose the Duke of Wellington, an unpleasant looking new place covered with slabs of something grey and prefabricated. I have a pint of Bass, a corned beef sandwich and a pickled egg while contemplating the clientele who, unlike the building, are highly traditional, mainly men of all ages, with many a flat cap and pint of mild. The ultra-modern, technicoloured video fruit machine in the corner tempts me to thoughts about how little difference technology can make. But one mustn't generalise.

Back in the streets I note some unusual refinements on the terraced houses: Georgian lintels over some doors, and later, doors arranged in pairs with two (perpendicular) arches and three pillars. (Sir Gilbert Scott's version of a terraced house?) Prince Amin's mobile ice-cream van stops right beside me, the first Asian ice-cream vendor I have seen. Essaying a large '99' I find it less sweet than most ice-cream, an unusual taste.

It is time to make some serious progress and I turn northwards on the A50 towards Hanley and the city centre. A startling contrast: everything along the road is new, box-like and spread out. It is a main drag which would grace any sprawling Californian town; new factories, warehouses and showrooms and a pristine sixth-form college. The Used Car Centre has acres of cars with prices on the windscreen and after that is a showroom where you can buy a Rolls

Royce straight away in any one of six colours. A little later a parade of new JCB digger-tractors, all yellow. Going up the hill into Hanley presents another throw-back: three barges are waiting to be loaded at the wharf outside Johnson Brothers pottery.

There now begins a complex and confused detour. In order to find the centre I set off, backtracking slightly to the south-west toward what is marked on my OS map as Stoke-upon-Trent. This takes me round Hanley Park, an area which is well-established, leafy and prosperous. There are the predictable Edwardian villas overlooking the park and some smart twentieth-century factories in the garden city tradition. Also a tall modern building with 'YMCA' at the top, a building so imposing that it must be the one in the song. The centre of Stoke-upon-Trent is cut completely in two by the modern freeway version of the A50 and the Trent and Mersey canal. You cross this concrete complex in a tunnel under the road, a bridge across the canal and a sprint across the slip-road. The tunnel, of course, has the graffiti, virtually the first I have seen. DISCHARGE is written many times and 'I ain't going to work on Maggie's farm'. On the west side of the freeway are a few shopping streets and on the east side the railway station, the North Staffordshire Polytechnic and a Suzuki showroom where couples in black leather are admiring pristine, polished machines. I conclude that this is the most pathetic town centre I have ever seen when I realise that it isn't the centre at all. It is merely the centre of diminutive Stoke-upon-Trent. The centre of Stoke-on-Trent, the conurbation, is in Hanley and I follow the signs to it.

The real city centre is a great deal more impressive, with all the normal functions of a city centre, though only a few towering office blocks on the edges to show that this is the centre of a conurbation, rather than a market town. In front of the library is a remarkable stainless steel statue of a steelworker 'created to commemorate the struggle by the Shelton Steel Workers to preserve the future of their works for the good of the community, 1976'. Now comes the intrigue. Just to the north of the centre the map shows an area called the Central Forest Park. My step quickens, accelerated by curiosity as to what such a place can be. Across a car park, past a block of flats and there is the entrance marked by a huge wheel. The park itself rolls away to the north, acres of rolling grassland, reclaimed from the old collieries. The 'forest' aspect is explained on a notice; indigenous trees have been planted which should mature into a forest in the nineties. The project was started in the late sixties and the notice dates from 1975. Already, it says, the fieldmice, and the rabbits and the birds are returning to the area. The land falls away to a lake and the horizon is dominated by three hills which used to be slag heaps. The central one is the biggest, perhaps three hundred feet high, with two peaks like a woman's breasts. Frankly, the 'forest' seems a little optimistic; there don't seem to be as many saplings as the plan would imply. But the place is still extraordinarily exciting. It must excite children because it is a landscape adequate for any military or cowboy game the mind could devise. It excites me because it represents the triumph of grass, the return of green, the most inspired recovery from dereliction since the Norfolk Broads.

At the top of the twin-breasted hill, after a stiff walk up the steep grassy shale, I can see the whole of the Potteries. There is no sense of being in a city; the amount of green space is vast. It would be wrong, even, to call it a conurbation. More accurately, the landscape is many different communities and industrial activities spread out and interspersed among the land that they have exploited, the collieries and clay pits and farms. Three small boys, about ten or eleven, are throwing pieces of shale down the hill. I remonstrate with them, putting conventional arguments about their own feeings if they had an eye injured by a piece of shale which somebody threw. They are suitably deferential and the biggest one says, 'We were only trying to get them in the lake', in that curious accent which seems to be part Brum, part Scouse, and part Manchester and to vary from one part of the Potteries to another.

On the north side of the park, passing some old miners' cottages, I enter Burslem or, rather, Burslem cemetery. It is a large and dignified place to be buried. The graves are well kept and many have fresh flowers. I am saddened and impressed by one which looks as good as new which says simply, 'My wonderful husband died at the age of 38' and then a date in 1944. The wind murmurs in the trees. To the west, overshadowing the cemetery, is another slag heap, now well-grassed, which looks like a southerly afterthought of the Pennines.

I walk across a neat and well-ordered park in the direction of the lights of the Port Vale Football Club. The park has an area reserved for skateboarding, but fashions change quickly and, though it is a fine day and a school holiday, there is not a skateboard in sight. Port Vale itself is a place of horrid memory for me: an afternoon spent watching the home club knocking Burnley out of the cup, and our lot didn't even have the grace to look surprised about it. It seems a very different place on this blustery, sunny afternoon and a market is taking place in the grounds, outside one end of the stadium. At the 'American Snack Bar' I have a hot dog and a Vimto. An 'American Snack Bar' with Vimto, I reflect, and cannot resist a smile, despite the slightly nauseating qualities of the tinned sausage and burnt onions.

I set off for Tunstall along the 'greenway', or disused railway. It is in splendid nick, unlike many of them, a beautiful walking surface, good quality green grass, no litter. The tunnel seems far too small to take a train, but I suppose it must have done. There is the boiler of an old engine, mounted on brick, another sign of the local official enthusiasm for industrial archaeology. First views of Tunstall are dominated by a large church, which turns out to be the Catholic Church of the Sacred Heart, on the ridge. It is built in stone, now blackened, with a tall square tower and several pale green copper domes. On one corner is an appended round tower in Scottish baronial (or Gorbals) style. Tunstall, too, has its own centre which even boasts an underpass, strengthening the impression that these towns are genuinely separate places rather than mere neighbourhoods or suburbs.

North of Tunstall I come to the realisation that, in following the road toward Kidsgrove, I am going in the wrong direction. My pick-up is in a village near Leek, due east, and there is no obvious way of getting there. So, in desperation, I simply strike out away from the sun, down a scruffy little lane, across a housing estate and then out on to open grassland. It seems odd that one can just pick a direction and walk without manoeuvre or hindrance on the edge of an urban area in England. but this is an exception, an unusual place, a new, even revolutionary landscape. From Sandyford to Westcliffe and over to Fegg Hayes I walk straight across the new pampas created from the old mineworkings. Thousands of acres gleaming with a pre-Raphaelite green in the evening sun interspersed with small developments, old mining villages and new suburbs. The sense of space is astounding. At Fegg Hayes I have to go straight over the huge slag heap where the grass is half-way to winning its vital battle against the shale. It is a landscape which inspires optimism because it is a bonus, a recovery, a victory over the past. I reflect on the riding and jogging and the summer evening games, in short, the wealth of sensation, which this land should provide in the future. It should be better again in ten, then in twenty years.

Over beyond Whitfield and Norton Green the countryside takes on a more familiar look – stone-walled fields, grazing cows and patches of old woodland. On the other side of Leek the evening sun is illuminating the first ridges of the Pennines. But that sight, familiar and pleasant as it is, does not drive from my mind the memory of the man-made hills of the Potteries and all the possibilities they suggest.

5 *In the deep Fens*

(August 1980)

Because of the difficulty in getting from west to east in most parts of England it is after midday when I reach my starting destination: Welney, Norfolk. I had thought it was in Cambridgeshire, but the index of my map says Norfolk.

Welney is hardly a village, despite having at least three pubs. It is closer to a hamlet, spread out in a broken line along the road, unprepossessing yellow brick houses with great flat fields lapping up behind and between them as if the houses were so many boats moored along a jetty.

The village sign has a faded picture of skaters on it. I want to walk north-east to Downham market and I have four possible ways of doing it: either side of the Old Bedford River or of the New Bedford River. I decide to start on the nearest, the west (to me, left) bank of the Old Bedford River. A young woman is standing waiting for a dog so I ask her if it is possible to walk to Downham Market this way. 'Don't know, really,' she says, in a rustic Norfolk accent, 'I know you can get at least four miles.'

I decide to press on. I pass a man scything down the reeds along the bank, naked to the waist. He looks up, takes a breath, wishes me a very cheerful 'Good-day' and continues with his work. Ahead of me are a young couple with a baby and a bulldog and a lot of horses, spread out along the bank. The man is worried in case his dog molests the horses and his insistent call of 'Come here, Thomas, come *here*' pursues me for a couple of hundred yards. Actually, Thomas is more interested in me, in a friendly sort of way. But I am glad to get them behind me and be alone with the landscape.

It is a landscape which stretches in front of me to the horizon in five great strips. To my right, on the other side of the river, is a long green bank. I can see nothing beyond that. Then the river – at least it's called a river, though it is really a canal – seventy feet wide, smooth as plastic and reflecting the blue of the sky when the sun is out, which is about half the time. The bank I am on is perhaps forty feet high and a hundred yards across at at its widest, sloping down to thickets of elder and hawthorn on the left. Beyond these are small patches of grass, sometimes vegetables at first, clumps of tall willow trees and some thick undergrowth of a form of wild parsley, sometimes as high as seven feet. Then a drainage ditch and beyond that, rivalled only by the sky in their scale, the Fens themselves in huge squares of yellow mustard and green beet leaves and cereals of various colours giving way to a very distant tree-lined horizon.

It is a landscape which makes me a little nervous. There is, of course, the uncertainty about whether I can get anywhere, coupled with the very unfamiliarity of the shapes around me. Then there is the matter of the horses. Many of them are mares with foals. I try to remember what I know about mares with foals. For the most part the foals are lying on the ground, motionless as if dead, exhausted from the business of being born, their mothers licking them protectively and patiently. Although I go round them carefully and quietly, the foals often start and get up and stagger away from me, spindly, wary and elegant.

I divert to the path at the bottom of the bank on my left between the thickets and the wild parsley. Two of the fattest wood-pigeons I have ever seen explode into flight from a hawthorn about a yard away from me, causing me to jump. Something big moves in the undergrowth to my right. On the path are the remains of a hen pheasant which has been comprehensively terminated, possibly by the something big in the undergrowth. There is almost silence, hardly broken by a murmuring of insects and a twittering of larks, with the occasional raucous intrusion from a pheasant in the fields. The sounds of deep country, you might say, and it comes as a timely reminder of what this land really is to see a neat, modern, red-brick pumphouse linking the 'river' to a broad channel which runs at a precise right angle away through the fields.

There are no people about. Four times within a couple of miles I see a caravan among the willows or under the hawthorn hedge away to the left. All of these caravans are old and rather tatty; they are all well-hidden. There is a pound to a piece of parsley that the Local Planning Authority doesn't know they are there. But why are they there? Hideouts for Cambridge moles? Lovers' meeting places? (Or 'knocking-shops', as we used to say in my youth?) A more mundane explanation is that they are there for farmworkers to shelter and have lunch. However, the intrigue is maintained because the fourth caravan has an open door and through the open door, I can see a big book, about the size of the Shorter Oxford Dictionary, lying on a blue plastic bag.

I soon rid myself of my vague prejudice that the Fens are a lifeless kind of place. They hum with life. Rabbits bolt into holes along the bank. Frequently a pair of ducks will rise off the river like fighting planes or a moorhen will panic through the reeds. Several swans aloofly ignore me. A pair of yellow wagtails flirt in mid-air above the ditch and an unidentified small bird (sedge warbler?) hovers and sweeps around the tops of the long grass. Most impressive of all are the herons, which occasionally rise out of the river beside me and flap away with a huge, slow, prehistoric dignity. There are no hedges, but the ditches have as much life as any hedge: coots bustle among them, dragonflies idle above them and the smaller birds perch in the reeds.

All this makes up for the poverty of the direct human contribution to the landscape. A line of pylons stalks diagonally across to the north-west and sometimes a military jet roars in the distance. There are very few farmhouses, those there are being plain, modern and brick-built. The main buildings in sight are corrugated barns, black and red. Occasionally I see men hoeing in the distant fields. I can hear two, working, calling to each other and then I see three, resting together on their hoes and talking.

Quite frequently there are bullocks along the bank. This is common sense, really; the Fens themselves are too rich for grazing land, but the bank is a hundred yards wide and unsuitable for growing anything except grass. A few miles of this and you have a decent-sized farm. As I get farther from human habitation I come to bullocks which rarely see people and which show an excessive interest in me. At one stage I can hear a herd of fifty gathering pace behind me. Now I know, reflectively, that they are only curious and playful and that if I turn round and go at them they will back off. But some deep instincts are aroused by having fifty large animals break into a trot behind you and I take the easy way out and dive under an electric fence which bars their way.

This leads me into several miles of utterly quiet country. There are no longer any bullocks so the grass is long, almost waist-high, and the going slow. Three or four times I form the impression that a channel of water completely blocks my way. I make a contingency plan: I will take off all my clothes, put them in my bag, throw it across the channel and then, bollock-naked in the huge landscape, swim or wade across. It is a plan which has a certain sensual appeal when the sun is out, but very little when it is behind the clouds. Anyway, it never has to be implemented.

Some miles further on – I must be quite close to Downham Market – I cross a fence and I am back on grass that has been grazed. The way is blocked by a herd of bullocks of a number of different breeds. What is worse, three well-horned, virtually full-grown, bullocks break off from the vigorously playful sparring in which they were engaged and trot purposefully towards me. Now is the time for knowledge to conquer instinct. Remember the rules of childhood! Remember who's top species round here! I walk vigorously straight at them, slapping my thigh and, of course, they back off and trot away.

In a field on my left is the largest group of people I have seen, a group of three men and two women who are hoeing slowly across in a close row. The women are in old-fashioned summer frocks and headscarves. They seem to be sharing some huge joke: one will nudge another as if reflecting on a new aspect of the joke and they will double up with laughter again. They wave to me as I pass.

I come to the Salter's Lode Lock where my 'river' and another cut meet the Ouse, flowing fast between its steep, high banks. The lock is beautifully cared for, surrounded by red-hot pokers and decorated with plaster gnomes and mermaids. I alternate between the river bank and the A1122 into Downham Market. It is an uncompromisingly workaday agricultural town; the first thing I see is a big sales yard with rows of neat tractors and harvesters and the second is a very big flour mill. The main couple of streets are on a small scale, with many pre-Victorian buildings and bunting flying between them. A substantial minority of the buildings are in a combination of material unknown to me, brick frames filled with layers of dark brown flintstone, each stone about an inch across. It is a rich town, though. There are quite a few Rolls Royces and on the north side of the town are a scattering of very large, new, mock-Georgian houses. I eat a snack on the hoof, as it were: my wife's shortbread washed down with a can of iced Coca-Cola.

I am always impressed by the way in which the whole mood and atmosphere of the English landscape can change almost instantly. The north side of Downham Market is quite different from the eerily empty drained lands to the south. The land rolls and is thickly wooded with tall trees, both clumped in the wheatfields and in woods of many acres. It is a settled, rich land; at discrete intervals the towers of Norman churches stand squarely up to indicate villages. I find myself walking on the very fast new, by-pass, version of the A10. I make good progress and the appalling expression, 'trade-off' comes to my mind because it is fast walking, but boring and unpleasantly dangerous: the average speed seems to be about eighty miles an hour and the draught from the lorries almost blows me over. I spot a sign with the mileage to King's Lynn. Great! It's in single figures. But, damn, as I get closer I am convinced that it is a 9. I am right. Time is pressing. What to do? The dilemma is solved when a blue Ford Escort stops alongside me and offers me a lift. The driver and sole occupant is a blond, bearded man a little older than me. He is amused by my answers to his questions and when he learns how far I have walked. He tells me that the Fens through which I have walked are flooded in winter and inhabited by thousands of Bewick's swans from Siberia. He leaves me in his home village of Watlington, with instructions on how to walk along the minor roads to King's Lynn. Watlington is a leafy, unchanging sort of place. The combination of woods and trees and gardens gives the impression that it is entirely surrounded by forest.

The six miles into King's Lynn is, frankly, a bit boring and annoying. The land is utilitarian: great rolling fields of wheat, peas and beans with few features. The road from Watlington to Wiggenhall St Germans is flanked by crab-apple trees for a while and then by giant blue-grey thistles taller than I am.

There are some deserted farmhouses though once, when I am peering at a run-down and apparently deserted cottage, an old man with white hair and moustache puts his head out of the ground-floor window and waves earnestly at me, as if glad to see someone. The annoying part is that I can see what I take to be a colossal flour mill which must be on the edge of King's Lynn, but the road will not go straight towards it, tacking west, then east and only going north in the last analysis. A green van passes me and I watch the top of it slaloming into the distance, depressed by the unnecessary furlongs I am going to have to walk. It is clouded over now and quite dark. As I never carry a watch I can no longer even estimate the time. So I try to walk very quickly at a pace rising up toward the Olympic, hip-swinging style.

From an agricultural point of view, the land is extraordinarily impressive. Contemplating twenty acres of peas I wonder why the birds don't eat them as they do in my garden. There is a kind of automatic firework which booms away every thirty seconds, but I wouldn't have thought that would frighten the average pigeon. Most of the cottage gardens are mini-farms of intensive cultivation with strawberries and every kind of vegetable. Strange: you would think that having twenty acres of peas on the other side of your garden fence might put you off small-scale growing. But this doesn't seen to be the case. Many gardens have elaborate scarecrows with pumpkin heads and one has a walking stick. I reflect that this is a uniquely agricultural part of England. In most other places agriculture goes on – prosperous and important, but a minority activity. Here, life is about agriculture.

First sight of King's Lynn confirms this impression. Outside the outer wall of the city, the new trunk A17 is an industrial estate dominated by the huge British Sugar Corporation plant which I had taken for a flour mill. Dark blue tankers marked 'Liquid Sugar' come and go. Between this new wall and the old wall is a Fison's warehouse so big you could fit some cathedrals in it. The area between the walls consists of dingy, drab little Edwardian houses and whitewashed council semis from the thirties. Inside the old wall, through the arched city gate, King's Lynn is more what I expected. There are many Georgian buildings in the dark brick I always think of as being London brick. But they are often dirty and poorly kept; the town is not as impressive as its place in the guide books would seem to imply. But I am hardly in a position to be fair, being tired and thirsty. I take a quick look at the docks and river before seeking refreshment.

Both are much bigger than I imagined. The Ouse is a majestic broad river at this point: you can see the great expanse of the Wash beyond its mouth. There are big modern harbours with medium-sized cargo vessels from all over the world and little, slimy, muddy inlets with pleasure boats and fishing smacks stuck on the banks. I find a roughish modern pub near the docks and quickly murder a pint of Norwich bitter, too fizzy for perfection but very refreshing, nevertheless (six out of ten). There are a number of small hotels and guest houses around advertising cheap bed and breakfast. Lorry drivers I imagine. Do people go on holiday to King's Lynn?

Finally, before finding the road west, we have fish and chips. I have a double portion, because they are very good, far better than I am used to. One crucial factor is that they are fried in dripping and not in the odious cooking oil. They ought to be good, though, I think to myself. There's lots of potatoes just down there and a lot of fish just up that way.

6 *The road to Bristol*

(September 1980)

I start to walk up the Avon Valley from a container park overlooking the Bristol Channel. It is a blustery autumn day; the channel itself is brown and choppy, the Welsh coast on the other side alternately glowers under cloud and has a pleasantly pastoral lightness when the sun is out.

There cannot be a more uncompromisingly utilitarian place than the industrial part of Avonmouth. As I cross over the railway on a bridge I have a general view of it. Rows of storage tanks, neat lines of containers, pipelines which carry unnamed substances from ships to trains, distant cranes. It is a functionlist's dream, a place where everything is designed simply for effective use. As I walk down the main road, parallel to the coast and towards the docks, I am, strictly, in an urban area; there are buildings on either side of the road: long, low storage and processing plants. Yet there are no people and there isn't even a pavement much of the time; where there has been one, it is broken and made useless with grass and puddles, as if some committee has decided that people don't walk here or, anyway, they ought not to. This is one of the places which we have increasingly hived off in the last generation as an uninhabited, undecorated repository for our necessities; its centres of activity being strictly modern and fundamentally important. They include smelters, oil storage depots, cold stores, chemical works and fertilizer plants.

The only grass is long and dirty, invaded by such tough weeds as thistles and teasels, remaining in those patches by the road or between the buildings which are rendered useless by size or shape. The most colourful thing I can see is the consistent stream of smoke which comes out of a tall metal chimney and blows away inland. It is a deep orange-brown colour and attracts my eyes just as it repels them, like some attractive and exotic poison.

The first signs of inhabited Avonmouth are surprising. The industrial cottages and hotels are far older than the industry, so that the whole seems like some modest little port or resort which has been surrounded and overwhelmed by something on a wholly bigger scale. I see my first people, three teenage boys walking down a side street towards me with a football. In the tradition of the old Punch cartoon one of them heaves half an apple at me as I turn my back. It misses by a long way, but I instinctively slow down as if to establish my right to be there.

I had thought of walking out to the piers and the harbour entrance, but at the dock gates a young policeman tells me that the public are not allowed in. When he sees the deference with which I treat this news he sort of changes his mind and starts suggesting ways in which we could square my visit with the Port Authority. No time for that. I make my way inland and am looking at the Indian and Pakistani Seamen's Centre when I am almost decapitated by the automatic level crossing gate of the railway I am trying to cross. The Centre looks unused and I presume it dates from the days when many British merchant lines employed entirely Asian crews (and called them all 'Laskers').

I walk towards Bristol. Navigation is no problem because it is obvious that the road must go under the most prominent feature of the landscape, the colossal curving bridge on which the M5 crosses the Avon Valley. Everything is new: the road, the motorway and the box-like coloured houses which adjoin the road. The pleasantly empty wooded hills on the other side of the valley look as if they belong to another dimension. I cross the strange no-man's land under the motorway, where no grass grows. There are several signs to the Robin Cousins Sports Centre. (What status at such a young age. I reflect with grim equanimity that I am no nearer than I ever was to having a sports centre named after me.)

Walking on the A4 is intolerably boring. I am on a perfectly adequate pavement, but sandwiched between swiftly moving traffic and utterly repetitive red-brick semis. So I strike away from the main road and river and, aided by a slightly difficult conversation about directions with a deaf local resident, pick up the Shirehampton Road to Bristol. This is a vast improvement, English suburbia at its best. In fact, it is so pleasant it might as well be called *superurbia* so different is it (and as superior as it is inferior) to genuine town or country. The road goes up and down rolling hills. It is a well-treed landscape, it has a well-maintained and varied architecture of prosperous houses and schools and is interspersed with great swathes of wood and parkland. The first of these is Shirehampton Park, sloping away towards the river, well-manicured and gleaming greenly as only English grass does in the sun after rain. Every impression of this sleek landscape is confirmed as I pass the Shirehampton Golf Clubhouse and a metallic blue Rolls Royce passes me and turns in to the car park. It is Saturday in the suburbs, a day for activity: golf, rugby, young girls playing tennis, an overweight jogger who looks a bit of a novice at it, a game of football between the sky-blues and the canary-yellows with a backcloth of dark, tall trees which surround the pitch.

By this route I reach Bristol almost imperceptibly, crossing the great expanse of grass of Durdham Downs and Clifton Downs before it is finally established that I am in a city. The Downs are flanked by huge Georgian mansions, many of which seem to be called Downside, a Downside guest house, private hospital, and so on. The street I choose to make my way to the city is flanked by two ultramodern churches in very similar styles. All Saints (Anglican) and the Catholic cathedral stand a couple of hundred yards apart, and, constructed in identical glass and concrete with metal erections above, seem a little like two women who have turned up to a party in the same dress or as if the rivalry between the two churches had reasserted itself as a competition in sixties modernism.

In general, this area of the city, Clifton, is astonishing, superb. It is, essentially, a vast display of Georgian architecture all on the same scale and in the same mood of mellow and spacious prosperity, but with attractive differences of style and materials, like variations on a theme. I see even more of it than I intended, pursuing a zig-zag course toward the suspension bridge, punctuated by several enthusiastic directions. Apropos of nothing, I notice a thick layer of moss growing on a *car*. I mention it simply because I have never seen such a thing before. It is, of course, a Morris Minor Traveller, the traditional English 'Tudor' car, and the moss is growing out of the wood. I am diverted briefly by what sounds like a riot or demonstration, but it turns out to be a schoolboy rugby game.

Every city should have a place like the Clifton Gorge, an area so physically predominant that it makes the people and the buildings of the city seem an acceptably small and integral part of the land. I pay my twopence along with many other visitors and make my way on to Brunel's bridge. I have been here before, but my memory does not do justice to it, nor even to the sheer scale of the three-hundred-foot limestone cliffs, the apparently virgin woodlands on the south bank stretching toward the westward horizon and the river itself, far below, flowing calmly through acres of sticky mud. Eastward I can see much of the city, Georgian terraces at the top and bottom of the cliff in the foreground, a great mass of churches, houses and roads in the middle distance with the ridge of the Cotswolds forming the horizon.

Back on the inhabited north bank, I find myself in Clifton's shopping area. My introduction to this is a Georgian street with a lot of small shops, bistros and so on which appears to my eye to be inhabited by a number of astonishingly good-looking women strutting about. They obviously want to be looked at, and I like looking, so we are in harmony. There are several streets like this and they give me the illusion of being in a small-scale, intimate and entirely middle-class city. The pace seems very relaxed and there are no large shops. A line of conversation sticks in my mind: a young man wearing an Aran sweater and a scarf is saying loudly to an Asian girl in expensive Western clothes, 'I've been using some of my proverbial.' She looks as mystified as I feel.

I want to see the real city centre and I ask directions to the cathedral from a tall middle-aged lady. In reply, I am treated to a monologue of civic pride in a strong Bristol accent, with the elongated vowels like so many micro-syllables. She gives me a long account which tells me I will be going 'pa-arst the longest crescent in Europe . . . and then parst ole Brunel's boat', until, eventually noticing my expression of bewilderment she adds 'Ut may not be the mos' direc' route, but it's got a lot of untrestin' things onnut.'

I do manage to follow it, descending the cliffs and walking along the river through the old docks. After Avonmouth, it all looks clean and small and rather like a museum with the masts and broad black hull of the *SS Great Britain* as its most famous item. The cathedral is plain and dignified, much smaller than it looked from a distance and almost entirely without stained glass, so that it is like a large Cotswold parish church. Inside, the choir is in full rehearsal with and audience of perhaps forty or fifty sitting and listening.

North from the cathedral across the real city centre. There are some interesting buildings and some attractive streets, but much of it suffers from the standardisation that has affected English city centres through the course of this century: the same inter-war department stores, the same post-war office blocks as can be seen in Manchester or Nottingham. But this criticism is not a complete condemnation. Pausing for a rest in Broad Quay, my eye traverses a great variety of buildings from the old warehouses across the river which are now the Bristol Industrial Museum, through an office block, and early cinema and some terraced Georgian offices, to some shops so small and old that allowing them to remain seems best justified as a visual joke.

The mixture changes markedly as I go into an area of complete redevelopment including office blocks, the Broad Mead Shopping Centre and ring roads. Three times I can only make progress by going underground, and the third time when I emerge it is to a shock: I have left the city centre and entered what is euphemistically known as the inner city. It is not shocking by the standards of Liverpool or Glasgow, but I am shocked simply because I have walked for a dozen miles without seeing anything, of any great size, that is not prosperous and well preserved. Yet here are all the symptom of advanced decay, empty shops and an old hall which is tatty but still used, all being covered with various posters. The most thriving business is a spectacularly old-fashioned pawnbrokers with its three polished balls and everything from T-shirts to gold watches in the window. And then there is the matter of race. Until I got to the (real) city centre I saw only a handful of non-white faces. Now about half the faces are black and the shops are selling chitterlings and yams and ginger.

The area of dereliction ends abruptly with a new road and several blocks of new flats. Crossing these (underground again) I enter the area of St Paul's, recently notorious for its race riots, spectacular ones, by English standards. The area seems about seventy per cent black, rather more in some of the streets, rather less in the shopping area. I had thought that, given the absence of black faces from other parts of Bristol, the problem might be one of a ghetto. But everything I see acts against that guess: in every case the predominantly black groups of children and of teenagers that I see contain at least one white face. Nor, by any extension of the language, can most of it be described as a slum consisting, as it does, mainly of streets of perfectly respectable Edwardian houses with ordinary cars parked outside in the ordinary way. Nor do I feel any sense of hostility; the few black people who give me a look at all seem positively friendly. (Quite a contrast with Avonmouth, for instance, where, apart from apple throwing, I was the object of several aggressively curious stares.)

There come several times in the life of any long-distance walker when he must just switch onto automatic pilot, using the eyes only for necessity and allowing the mind to wander in pleasant fantasies. Just cover the ground. For me, leaving St Paul's, I go into one of these phases. Without noticing detail, I cannot avoid the impression that the eastern half of Bristol is quite different from the western half. It seems an interminable domain of the respectable working class and their crowded and repetitive English houses – the Edwardian villa, the thirties semi and the modern box. I swing east from Eastville through Speedwell and Kingswood, each of which seems enormous. A slight disappointment – this is Saturday evening – is that I cannot get a sports paper. Apparently, they stopped printing the 'green 'un' because of lack of demand. Finally, going down a steep hill toward Warmley, I can see the ridge of the Cotswolds in what remains of the light. At least my destination is now within the horizon, if not by much. It is the village of Wick on the edge of the Cotswolds. Getting there, as complete darkness falls, is neither plasant nor memorable. But I get there.

7 *Aberdeen in winter*

(December 1980)

Balmedie Beach, Gordon District, Grampian Region, Scotland, on the shortest day of the year. I am standing on a sandhill, part of a range that stretches indefinitely north and south. It is not yet dawn. In the west a full moon, low and bright, still shines over the sparse, low-lying countryside dotted with simple white farmhouses. In the east the sun is reddening wisps of purple cloud above a sea neutralised to a flat calm by a west wind. Beneath my feet the sand is frozen and has a crisp, powdery texture. Directly above me a helicopter, two headlights shining in front of it, makes its way north-east to the rigs. Then another and another within two minutes, following exactly the same path. They are coming from Aberdeen, which is dimly visible to the south as the top halves of a set of tower blocks.

There is something exciting, almost illicit, about being here. I rarely see the dawn; I have never been to Scotland except in summer. I had a clear sense of going somewhere different as the 125, a kind of huge sports car on rails, accelerated out of Berwick and past the sign which marks the border. Already it seemed a bigger, wilder, tougher country. On the left were little frozen valleys which had never felt the impact of the winter sun, now setting huge and red. The hills were covered in snow and the coast above Berwick is much more rugged than the Northumberland coast. Such building as can be seen is distinctively Scottish in style. The train was mainly empty and most of my travelling companions seemed to be those young Scots, soldiers and itinerant workers, ubiquitous on British Rail, who sit chain-smoking and examining their tattoos with eight cans of McEwan's Export in front of them. Perhaps it is my imagination, but their manner seems to change north of the Border; they assume a kind of tartan swagger when they go to the loo.

I am here to visit Aberdeen. I already have a composite image of the place: granite, shrewdness, civic pride, fish, prosperity, cold, grey, oil, Americans. By now the sun is up, re-emerging, as it disappeared seventeen hours ago, as a great red ball. I have collected my thoughts and start to walk south along the clean, flat, golden beach. It is a bracing, exhilarating walk as the sun turns from red to yellow and creates a dazzling series of reflections across the sea. There are many boats, in various stages of decay, beached along this stretch. Two of them are both large and new, including the Coastal Emperor (Aberdeen), over a hundred feet long and rusting away in a dignified, upright position at the top of the beach, an 'adventure playground' designed by fate. I assume that nobody dies when a ship beaches on a coast like this and that the cost of re-floating is prohibitive. I have my own problems. Three times I have to cross rivers too deep and wide to jump or step across. Shoes and socks off. We all know this is a jolly wheeze in summer, but in winter, as you run through the ice-cold water and then continue, shoes in hand, along *frozen* sand wondering how long it takes to get frostbite and whether the water will dry before it freezes, it is no joke, at least not until shoes and socks are back on.

First sight of Aberdeen, from a sand ridge between a golf course and the River Don, is not pretty because half a dozen tower blocks dominate the middle distance. A foghorn booms away from the lighthouse on the north pier, though it is a clear day. I make my way upstream past some drab council houses, painted white but stained with damp and moss. Ordinary, domestic architecture in Scotland – which means primarily the council house – is markedly drabber and drearier than its equivalent in England. It is partly that so few in Scotland own their own homes and that there is a long tradition of low-rent, low-cost accommodation. But they do less to decorate houses than the English do. Yet dignified buildings in Scotland – hotels and town halls and the like – are often far more elaborate and decorated than in England.

I ignore the road bridge which takes the A92 traffic north towards Peterhead and follow a path up the river. The Don is very wide and still here with steep, wooded banks and an island in the middle. It reminds me a little of the river banks in Durham. But the river suddenly narrows and I cross it by the high, narrow, stone Brig O' Balgownie which has been there since 1320. South of the bridge is what seems like an ancient highland village with cobbled streets and old stone cottages, the illusion preserved from the sight of those tower blocks by the height of the river banks and the trees. A new mini-van, labelled 'Women's Voluntary Service' drives away up the steep street.

I follow it up Don Street and then go through a gap in the wall to get into Seaton Park. There now happens one of those great bonuses in the life of a middle-distance walker which make up for such things as ice-cold rivers. As I negotiate my way carefully down the steep and greasy steps which lead into the park through the leafless trees and the cawing rooks, I realise that the competence, fitness and smart scarlet tracksuits of the men playing football in the park below can only mean one thing. Right in front of me, obstructing my line of progress, is the entire squad of Aberdeen FC, the Dons, champions of Scotland.

Almost immediately I become involved in an intense argument.

There are about a dozen people, true fans, watching the practice game, in which one side wears neat green bibs over its tracksuits. I ask an old man to identify some of the players for me and he does so enthusiastically, then continues to talk about football, offering the opinion that Aberdeen would be 'murdered' if they had to play in the English First Division. This enrages the man standing next to us. He is in his late twenties, a short, stocky, handsome man with black hair and a moustache and wearing a scarlet, padded waterproof. He is standing with his small son and he turns to us and mouths the word 'Crap' with angry emphasis, though in the style of a man driven by intellectual conviction rather than aggression. An argument begins; it focuses on the recent European Cup games between Liverpool and Aberdeen. The structure of the argument is as old as sport itself. Did Liverpool win so easily because they are fundamentally better and for immutable reasons (the old man's view)? Or was it mere contingency, a consequence of injuries, fouls, refereeing decisions and Liverpool's luck in getting ahead (the young man's view)? It is, of course, irresoluble, like most good arguments and it takes some time to fail to resolve it.

Their different levels of faith are repeated in their views of the players. The young man tells me, 'There's guid young players here, really guid; players that are goin' ter be the greet names o' Scottish fitba'.' We watch Gordon Strachan, the wee man, and already a famous player, tackling back in his own penalty area as if he were playing against England. But then another player, slim and dark-haired, is pointed out and the young man tells me that he has 'more skill than anyone ah've ivver seen. More skill than Charlie Cook, even'. But the old man says, 'Ach, he's makin' nae progress, man. He can play on a Mondie mornin', he cannae play on a Sat'die.' I learn a lot about Scottish football in this conversation and one thing that is agreed is the lack of an adequate reserve league in which Aberdeen's youngsters can learn their trade. As we look at the tall and elegant figure of Marc de Clerck, the reserve goalkeeper, the young man says, 'He's in the Guinness Buk o' Records, ye ken.' Of course, I ask why, and am told, 'In the hist'ry o' fitba, he's the only Belgian goalie tie score a goal for a Scottish side in England.' Apparently it happened during a League Cup match at Berwick when de Clerck netted with an enormous punt.

Overlooking Seaton Park on its south side is St Machar's Cathedral with its dumpy twin spires. There is nobody around and I am alone inside, its eerie twilight and Presbyterian plainness contrasting dramatically with the fine day outside and the hustle of the football only a quarter of a mile away. This is the beginning of Old Aberdeen (known as the 'Auld Toon' if you own a teashop) and I go south down its main artery, which starts as Chanonry, becomes High Street and then College Bounds. It is a peaceful, prosperous, eternal sort of place. It reminds me of the vicinity of some English cathedrals when there are no tourists, except that the grey granite is distinctively Scottish. Like the rest of the town, Old Aberdeen is almost entirely made of it, with occasional decorative intrusions of the pink granite from Peterhead. But it is more varied in the old town, a riotous symphony of grey. There are low courtyards of cottages, large, stern, manse-like houses and intermediate friendly little terraces. Then there are the more elaborate buildings of the University with their gothic arches and cloisters. Walking into the quadrangle of King's College, I am reminded immediately of Oxford. The porter is called a sacrist and the stone is grey instead of golden brown. And the impression is intensified by the two people I see in the quadrangle. One is a plump, middle-aged academic, the other a slim young Chinese. As they pass, the don says, in an English accent, 'How are you? . . . Not too cold for you, I hope'. The traditional call of the dutiful teacher to the foreign student. The Chinese boy beams and nods and walks on.

Further south down Spittal the gaps between the houses to the east reveal views of Pittodrie football ground, the gasworks and the sea. What with the architecture and the calls of seagulls and the view, I am constantly assuming that I am in a seaside resort rather than a fairly large city. At the bottom of Mounthooly there is a huge new roundabout overshadowed by blocks of flats with fourteen storeys so the Old Town is entire behind me. I follow King Street to the town centre. It is broad and busy, flanked by uniform, tall, plain grey buildings. There is a strange brightness because the sun is shining on the dampness of the road, now that the frost has melted. Apparently the plainness has nothing to do with culture nor religion, but is simply because the granite is so hard and difficult to work. In Castle Street, though, is a contrasting elaboration in the Scottish baronial grandeur of the Town Hall and the Salvation Army Citadel.

I walk east and Aberdeen suddenly becomes a resort,the Amusements and cafés surrounded by the grass of the Queen's Links. As in other resorts dogs are being walked briskly along the promenade and some people are just sitting in their cars looking at the calm sea. A fat man smoking a cigarette in a turquoise Rolls Royce looks very bored. Then, at the tip of the north side of the Dee I reach the amazing Footdee (pronounced Fidee). It is a little Hebridean fishing village of low cottages and narrow cobbled streets and in it old ladies potter round tiny gardens. But it is right next to the docks and the ends of some of its streets are literally overshadowed by oil storage tanks.

The docks themselves seem busy and important. The *Ben Viking* (Kristiansand) is leaving, its stern half a tangle of mysterious pipes. Lorries come and go and strange machinery is being welded on the quay. It seems rough, tough and prosperous, but there is also a lot of dereliction, big areas of scruffy, unused ground and blackened stone buildings which are falling down.

I am hungry now and I find a small 'caff' in what seems a poorer area on the south side of the Dee. Everything is half-cooked and re-heated and I choose Scotch pie, beans and chips, 75p. It is hot and the portions are big; across the road on an unused shop I can see posters which show Mrs Thatcher as a laughing vampire with the slogan: 'NO WONDER SHE'S SMILING. SHE'S GOT SCOTLAND'S OIL'.

Across the road in the Victoria Bar I impulsively order a pint of light. It is the worst beer I have ever tasted, thin, fizzy and metallic. Then I realise that all the tables have decanters on them and that it is normal to drink chasers. I order a malt whisky which makes the light taste better. Due to a legislative miscalculation Scottish pubs can open all day now and there are people here who have no intention of leaving. The largest group of men is swearing and talking about racing in an incomprehensibly thick accent and the woman next to me is saying to one of her male companions, 'Ye've nae soul, Charlie, ye've nae soul.'

In the short afternoon I go up Torry Hill. At first I am confused by this area. The people and the cars look thoroughly working-class, but they live in great, grey detached manses. But then I realise that each front door has two numbers on it and there are different numbers on each of the side doors. Yet another peculiarity of Scottish housing. On top of the hill there is a panoramic view south of industry with hills as a backcloth, from the new sewage plant they are building on Nigg Bay, across the modern industrial estates of Tullos and Altens. Down at the bottom of the hill I finally find the smell of fish (for whch Aberdeen used to be famous) in the little fish warehouses and packing plants of Ferryhill. Predictably, two Yorkshire lorry drivers ask me the way.

I go back to the city centre, to the lights and big shops of Union Street. It is dark now and I am tired, in no mood to jostle with the big crowds of shoppers. The evening paper says that an Aberdeen skipper had been detained for using illegal nets in the Faroes. A middle-aged man reprimands a passing youth for swearing. In a quieter part of the street, the A1 Employment Agency has vacancies for tool pushers, mud sprayers and the like. But you need experience.

What of the Yanks? Apart from the odd accent and a stetson near the station (which might belong to a Glaswegian) I have seen no evidence of the American presence in Aberdeen. On the whole, they play little part in the life of the city, having their own school, newspaper and shop. So I make my way past dignified Georgian granite houses to the American Food Store in Midstocket Road. It is a small supermarket where you can buy Taco Shells and Hershey bars and Little League baseball bats. For old times' sake, I buy some tortillas, but, having done so, I calculate that I have paid approximately *twenty times* what I used to pay for them in California.

Finally, long after the sun has gone down, I visit one last corner of Aberdeen, the Winter Gardens in Duthrie Park. It is a botanical garden, a complex of greenhouses not unlike those in Kew and Edinburgh. But it is dark now and the tropical foliage is lit by hundreds of tiny night-light candles, some lining the paths, some carried by children and some floating on the ponds. A brass band is playing near the entrance and the place has the atmosphere of some fantastical, tropical grotto, a strange and, perhaps, intentional contrast to the hard, grey, ancient, modern, proud city which owns it.

8 *Down the Rhondda*

(March 1981)

It is a crisp winter morning. The mist has cleared, unveiling a blue sky and brilliant sunshine. Across the road could be almost anywhere at this latitude, from Canada to Siberia and back again the other way, because there are just fir trees and snow and the last of the mist clearing away from them. But the near side is unquestionably Welsh, even if you did not know that this place was called Mynydd Beili-glas. The long steep ridge of Craig-y-Lyn stretches away for a couple of miles, pristine and pure white except where it is so steep and rugged that the grey rock speckles the face. Below that is the black–green forest, striped with white where the snow lies in the firebreaks. And then brown grassland, dotted with mining villages toward the horizon and, beyond that, Merthyr. But the real giveaway is the sheep which, while I am looking at the view, has wandered up to within a couple of yards of me and is staring quizzically at me. This confirms one of my prejudices about Wales. In England people think sheep are silly and harmless; in Wales, it is the other way round.

I go south, into the Rhondda. It is like walking into a huge monochrome abstract painting. There are great stretches of conifer in various stages of growth, giving way to the valley, two miles across, the sides almost sheer like a great trough. There are sheep pottering busily about: although it is an 'A' road there is no traffic. In fact, there is complete silence. Three sheep come to look at me, looking over the rim into the valley. I am looking down at the first sign of industry, a drift mine, like a black amphitheatre, where a tractor is moving far below. One sheep crosses the road, the other two think about it and then follow. They have clever faces, these sheep.

The road, which has been running along a ridge, finally hits the valley bottom at Treherbert. By now the valley has filled out with a great swathe of man-made shapes, dominated by the immensley long lines of grey terraced houses. It strikes me that this is a form of life which is manifestly 'industrial', but certainly not urban, in any recognisable sense. Nobody in Treherbert lives more than a couple of hundred yards from the mountainside. I start to walk down the valley, on the main road.

Mediocre writers often get themselves, or their characters, from one place to another by implying that it is the place which changes rather than they who move: 'France became Italy' or 'Leicestershire became Nottinghamshire'. It is a usage I find irritating, but it seems unavoidable here. Treherbert *does* become Treorchy, somehow incorporating Pen-yr-englyn and Ynswen on the way. Between the two, the terrace only relents for perhaps three hundred yards, and, then, only on my right. The centres of places, if they can be called that, are only distinguishable by a higher concentration of shops. Extrapolating from the map, I begin to think of the Rhondda as one long terrace, twenty miles from end to end. Then this thought turns into a fantasy, of the whole of Wales being a single terrace, hundreds of miles long, with no two adjacent window frames painted the same colour. The whole landscape is similar to the valleys of North Lancashire and West Yorkshire, but this seems to be the extreme version.

There are few pubs, but quite a lot of clubs – most of them are called 'workingmen's' clubs – but the biggest and most prosperous in appearance, after Treorchy has become Pentre, with Ton ranging up the hill to my right, is the Ton and Pentre *Conservative* Club. This seems to bely the radical image of the Rhondda, the huge Labour and substantial Communist traditions. But then I remember what several Welshmen have told me about the Con. clubs of the valleys: 'See, you don' ave to *vote* Tory, do you? But they always 'ave the best snooker tables.'

I have passed through Ystrad Rhondda and Llweyn-y-pia and reached Tonypandy. The valley has become wider and flatter now. There is less snow on the surrounding hills, but they are as rugged and steep as before. It is after midday. I relax my pace a little and saunter round Tonypandy. Now, I already know something about Tonypandy, about how a series of riots in a prosperous, raw, new mining community in the early years of this century became mysteriously transformed by rumour and the passage of time into a symbol of class struggle, remembered long after any genuine class conflicts were forgotten. But there is no evidence to be seen of either the myth or the historical truth. Tonypandy seems like a quiet and prosperous country town. Beyond the tall grey solidity of the Edwardian shops in its main street there are the wooded hills, glowing a pale brown in the sun. It is the sort of place where you expect to see English tourists buying anoraks and walking boots. There are few graffiti, except at the railway station, and very little dereliction or unoccupied building. There is an empty shop and what used to be a bookie's and a derelict chapel with the roof coming off which has a 'SOLD' notice on it. There are a handful of youths standing talking in the street, but no more than you see anywhere these days, and many women going about their business exchanging quick, cheerful comments with one another. I buy some new bootlaces from a man who calls me *bach* which I thought real Welshmen didn't do.

I make my way to the White Hart, a solid, town-centre sort of pub. There is a single big bar inside, but there are only half a dozen people in it, even in the middle of lunch time. I order a pint of Welsh Bitter, which is clearly descended from a liquid which used to be advertised, with proper modesty, as 'RHYMNEY BEER: THE BEST ROUND HERE'. It confirms another prejudice. Next to me, as I sit, is a notice where three names have been put down to travel as supporters with the White Hart RFC. Opposite that is a notice which says 'DON'T HIT THE LANDLORD. HE'S ONLY A DWARF', though he seems very little shorter than most Welshmen. One man by the bar is saying, 'Excellent prop forward, 'e was' and demonstrating a rucking technique. I think to myself that I could have written all this without actually coming here.

After a while, more of a crowd develops round the bar, a collection of dark-haired, stocky men in anoraks and rugby club sweaters. The news is on, very loudly, on the big colour television. Nobody pays any attention to it, not even when Joe Gormley is interviewed about the future of the coal industry. Nor do they pay any attention when the Welsh news comes on, first in Welsh, then in English with what seems to be an interminable list of Welsh factory closures. There is more attention, though, and some raucous laughter, when Crown Court is on, with a witness describing the fight he had with his Irish wife.

A chunky, dark-haired man with tinted glasses joins the group. In reply to 'How's tricks?' he says, 'We've never 'ad it so bad, man', and repeats 'Never 'ad it so bad' with a huge beaming smile as if he had just said the opposite. I have a strange sensation of reality being at two levels, which is reinforced by the television weather forecast. This includes an aerial photograph of what would be the British Isles, except that the whole thing is covered with cloud. But my eye can simultaneously take in the pub window and the brilliant blue sky outside.

Leaving Tonypandy, I climb the side of the valley into Pen-y-graig where a number of rows of terraces stand at different angles on the hillside. Two boys are kicking a rugby ball on one of the streets. There is something marvellously random about a rugby ball on a steep cobbled street. If it is allowed to land, anything can happen. It can stand straight up, so that my granny could catch it, or it can dart away round your ankles down the hill, or dangerously close to a window.

I am out in the Rhondda Valley now in the narrowest sense and into a subsidiary chain of dwelling. This takes me to places with the surprisingly English names of Williamstown and Edmondstown. These seem to be rougher and poorer places. Much of the way, the terrace faces across the road to the sheer cliff of Mynydd Dinas which towers seven hundred feet directly above the houses. The bottom of the hill is an area in which the people in the terraces use for all sorts of purposes. There are pigeon lofts and old cars in various states of decay, chickens scrabbling about and a couple of rather down-market ponies. Such cars as are parked are very old and corroded. The people look poor, too, both the adults, standing and talking, and children, sitting on the steps of the houses. All in all, it is a bit of a shanty town and reminds me of parts of Lancashire that I know.

Up beyond Trebanog I decide to cut across the hills to Pontypridd so I leave the road and go into Rhiwgarn. This is a new estate, higher than almost any other settlement in the Rhondda on the edge of open country and what is, today, the snowline. It seems bleaker by far than anywhere else I have seen. Not only is it high and exposed, but the brown, pebble-dashed houses and flats lack that sense of solidity and cosiness which the old terraces have.

I make my way through a hole in the fence, out on to open country and toward the top of Mynydd-y-Glyn. Soon I am completely alone, beyond the marks of any other footsteps and ascending a great, bare plateau of snow. There is no sound except for my boots crunching into the crisp snow. Turning round I can see below a great sweep of the valley, perhaps eight or nine miles long, the endless chain of terraced houses being sometimes thick, sometimes thin, but never completely broken. I stumble on a hidden rock and my feet whip away from under me on the hard snow. I land quite heavily, but there is no harm done. It occurs to me that if I had broken my leg I might have lain and died of exposure within sight of thousands of houses. These hills are like the Pennines, only more so; the intimacy of the inhabited valleys and the wildness of the hills are both more extreme than anything in lowland England. As I sit there for a moment I notice that the other side of the valley, probably because it faces south, has less snow. It looks as though someone had decided to paint the hills white and just finished off the dregs of his old tin of paint on the top and gone off to buy another one.

In order to descend into Pontypridd I have to go through a mature forest. By local standards it is small, about three square miles, but the trees are packed so close that it is only possible to make progress through the firebreaks and felled areas, so I zig-zag, making slow progress, down into the valley. I do not like such planted forests; they lack any sense of life and character. And to me, they are made slightly sad places by the relics of the open countryside which they contain: often a bit of dry stone wall, usually collapsed, and once the remains of a farmhouse.

I approach Pontypridd through another kind of shanty town, with horses and pigeon lofts and little vegetable patches on the edge of the woods. I pass a rugby pitch with sheep grazing on it and then into a part of town which appears to be called Merlin: at least there is a Merlin fireplace factory and a Merlin School of Motoring and a Merlin pub which has an enormous plaster statue of the wizard, about eight feet high. On my way into town I pass Pontypridd Rugby Club with its new stand and its tall posts, striped black and white. The town itself seems somehow more urban than the rest of the valley, a miniature of one of the great industrial cities, dark and intimate and rather shabby.

I sit on a sheltered seat in the park to jot down a few notes. A man of about my own age suddenly joins me. He is small and wiry and wears a lumber jacket and those shoes, no longer fashionable, with big toecaps and heels. He thinks I am lost because I am looking at the map, but I explain that I am looking at where I have been. But he sits down next to me, anyway, drunk in a mellow sort of way and smelling of stale beer. He becomes fascinated by my Ordnance Survey map. 'Good map, this, eh?' he says. 'What? Bloody good map.' He points to many places on it pronouncing the unpronounceable names in a fluent, sing-song voice and seems intrigued that they are, on the map, where they really are. He is from a farm which he calls 'Gethlyooch. . . up the back o' Ponty'.

For a time we sit and talk about life and farms and forests and jobs and money and beer and houses until it is getting dark. Then he wants me to go with him to see something. But as we walk it occurs to me that we are going very much in the wrong direction for me. In any case, where is he taking me? And why? I have suspicious thoughts, but my judgement is that he is lonely and bored. I tell him I want to go back and catch the train. He looks at me in a pained way and we part.

Actually, I want to continue my notes and I do so on a bench by the bowling green in the last of the light until, to my surprise and embarrassment, he comes up to me again. We resume our conversation as before, but it is interrupted by the park-keeper who is closing the gates. He shouts at my companion, 'Get out, boyo,' he says, 'You're not allowed in 'ere. You 'ad me once, but the bloody dog'll 'ave you next time.' 'What did you do?' I ask, as we get back to the street, walking briskly. 'I 'it 'im once, see,' he says. 'Well, not so much 'it 'im really. Pushed 'im a bit. Cheerio for now.' And he turns away as I go to leave the Rhondda. A middle-aged woman is saying to her companions, 'Course they'll 'ave to give us a bloody 'oliday, now. 'E's the Prince of *Wales*, innee?'

9 *On a damp day in Dublin*

(April 1981)

'Soft, refreshing rain', the harvest hymn calls it. This morning it seems to fill the universe, persistently vertical as it leaves the sky, dripping off the trees and the goalposts and forming little rivers on the black tarmac path. I (and I alone) am in Marley Park, where the prosperous suburbs of South Dublin meet the mountains, which are dimly visible as three or four hundred feet of brown hillside under the cloud.

I begin to walk towards the city on a road which runs through damp green fields and estates of big white houses. This is called Ballinteer and steadily the houses become more numerous and the fields smaller. A shopping mall called 'SUPERQUINN' has a covered walkway and offers an opportunity to get out of the rain for a few minutes which I accept, gratefully. It allows me to satisfy a long-standing curiosity. I address myself to the question 'What do Irish children read?' in the newsagent's. The answer is, unequivocally, British comics. They read about Brits playing football and shooting Germans and the girls have magazines with pictures of Lady Diana. The adults are different from the British, though. On the sort of bookstand which, in England, would be devoted exclusively to popular novels, there is a large selection of books on Irish history including a very dull collection of essays by academic historians which I happen to have read, the sort of thing which wouldn't be found outside a fairly large library in England.

The sweet, gentle quality of the music coming out of the nearby supermarket is beginning to make me feel violent, so I leave. Something has changed. To a Lancastrian connoisseur of rain like myself there is a perceptible difference in the quality of the clouds and the rain, a certain brightening. Cautious optimism can be added to resigned acceptance.

South Dublin suburbia is solid and spacious. There are great swathes of parkland surrounding colleges, schools and hospitals, usually enclosed by long, high stone walls and anomalous squares of rich, steep meadow patched with brambles. In Dundrum it becomes more like a town, the bars and shops of the main street forming a terrace of brown brick. A man asks me, 'Now, where did they move the bank to?' In Milltown, I swing right on the path by the River Dodder which is full and foaming brown and white. It has stopped raining now and the air is left damp and fresh. At some stage the character of the place has stopped being suburban. There are no more new white houses and the dominant architecture has become the Georgian terrace. I go on through Donnybrook towards the centre of Dublin.

Walking through this southern half of Dublin leaves me with two overwhelming impressions. The first is of the complete predominance of the Georgian style, the long terraces of brown brick houses with their square windows and round-arched doors and iron railings. I find myself asking: Is it Irish? If I were just to be put here and open my eyes, would I know I was in Ireland? Is there such a thing as Irish architecture? (In Scotland, the answer to the equivalent questions would be yes, almost anywhere.) At first my answer to these questions is no, but then I think maybe there is a quality which these buildings have which marks them out from the equivalents in London. Certainly, the concentration of this style is unique to Dublin.

The other impression is of a grimmer, sadder subject. It is of the impossibility of ignoring the Northern Question or the English Question as it really is at bottom, always provided one can read. There are posters everywhere about H-block and Bobby Sands and excessive foreign influence on Radio Telefis Eireann and huge writings on the stone walls: 'BOBBY SANDS IS NO. 1, TRAITORS BEWARE' and 'RTE – BBC?' Many have been erased, but are still legible. Others are freshly painted. Moreover, although I do not want to dwell on these matters, I cannot help but see myself as half-alien, half-enemy in this place. It is not foreign, like Paris or Rome. The buildings, the cars, the products in the shops, the language, the clothes, the driving on the left, are just like England. Some things, like a double-decker bus with pictures of Smarties all over it, seem more Engish than England. But the posters and slogans and the movement they represent are more hostile to England than any other on earth. This great cultural Janus transcends the politics and life of Ireland as nothing does in England. As it happens, my only other visit to Dublin was in 1967, during what we now know was a curious lull in the intensity of the Anglo-Irish problem, when the whole thing seemed to be disappearing into the mists of history. It was easier, then, to walk round Dublin and ignore it all.

I walk along the Grand Parade by the canal. Across the canal, to the north, is evidence that Dublin is a developing, prosperous city; there are established office blocks and some still going up, including the huge offices of an antipodean insurance company. Then I turn down Leeson Street, following the signs for St Stephen's Green. Here the brown brick terrace is higher than ever and there is a strong sense of a chic professional class: the offices of advertisers and lawyers and accountants, French and Italian restaurants in the basements, neatly suited men and elegantly dressed women. For a while I sit on a bench in Stephen's Green watching the people as they hurry across in the freshness of a cold spring day and dodge the spray of the fountain when a gust blows up. I examine my map with the anticipatory pleasure of a free explorer. I am here, now, where I want to be. In adolescence I absorbed a good quantity of Irish history and literature, of Pearse, and O'Casey, of Collins, Joyce, Connolly and Yeats, so these places mean something to me.

Exhilarated, I begin a great zig-zag tour of central Dublin, down York Street and over to St Patrick's cathedral, as cool and grey as Aberdeen, and locked up. Then up Nicholas Street to Christ Church Cathedral, which is built in the same grey granite, marvelling at the further extension of the Irish paradox which gives this city two Protestant cathedrals yet no Catholic one. Through the castle, which is no castle at all, but an eighteenth-century office block with modern additions and government offices and a sort of fortified structure in the middle. Down busy Dame Street to Trinity. All of these civic buildings are in the same monumental grey stone. Trinity seems to have one great stone quadrangle after another, all of them bustling and full with students and American tourists and working Dubliners striding about their business. On to Pearse Station and over the Liffey by the Custom House. I stop on the bridge. Looking downstream I can see the ships moored along the quays and see and smell the open sea.

The classical civic buildings of this city are mixed up with scruffy little old streets, often dirty and with shops, cobblers' shops particularly, which look as if they have not changed in thirty years. One in particular intrigues me with its faded, old advertisements and team photographs from 1952-53. The door is open, but I have no possible reason to go in. Connolly Station is neat and attractive, a grey stone exterior and tiled platforms. I half expect to see the Fat Controller talking to the engines and I feel tempted to get on a train and get off again at Mullingar or Sligo.

After going north up Amiens Street and turning west towards O'Connell Street, I find myself in a very poor part of Dublin. In fact, I am not expecting the sudden and dramatic poverty of these slums; it is like steppng back into a play by O'Casey, except that things have gone downhill a bit. The brown brick tenements are in a poor state here, some half knocked-down and some just falling down. In some places they have been replaced by blocks of flats of about the same proportions as the old tenements, but there are areas of mud and rubble and puddles and litter. I am crossing one of these when I see an old woman slowly and laboriously pushing a small child in a pushchair. This is a sight – there is nothing especially Irish about it – which always makes me feel sad and emotional. Rightly or wrongly, I always assume a desertion by the parents which leaves grandmother and grandchild alone together.

I try to get a drink in a small bar in Summerhill Road. But the barman explains, with great charm, that it is the holy hour and they are closing up 'for an hour or so'. I carry on walking west. This is urban decay, inner-city, multiple deprivation – whatever jargon you prefer – as seen in England or Scotland or America with all its classic symptoms of rubble, empty buildings, and shops protected from attack by iron frames. And, of course, the writing on the wall. This is more prolific on the newer flats. But in this part of Dublin, the Dublin of the poor, the sentiments are not about nationalism, but about love and lust and strikes and evictions and Manchester United Football Club.

I stop to examine a plaque on a small street about Matt Talbot (1856-1925) who lived in a single room on that site for twenty-five years. In 1971 he was made a saint, but there is no indication why. I make some notes in order to be able to look it up, when I am surrounded by four small boys with crew-cuts who demand, 'Whatcher writin' mistehrr?' in their tough, harsh, Dublin accents which are more like Scouse than like the classic Irish 'brogue' and which make them seem streetwise and formidable. I tell them what I'm doing and one of them says,'Yerr from England, intcherr?' But this excites no enmity. In fact, one of them goes '*England* – clap-clap-clap' and they tell me about their various cousins in England. They introduce themselves – two of them are called Jimmy like my eldest son – and we talk for a while. Having found me, they seem reluctant to let me go, but they are immensely good-natured and as they clamour round me, talking all at once, one of them even asks me whether I mind them pestering me. I don't really, I enjoy it, but I must get on.

It is not far to O'Connell Street which is full of people and a complete mixture with everything from posh hotels to scruffy 'caffs' and, of course, that post office, the one with the bullet holes and the green, white and gold flag standing out in the stiff breeze. I have a packet of plaice and chips fried by two Sicilians and a quarter of Turkish Delight. For a few minutes I play on Blackjack and Poker machines until I have lost 70p. Then I turn west along the Liffey by Bachelor's Walk and the Quays, past many ill-kempt and intriguing 'rooms' full of furniture and antiques, past the Guinness brewery on the other side of the river, and past the Courts on my side and after them the Collins Barracks, where some very unfit-looking soldiers are doing fatigues running round their field in their boots, and where I ponder whether there is an reason for the green paint on the iron railings to be splattered with red patches.

And from there to Phoenix Park which begins as an arrowhead of green between Conyngham Road and Infirmary Road and then broadens out into an enormous park, so that is seems to be a wedge of the great vastness of rural Ireland pushed right into the heart of Dublin. I have heard that it is the largest park in Europe, but I would think that, like most fascinating facts, this claim would vanish, under examination, into a mist of semantics. As I sit for a moment on a wooden bench between the Polo Ground and the Zoo the sun comes out, completing the transition of the day. Blue sky is increasing by the yard now and the mountains are clearly visible beyond the city. The park sparkles with a vivid damp green in the sun.

I go north, through the polite, comfortable semis of Ashtown on the edge of the Park and over to Cabra and then Finglas. This is brand new Dublin, industrial estates and hundreds of neat, white, identical houses like an English council estate. But, there are some special features; I have never seen so much litter, nor so many children, nor as many graffiti, here of every kind, 'ASTON VILLA' right next to 'BE IRISH: SUPPORT THE I.R.A.'. Then I go over to Balymun, Dublin's only high-rise residential development on the edge of the open country and like those in Birmingham or Berlin but rather less kempt than either. Here, at last, I have a pint of Guinness in a place called 'The Towers' next to the Garda Station. It is a huge place, more like a club in Northern England than a pub and now, not yet seven o'clock, it is already full, not a woman in sight and a Paul Newman film showing in the corner on a small cinema screen. So much is Guinness the norm here that I do not need to order a drink. The barman just gives me one and says 'Point? 72p.' And one final thought, as I ingest the smooth bitter liquid. Dublin is as class-divided a city as I have ever seen, with the working class living in the north, and those great varieties of people called the middle class living in the south.

10 *Cowes that cannot be milked*

(July 1981)

At the very last minute, legislatively speaking, the House of Commons amended the 1972 Local Government Act to make the Isle of Wight a separate county, England's smallest. In doing so, they took away a personal record which I had held since childhood, that of having been in every English county.

Now, after a dignified pause, I have come to reclaim my record. So I am standing on the top deck of the *Cowes Castle* from Southampton, along with coach-loads of German teenagers and a boys' cricket team, from Dorset, by their accents. Our ship is constantly hooting to warn the innumerable small yachts which fill the mercifully narrow, choppy stretch of the Solent between the calm of Southampton Water and Cowes. The Germans are beginning to sing, even though it is still quite early on a grey summer morning.

This particular boat stops first at (West) Cowes and then at East Cowes. This gives us the chance to see the West Cowes waterfront as the ferry glides into its mooring. It is a fine mixture of a place: little landing stations, old cottages, a very modern white hotel which belongs by rights in a campus university, garish pubs, a modern house with a swimming pool and a huge pink boathouse with a colossal figurehead. East Cowes is more modest; as we swing towards it the waterfront is dominated by the hangar-like building of the British Hovercraft corporation. We disembark with a speed and efficiency born of routine. Two of the cricketers immediately in front of me are looking at the sky, at the layer of low, grey cloud, immobile but probably innocuous. 'We sh'll getta game, oi s'pose,' says one,' 'but the loight won't be too good.' 'Ner moin tha', what 'bout this disco?' his companion mutters.

As a walker I find that my mind has certain rhythms of desire. Go fast. Go slow. Get away from the people. Move towards them. Now I want to get quickly away from the quay and the people, up the hill past the big, detached brick houses and towards Osborne House, which could be seen from the boat and which was built by Cubitt and the Prince Consort for Queen Victoria. On my map there is a road which leads south through the grounds which will allow me to see the house *and* move on south. The notice on the gate says that the public can visit the house, but that part of it is used as an officers' convalescent home. I check on my plan with one of the guards on the gate. He is wearing a black uniform and is handsome and dark-skinned with a jet black beard. To my surprise, he replies in a South African or Rhodesian accent. 'Ah no,' he says, 'that is private property.' 'But there is a road marked,' I persist. 'It is private property,' he repeats, as if that was all that could be said. For a part of a second I have a strange feeling that I have come further south than I intended.

I make my way to the house. At the turnstile I persuade the lady in charge to let me in to see the house and take a picture without paying the full fee to go round. She agrees, adding cheerfully, 'You'll get me lynched, dear.' It confirms one of my rules of thumb; you can get English officials to bend the rules for you, provided you never assert any right to have them bent. The house itself is unnattractive. I can see its plain, grey, Italianate towers across the lawn and through the cedars. Albert's hand in it was probably a heavy one.

So I have to retrace my steps and carry on south by the main road. I cannot resist the next available diversion, this time to Barton Manor Vineyard. I have a mind to try the local product, in the manner of travellers in vineyards throughout the ages. So I make my way up through a field of maize, the Osborne tower and its Union Jack still visible in the distance, and follow a path marked 'pedestrians' through a wood. Then on a tree there is a notice, written in a more direct style than these things usually are. It damns English licensing laws, then it damns the miserable summer of 1980 and says that what little they were able to make has already gone. I follow the path to a kiosk where you can pay 80p to see round the vineyard. A family from London in front of me pay and go in. There is no one else about, except the occupant of the kiosk, a burly, aristocratic sort of chap whom I would expect to run a vineyard. I do not have time for a tour, but I ask him about the vines. They are, he says, waist-high and flowering: should be a lot better than last year. Then I ask him about the road which, on the map, runs south from his house. Not a right of way, apparently. But could I get through? 'The farmer would probably shoot you', then, as he sees my face, 'Nothing to do with me, I wouldn't shoot you'. So back to the main road, feeling somewhat frustrated. It is busy and boring.

But after a few hundred yards I do find a satisfactory way to go south. I make my way down towards the river, following the signs for the Folly Inn down a narrow road between shacks which are described as 'mobile homes' which which are no longer mobile and are unlikely to be thought of as home. The inn itself is a modern, white pub down on the broad estuary of the River Medina. There are a lot of cars round it, but not half so any as there are boats. There are boats moored right across the river, and boasts on the mudflats and boats on the grassy banks. There is that rattle you get around yachts, a rattle of steel coil flapping against aluminium masts and similar contacts. I think to myself that if they re-run Dunkirk we'll cream it. (Ah! But have the chaps got the moral fibre?)

In walking terms the world has come right now, because I can follow the Medina Trail south to Newport. It is a good clear path which runs through thickets sandwiched between fields and the mud-banks. There is a strong estuary smell of fish and salty rottenness which make me fancy a plate of shrimps with lemon juice and pepper and brown bread and butter. Every few hundred yards there are men in wellies digging for shellfish. In general, the river has a workmanlike air to it. There are medium-sized boats, barge-sized and tug-sized along the far bank. Then, on my side, there are two big paddle steamers laid up. One of them, the Medway Queen, looks to be decayed well beyond any possibility of salvation. But someone is trying. There is the chug-chug of a diesel-driven bilge pump and water slurping out of a red pipe which protrudes from a hole high on the hull.

The Medina Trail is a real pedoway; it has wooden bridges over every stream and swamp. Even so, I see only two groups of people on it, both middle-aged and sun-tanned, wearing yachting shoes. Newport, when I arrive, seems at first like a toytown version of the East End of London, because I arrive in its port, with its crumbling wharves and small factories and warehouses related to the islands' need to import. But, crossing the river into Quay Street, I find what I had expected, busy Georgian streets and the sense of a rustic capital. 'MAN DIES IN PARKHURST STABBING', say the billboards. I queue for fish and chips in St Thomas's Square, behind three boys who are struggling to work out whether 3 x 17 = 51. One thinks it makes 54. I leave them to it. I eat cod, chips, pickled onion and a curry roll on a bench by the church. The food is pretty good, but the ice-cold can of lemonade gives ecstasy as it slips over my throat, dry with the morning's exertions.

Further on, in the High Street and Castle Street and St James' Square, there are shoppers, moving briskly, and tourists wondering what to do next. The town remains charmingly small-scale, its business conducted in the neat Georgian terraces of shops, hotels and offices. The finest building is Nash's elegant little Guildhall. I think about popping into a pub, but decide to leave it and follow the signs for Carisbrooke Castle. I go up a steep road with the castle on my right. Charles I was imprisoned there (1647-49) and, as the hill becomes a ridge, I have a good view of its walls and mounds and cannons and car parks. I am looking for a long-distance footpath called the Shepherd's Trail and I find, it just where it ought to be, leading up the downs in an angle made by two minor roads.

It is not as I imagined, an open chalky path. Instead, it is a narrow path between two high banks, perhaps eight or ten feet high. The banks have small trees growing out of them and these trees overlap and interlock above the path. So it is like going up a long, ascending tunnel, dark and eerie, full of primitive vegetation like ferns and hartstongues. The sun has come out now, but my only sight of it is through tiny gaps in the foliage above. The experience of walking in this tunnel is physically unpleasant, being damp and enclosed and full of insects. But it is strangely reminiscent of childhood stories. The primitive part of me is excited by what might be at the other end of such a tunnel.

The answer is broad beans; a huge field of them on top of the downs and the sight of unlimited green, rolling country. Now the walking is of that unique downland kind, the easiest in the world, over firm springy grass. The first people I see are four boys and four girls – in their twenties, but feeling like boys and girls because they are playing leap-frog and rolling on the grass and laughing. Only yesterday there were riots in twelve English cities, so what is reality? My presence spoils their game; they move on, opening the gate to let me walk ahead.

I come to the higher part of the village of Gatcombe, but it is not recognisable as a village in the ordinary sense, just three large inhabited houses and a derelict farmhouse high and quiet among the wooded downs. A white horse stands motionless by the derelict farmhouse, as if he had been chosen to go with the scenery.

From this point I get lost. I follow a bridle-path up a valley, but then it stops and I pick my way up the thin line between wheat and barley to the woods and along the edge of the woods. I am enclosed by the downs which form a great horseshoe with cereals in the valley and woods along the ridge. It is deep country, an enclosed place and a man from the town alone here must feel alert, apprehensive. Five partridge chicks blunder out of the woods in front of me and then two rabbits make a dash into the woods. The valley becomes steeper and the crops end. From the sloping meadow perhaps a dozen rabbits run for the woods and then a group of twenty or more. I have never seen so many rabbits. But two big hares, who had been sitting upright close to the rabbits, refuse to panic and lollop calmly away in the other direction. They know a man without a gun when they see one.

Up over the ridge, following a trail of cartridge cases. Rabbits everywhere. At the top I am on a very steep ridge below which I can see a road and a farmhouse. And a *black* rabbit which moves away into a clump of thistles. Honestly! For several miles I follow the road south between fields of barley, oats, beets and sprouts, heading for the high ridge of St Catherine's Down. In the spread-out hamlet of Chale Green I buy two cans of cold Coca-Cola from the garage/general dealer. His newspaper stand says: 'ISLAND PETROL TO GO DOWN SHOCK'. His petrol is the most expensive I have ever seen.

St Catherine's Down is higher and rougher than the others, steep with much gorse. At the top is a fourteenth-century stone space-rocket called St Catherine's oratory, once used as a lighthouse. Up here, I have the greatest sense of having made it which I have ever had as a walker. Below me is the sea, shining and infinite in the late afternoon sun. From side to side stretch the cliffs of the south coast of the island.

Until evening I explore the Undercliff, a strange piece of country caused by the ancient collapse of the chalk cliffs. The cliff itself is now a steep ridge half a mile inland and thickly wooded. Much of the Undercliff is wooded, too, dotted with smallholdings and greenhouses. At Puckaster Cove I go right down to the sea on a barely discernible path through the densest of dense vegetation, an impenetrable mass of grasses, shrubs and brambles stretching across the broken chalk ridges to the thin sliver of beach. And the houses. Through gateways and down drives I can see the detached houses, neat lawns gleaming in the sun and the sparkling blue sea beyond the palm trees and cypresses and cedars. Retired people, I presume. It seems everything the word 'south' can connote, especially to a northerner; it is sleek, rich and warm.

As time is pressing I hitch a lift with a Geordie into Ventnor. He has moved down here, he says, but does not really respond to the feelers of my curiosity about why he has moved here (he is in his twenties) and what he does. I have always fancied Ventnor on the map, a remote place with a strange name. Nor does it disappoint me, being a genteel little resort exotically placed between the sea and an eight-hundred-foot wall of woods on St Boniface Down. I make a mental note to come for a holiday here sometime. But, then, there are a lot of places on that particular list.

11 *A long walk to the chip shop*

(August 1981)

Mountain is a place in West Yorkshire on the road between Queensbury and Denholme. Not that much of a place, really, but like a lot of places in the Pennines – some solid, black stone houses along the main road and occasionally behind. One of them is the pub, the Mountain Eagle, which gives the place its name.

I am on the cricket field which is above the road and the houses. 'Mountain' seems appropriate here, for the cricket field is the top of a hill flattened off, with consequent difficulties of retrieving the ball in almost every direction. The dry-stone wall at the far end behind the bowler's arm is whitewashed to provide an immovable sight-screen. Six boys are playing cricket on the outfield. Northwards I can see the moors. Behind me and to my right are the buildings of Mountain. But my eyes are inevitably drawn to the east, below the ridge, where, in the middle distance, the land begins to fill up with houses and mills: Bradford.

I am feeling personally as well as physically on top of the world. I had a good night's sleep. The day has suddenly revealed itself as a beauty, the last wisps of cloud disappearing in the sun. But most of all I feel good because I am back in the North of England with all day just to wander round. I am from Lancashire and this is Yorkshire, but there is a homeness, a familiarity about this edge of the Pennines which makes it all but indistinguishable from the place I call home on the other side. The hugeness of the view, towns and moors stretching away indefinitely. The tiny fields with their black stone walls. The great variety of flowers and grasses in those fields, which have never been ploughed. The plump, workaday ponies whch graze the fields and carry the young girls ponderously up and down the narrow lanes.

I follow a path which is an overgrown road down the hill towards Bradford. The path meets a metalled lane. It is a well-populated countryside, dotted with big stone houses and occasional terraces of cottages. The first person I see is a man getting out of a van. He greets me enthusiastically: 'Grand day, eh? Ideal.' 'Lovely,' I reply. Shortly after this I come to a pub called the Junction where my lane meets Carter Lane. I order a pint of John Smith's and sit outside the pub in the warm sun, reflecting that up here you scarcely need a map; you can always *see* the lie of the land.

But further down I lose sight of Bradford and am, for a time, in a quiet country valley. I see a terrace of cottages, shimmering in a heat haze on the far side of a rich meadow. Everything is made of dark stone. Everybody speaks to the passing stranger. Woman smoking cigarette in garden says, 'Lovely day, eh?' and I say, 'Grand.' Tractor driver says something incomprehensible through the roar of his engine. Boy pushing bike uphill says 'Alloh' breathlessly. Man who gets off back of younger man's motor bike says 'Tha'll kill thissen on that bloody thing, that's fer certain,' and looking at me and raising his eyebrows, adds 'Ah doant know.'

Bradford comes into view again, this time much closer, and soon I am in Clayton. It is an old, prosperous place. There are a couple of small mills, a few new houses, and some beautiful old cottages with their cobbled squares and back streets. In one of them, called Bank Fold, an old lady in black has taken her tables out into the square and is scrubbing them. At the roundabout which seems to mark the centre of Clayton it says 'City Centre 3', emphasising that strange sense of distance which you get in English conurbations.

On to Lidget Green, more suburban now, the solid Victorian and Edwardian houses enlivened by the garish colours of the roses in their gardens. Somewhere between Lidget Green and Great Horton or maybe Little Horton I buy a meat and potato pie, a thing filled with a beautiful brown gunge and tasting mainly of onions. On impulse I abandon all pretence of a planned route, and swing randomly away among the terraced streets, eating my pie. I am in an area of long, brown stone streets. From having seen only white faces for miles, immediately everyone is Asian. The houses are well maintained and the streets are full of children playing. Many of them are blocked to traffic at one end so they seem cosy and safe. Some are paved over completely. On one of these skateboarding appears to be having a revival and a small Asian boy calls out to another, in a thick Yorkshire accent, 'Ah'll see if ah can get our kid's skateboard.' But further down the road three older boys are talking in Urdu.

On a nearby playing field I note the almost exact racial mix of the boys as they play cricket and chase each other and lie in the sun. I have seen the same phenomenon in many English cities and in itself it seems encouraging, but will they grow up like this, or divide into warring factions of skinheads and black power fanatics? Social science has no answers. And the girls, anyway, do not mix on the streets. I pass the surgery of an Asian doctor, his immensely long name and complicated surgery hours painted in two scripts. Opposite, on the railway bridge, is the unfinished sentiment: 'KILL THE CAPITALIST SWIN.'

The railway itself is no longer used and the track has been removed. It is overgrown with long grasses and saplings and purple flowers. There are many things dumped on it, including much of the property of a Chinese-Malayan student at Bradford University (judging from his name, address and Malayan newspapers). I follow it for a while and then abandon it as impenetrable and return to the road. There is a park, grand and appealing, on the other side of the road, with its terraces of stone steps going up the hill and its vivid flower beds. Then I am alongside a high stone wall. There are some doorways in the wall, bricked up. Beside one of them is painted 'Boys 25p'. In a flash, I know what it all means. The road is Horton Park Avenue, once the home of Bradford Park Avenue Football Club, kicked out of the League in 1970. Round the side, where the wall has collapsed a bit, I manage to scramble up and, clutching the barbed wire, I can just see into the ground. It is still recognisably a football stadium, but the terraces are covered with rubble and weeds and the pitch with just weeds. It is a miserable sight, like a foretaste of the end of the world. On the other hand, Park Avenue *cricket* ground which I can now see to my left and where Yorkshire play four times a year has a big handsome Victorian pavilion and, alongside that, a high bank of new seats.

By Bradford College playing fields and within a mile of the city centre I seem to have returned to rural Yorkshire in an area called Horton Green. There is a grand Georgian house, now used as a middle school, with a properly cut cricket strip on its playing field and a row of stone cottages and an old dark manor house which must be four hundred years old if it is a day.

I approach the city centre from west, down Morley Street. There is a smell of curry from the restaurants and of spice from the shops. A man is crouching on a broad part of the pavement, his wares, dinner jackets and gas masks and Victorian family portraits and that sort of thing, spread out alongside him. Virtually everyone is Asian and their talk and these sights and the unaccustomed heat of the day combine for a moment to create an exotic atmosphere, as if I were thousands of miles from those small meadows and dark stone houses instead of a very few.

It occurs to me, as I rest on bench by the statue of Queen Victoria immediately overlooking the city centre, that if you came back to Bradford and hadn't seen it for thirty years, it would be unrecognisable. Immigration has changed its society and redevelopment has changed its physical nature. Never mind 'if', I used to come here with my mother in the fifties to do the Christmas shopping at Brown Muff's and Busby's and it *is* a great shock, this shining, modern multi-racial city which has replaced the old, dark, Yorkshire one that I know. It is dominated now by the elegant offices of the Provincial Building Society.

Actually, the view from Queen Victoria is slightly misleading. The provincial building also incorporates many of the council offices, presumably the result of a planning 'deal' in the sixties. Between that and the old, Germanic town hall there is a square of trees and flowers and grassy mounds. Today the redevelopment has finally come good. There are many young people lying and sitting on the grass, including a beautiful blonde girl, dressed for the summer, whose male companion cannot keep his hands off her. And the shopping streets are an improvement, too, being mainly free of traffic in the modern style. I find myself following a colourfully dressed group of Asian girls and I notice that Brown Muff's is now Rackhams. Naturally, it has a sale on.

Up the hill, east of the centre. After about half a mile I face an acute dilemma. My final destination is Guiseley, north of Leeds and Bradford, and I can get there easily if I turn north now on the Harrogate road. But this seems too easy and I have a strange desire to walk to Leeds. My climb takes me into a park, steeply overlooking the city, which is now bathed in a heat haze. Several games of cricket are going on among the Asian boys. One of them comes up to me and says 'Excuse me, would you do me a favour?' 'What?' 'Thump this idiot', pointing at a much larger boy. 'But he might be skilled in the martial arts,' I reply and they all laugh.

For a couple of miles I walk briskly by the busy dual carriageway towards Leeds and then I leave it when it becomes a new ring road. I follow the old road into Stanningley and along a scruffy little valley, small factories mixed with pubs and houses and tiny shops, like many such old valleys in the north. A pub called Halfway House tells me, or so I presume, that I am half-way to Leeds. There is a hill, grassy and flat-topped, so I climb it. It is no ordinary hill, the top is symmetrically flat and feels hollow, though well grassed, and has a television mast and numerous chimneys. To the north is open country, a lush green valley and high purple moors. To the south-east the city is still some way off. In the playing field on the other side I ask a man in his vest, fat and pink from the sun, what it is. 'They call it the reservoir,' he says, 'but, actually, it's a pumping station.'

Now I am in an area of tall terraced houses. They are made of a dark red brick, an oppressive shade which seems common in Leeds, but rare elsewhere. They lack the cosiness and the charm of Bradford's stone houses. To my prejudiced imagination they seem the sort of places where psychopaths and novelists might be born. It is an area of white people and somehow much more slummy, at least to look at, than anything in Bradford. The children are not smartly dressed and many of the adults are in vests, sitting on the steps or tinkering with their cars.

I pick up the main drag again, now with a clear view of the city centre. It looks the perfectly despoiled city, with much less charm and distinction than Bradford. There are deserted terraces of houses, in that ugly dark red brick. There are swathes of wasteland and new box-like factories and warehouses surrounded by wasteland. There are even two unkempt adolescents sitting banging things on a heap of rubbish as if waiting for the colour supplement photographers to show up. Quite frequently, the green and white buses pass, with the panel-length advertisement which says 'PUT YOUR' – and then a picture of woman's buttocks in tight jeans – 'ON A BUS'. I amuse myself wondering how many words I can put in place of the picture, get into double figures and then give up. An electronic screen on a modern tower gives alternate readings: 1632 (time, not date); 74°F.

Vaulting barriers and sprinting carriageways, I make it to the citadel of Leeds which is surrounded by a moat of freeways, underpasses, car parks and scrubland. It is far better, now I am in it, than it looked from the outside. The great main street of Leeds, the Headrow, is now largely free of traffic. It has a self-conscious grandeur to compare with any city in Europe. Especially that colossal town hall; most countries don't have parliaments to compare with Leeds Town Hall. Behind the Headrow is the elegant little Park Square, its Georgian offices overlooking a colourful display of flowers. I ask a newspaperman the way to the bus station and he tells me, adding 'It's a fair bit walk.' 'Not by my standards, mate,' I think to myself, and thank him.

At the bus station I catch the 733 to Ilkley, stopping at Guiseley. At Guiseley is the world famous Harry Ramsden's fish and chip shop, possibly the largest in the world and certainly one of the best. So as I take my seat on the bus, my mind is already lingering on the prospect of large haddock, chips and mushy peas with a pot of tea and bread and butter. Well deserved, too.

12 *A day in the forest*

(September 1981)

If days were chaps this one would be a moody, mad bastard of a fellow about whom a charitable headmaster might write at the end of his report: 'He does have a style of his own, though, and might be worth persevering with.' Fifteen minutes ago there was a purple-black sky and it was raining the kind of rain that soaks you to the skin in the time it takes to run up a suburban drive. Now the sun is out and the puddles are a shiny blue, the vast expanse of the Severn estuary is sparkling, though its underlying colour is still brown.

I am at Lydney docks where a canal from the industrial part of the town of Lydney meets the estuary. On the other side of the water is a low wooded ridge, the line broken by two big refineries. It seem unnatural that this enormous obstacle should merely divide two parts of Gloucestershire, but in some long forgotten battle of the dark ages those who spoke the Germanic tongues pushed the Celts across the Severn and have held on to this corner of land ever since. It seems equally unnatural that the long piece of string, stretched and unsupported between two distant pillars should be a *road* carrying a motorway. It looks elegant and fragile in the distance.

One man is visible, having emerged from the small office on the quay to stretch his legs in the sun and check that I am not a vandal. The harbourmaster (which I presume is his title) is a middle-aged man in a pale blue sweater who is picking brambles from a bush on the quay. He seems pleased enough to talk to me. No, there is no commercial traffic these days, he says, since the iron and coal in the forest stopped production about a generation ago. But quite a few yachts go up and down and the industrial estate still thrives using land transport. There is talk, though, of starting mining again, opencast, 'God forbid'.

I choose the higher, drier bank to go to Lydney, a dyke between the canal and the estuary. Nameless machinery is grinding away in the industrial estate on the other side of the canal and there is a pile of huge tree trunks outside one plant. Smoky black clouds have come up from over South Wales and for a time they subject me to the irritating sensation of being rained on from a blue sky as that is all I can see looking forwards. But then we part, the clouds taking their usual route, north-east to the Midlands. There are hundreds of bramble bushes, all covered with fat, black fruit. (If you are serious about picking brambles this is the sort of place, near an industrial estate, not somewhere pretty.) Between the town and the factories, by the railway, is a very distinctive, long terrace of houses, in grey stone with steep gables like sharp arrowheads over the houses and smaller but similar ones over the porches.

This turns out to be the most interesting building in Lydney, which is otherwise a pretty ordinary sort of place. There is an impressive market cross, though, with two boys sitting on its high stone steps. As far as I can see the oldest buildings are a couple of Georgian houses. Generalisation: do not expect to find interesting collections of buildings where wood has been plentiful. Take, for instance, North America.

One suburban street and I am in the forest walking on the 'B' road. It is a thick forest, virtually impenetrable on either side, varied and opulent. There are fat brambles, glossy black elderberries and yellow and green crab-apples. More unusually there are plenty of sweet chestnuts. At the cost of some pain I pick one of these green porcupines and manage to split it open on the road. There is a sizeable chestnut in it, not yet ripe. Now that is impressive. Usually in England they contain only skin and virtually no flesh. I have a powerful affection for them and considerable fascination. I like the taste, but also the image of collecting them in late autumn and roasting them on the fire. Legend has it that the Romans planted them here to make a special bread for the legions. The more boring theory is that landowners brought them back from Italy in the nineteeth century.

After about a mile the forest officially starts with a notice announcing the Forestry Commission's suzerainty and some of its regulations. Opposite that, a track leads to the 'Steam Centre' of the Forest of Dean Railway Society. It is a railway station with a ticket office and a shop. There is a lot of old rolling stock, much of which is unlikely to move again. This is not a 'steam day', nothing is going on, so there are four tourists, including myself, mooching round the platform and looking at the engines and the carriages. A young lad in blue overalls is in charge. He is sitting on the step of a carriage, taking the sun which shines through a clearing in the forest and gleams on a bright blue train. There is no sound except for grasshoppers and occasional birdcalls. For a moment I am not me and this is not Gloucestershire, but rural Russia long ago and I am a minor nobleman patiently waiting for the Moscow train to arrive. Still three days to go!

The next village, Whitecroft, is a good antidote for such fantasy. It is a workaday, modern place, not the idyllic English village at all. We are obviously near the Welsh border because a notice on the wire fence of a small industrial estate warns that 'ANY SHEEP FOUND TRESPASSING ON THESE PREMISES WILL BE IMPOUNDED AND THE OWNERS WILL BE CHARGED.' A small factory a little further on is Nash and Morgan, 'Coachbuilders' as their sign says; nowadays that means exotic cars. But my attention is drawn to another car for sale in Whitecroft, a rounded, grey A35, at least twenty years old because its registration mark has no dating letter at the end. I have many sentimental memories of A35s, the van version mainly, and I have recently nurtured a wistful desire to have one as a second car. So it is perhaps just as well that I have no means of paying the £275 asked.

There isn't much to Whitecroft. The edge of the village is marked by an ancient garage with modern prices and some apprentices playing football. Then back to the forest and some immensely tall trees, Corsican pines being the tallest of all. Just outside the village it occurs to me that I could have test-driven the A35, albeit on a slightly dishonest basis.

The next village, Parkend, is equally unromantic. So far, all the inhabited places have confirmed my theory about wood and building. This a a modern place and the largest artefact is a caravan sales yard. A lot of teenagers, many of the girls looking very attractive, are emerging, booted and anoraked, from a couple of minibuses. Introductory arboriculture, I surmise. Leaving Parkend, I also leave the road and make my way on a track through the forest where, after about a mile, I eat my picnic lunch. It is extremely quiet, an ancient tranquillity which tourists seek and rarely find.

After lunch, like a good citizen, I put my organic refuse among the undergrowth and re-pack the rest. Now begins the central part of my journey, an uninterrrupted five miles or so through the centre of the forest. Over lunch a couple of black clouds appeared and spat rain threateningly, but now the sun is shining brightly and with every sign of permanence. This helps to alleviate my main worry, the difficulty of keeping a sense of direction in the forest. At first, though, I am on a track which obviously corresponds to one marked on the OS 'Landranger' map and which heads due north, so the task is easy. The track appears to have once been a metalled road. The atmosphere is different from most other forests I have crossed, mainly abroad. For one thing there is no dominant species. There are ancient beech and oak trees and conifers of every size. Sweet chestnuts are very common, some covered in prickly nuts and some with none. There are many crab-apples; one tree has big, yellow fruit, so I try one, but it is as sour as any crab-apple, though probably excellent for wine or cooking. Curiously, only the sycamores, usually so tough and adaptable, are diseased: their leaves are covered with jet black spots as they are in many other parts of England. Jays sometimes call in the trees and there is a an incessant presence of grasshoppers by the side of the track. Perhaps I notice these two kinds of creatures because I am not used to them. On this evidence, nobody ought to accuse the Forestry Commission of creating gloomy, lifeless forests. More often it is private foresters who do that. Twice I see a rather exotic, largish bird with a yellow-green rump which may be a woodcock. Only once is it clear that the forest was once inhabited; a bit of old stone wall is clearly visible and the remains of a cottage can be barely discerned among the trees.

After I cross the B4226 (Broadwell to Cinderford) life becomes much more difficult. The path is dark and narrow and my rucksack catches on the trees. There are obstacles at fairly regular intervals, sometimes wire fencing, but mostly fallen trees. My guess is that these have been deliberately left to discourage motorcyclists. For the first time walking in these islands I regret not having a compass. Soon I recognise that track of the old railway and follow that broad highway for a while. It occurs to me how strangely encouraging it is that this forest is an ex-industrial area, bringing back arguments and ideas in Nan Fairbrother's *New Lives, New Landscapes*. Many a mining area could become like this; some already are – I remember that only recently I was in a forest in one of the oldest of the mining areas around Wigan.

Unfortunately, the old railway is not really going my way, so I take a path and cross the B4234 (Lydney to Lydbrook). There are a couple of walkers, the only people I have seen since leaving the road. We comment in the usual way on the improvement in the weather. Now the navigation becomes really difficult. Using the sun as a guide I try to go north-west, but there is no path in this direction and I have to zig-zag. Up a beautiful grassy path among ferns and oak trees, then along a broad track but it veers in the wrong direction and I try to make my way through the forest without a path. This is hopeless: I am cracking dead wood and wading through ferns. The author of *Scouting for Boys* would have a fit and the Boers and the Apaches or whoever we imperialists were supposed to be scragging would hear me coming a mile away.

But I never quite lose my way, thanks to the sun, and I emerge at last on the A4136 (Gloucester – Monmouth). I would like to go up to somebody and ask them, in a manner entirely appropriate to someone who has been wandering in a forest for several hours: 'Excuse me, where am I?' But there is nobody except people in fast cars and I have to back my own judgement that this is the 'A' road and that I should turn left. Before long, my judgement is confirmed by a sign to English Bicknor and I follow it. Another mile and the forest ends with a superb sunlit view of rolling hills, most of them in Wales.

There are several interesting things on the narrow lane to English Bicknor. There is Eastbach Court, a grey Georgian mansion with a huge cedar tree in front of it. And there is a curious milestone, three feet high, which says 'Gloucester 17, London 122', suggesting that this tiny, deserted road was once a highway of some importance. The village is everything which the villages of the forest are not. It is on a hill, with a square stone church and solid stone and whitewashed houses. There is nobody about except for two boys wheeling aimlessly about the main street like two seagulls in the sky.

I am quite close to the end of my journey now. Although I do not know it yet this mad, moody day has a strange adventure of the senses in store for me. I find the path, virtually overgrown, through the woods towards the Wye. The river banks themselves are dark and dank; they drop steeply hundreds of feet below me. It clouds over again and begins to rain. I scurry on through the woods, feeling a little like the White Rabbit in *Alice* (except that the duchess is my wife). Way below I catch a glimpse of the river suddenly gleaming in the sunlight. Then the world turns grey again and there is a deafening hiss of gales and heavy rain simultaneously. I have a fear that trees will fall or that I might be swept off the cliff, but it settles to heavy rain and I hurry on to Symonds Yat.

This is a very famous view or beauty spot, now organised as such by the Forestry Commission with toilets and a snack bar. As I get there it is raining heavily, but the sun suddenly comes out and I run across a bridge to the viewpoint itself. There, below me, is the river and the steep, wooded banks backed by purple clouds, except that the whole scene is now brilliantly illuminated by the sun and bisected by a vivid double rainbow. Two men with a camera, one English, one foreign, run up behind me, but they have almost missed it. The foreign one says 'Come quickly. Is beautiful, is incredible. Quick, the camera. Is fading.'

This mad day has had his moment of genius. All else is anti-climax, though there is considerable satisfaction in finding that the ferry across the Wye actually works. It takes me some time to hail the ferryman, standing in a field of maize and whistling at the pub opposite, but he eventually emerges, aged about sixteen and rather too well-dressed for the part, and pulls the flat-bottomed boat across the river with his mate to keep him company. The latter asks me, in a friendly, aggressive sort of way, whether I like the Kinks. I certainly do, but I point out that they are creatures of my generation rather than his. 'I like all tha',' he says, 'Beatles an' tha', but 'specially the Kinks.' I ask him if the other side of the river is in Wales. 'No,' he says, ''erefordshire, but most people think it's in Wales.'

This has a curious consequence, I reflect, as I make my way along the flat bank on the west side of the Wye. Whereas English Bicknor is in England, Welsh Bicknor is also in England. (It's true; I checked it.)

13 *The not-so-Black Country*

(October 1981)

The day has a taste of autumn as crisp and distinctive as a ripe Bramley. The sky is a smoky blue and the sun illuminates the vivid colours of the land, now at their maximum of variety: the copper brown of the ploughed fields, the gold and red and brown of the trees and the fifty shades of green of the grass and the evergreens. Strange that I should be here to visit the *Black* Country.

We are in the Clent Hills, a piece of Cotswold apparently imported at great expense to the south-west corner of Birmingham. I say 'we' because, for the first tiny fraction of this journey, I am accompanied by my family. My eldest son shouts 'nearly in the sky' as we ascend the hill while his brother, who can walk and run well enough though he hasn't yet managed a known word, points and shouts 'Gooerah' approvingly at the view.

I leave them and walk on up. The hills are over a thousand feet high and offer spectacular views. There is nobody on them now, but the massively broad and well-trodden path to the top offers evidence that this is a well-frequented place. The hills are, in fact, shared between the National Trust and a country park. But there is nobody here now, until I spot a couple in their motorcycling leathers sitting on a bench sheltered by a clump of pines near the top, their crash helmets beside them. They are about thirty years old and they are sitting hand in hand silently looking at the view south. It is a vast view of a land of woods and rolling hills, of indefinite mystery and opulence, receding to the misty autumn horizon. The only urban intrusion is a glimpse of a part of Stourbridge. Anyone who thinks that green belts simply do not work should start the testing of this proposition here. As for the couple, I cannot help but see their solemn silence on a weekday morning on a hillside as part of the romantic melancholy of unemployment. But, of course, they could be eccentric millionaires.

At the top I can see north for the first time and that glimpse of Stourbridge extends itself into a great conurbation. More than I expected, it looks like an industrial conurbation; there are chimneys belching smoke and from here can be seen a great swathe of dirty air above the city. A really cold wind gets up and whistles round my ears; it cannot be much above freezing here on the top, if at all. So I start my descent, in search of the Black Country. Like Eldorado, it can be said of the Black Country that most people have heard of it but that very few know where it is. In order to clear up any confusion I have an authoritative definition on a piece of paper. It is taken from the *Micropaedia Britannica*:

> *Black Country, The*, industrial area closely corresponding to the small south Staffordshire coalfield in the Midland region of England: its name derives from its pollution-coated industrial landscape. The Black Country extends immediately to the west of the city of Birmingham, which itself lies off the coalfield, and comprises the western part of the metropolitan county of West Midlands. . .

To my relief it is possible to get off the hills on the other side. I go down a steep path through the woods and arrive in a car park. There are two workmen in the car park and two women on horses. One of the horses is frisky and its rider is saying 'Stand still! Stand STILL!' to it and I hope she can control the nag because it is looking at me as if it would dearly love to kick me. So it is a relief to be alone again in a sunken lane with Hagley Wood on my left. Apart from a very old lady in a Mercedes, turning up the drive of an isolated house, I see nobody until I reach the A456, a dual carriageway. Just along the road the sign says: Metropolitan County of West Midlands, Metropolitan Borough of Dudley, Halesowen. I go up a lane to the left, pursuing my course northwards.

It is strange how a conurbation tentatively envelops you if you walk into it. In this case I catch a glimpse of Halesowen, but retreat back into open country. Then there is a detached house or two followed by an estate of modern, 'executive' houses and a whole ridge of hundreds of semis in the distance. Then back to just country again in a valley full of sprouts and potatoes and hedges clipped savagely short by the council machine. Up a hill through scrubby woodland on what was obviously once a mine, past a rather grandiose scout hut. Then suddenly and finally I am really in it. Below me is a street of semis and then two blocks of flats and a rolling landscape crammed with flats and houses and little factory chimneys for miles ahead. This first part is called Colley Gate and near its village centre I see the first of the little factories for which this area is famous. Beaconsfield Industries: it is literally a cottage industry because its office is in the front room of a medium-sized 1853 terrace and its activity is in the sheds in the yard, which is piled high with gas cylinders.

On the other side of Colley Gate there are many more factories, though not quite so quaint. But, like many places in England, there is complete nonconformity to the 'urban' stereotype. On my right, Henley Foundries; on my left, a little country cottage in a hollow backed by a wood. A whole estate of factories, Rhodes and Cartwright, John Hall Refactories, Midland Iron, IT workshops, AEI Power Cable Division. Even the biggest of them is small by the standards of factories in Coventry which I am used to, suggesting a more human scale and, just possibly, a greater potential for survival. I am jotting down some impressions on a piece of waste land when a middle-aged man approaches me with great good humour and says something. He says it twice, but I only recognise 'Yow'm' (which is Black Country for 'you are') and 'good job' in quite a long sentence, so I am reduced to smiling amiably like a foreigner.

In Cradley there are many more factories. Intriguing places, not only for what they make but, for the non-engineer, for what you would do with what they make. For instance, the City Forge and Engineering Co. Ltd makes Bars, Blanks, Rings, Shafts and Boss Blanks. The one next door even has a vacancy, for a forgeman. Northwards from Cradley and through Cradley Heath. It is a land of complete clutter. There are mainly new houses and some old as well as both old and new factories. And, of course, dereliction, the odd abandoned shop or house and patches of land that just grow weeds. All in complete, colossal disorder, straggling around the rolling hills like Brobdingnagian litter. Occasionally, it reminds me of San Francisco, just the hills and the shape of the place. There are many black workers as well as white. At one point a group of young black and white workers cross the road in front of me, laughing and joking on the way from the pub to the factory like some ad. for how it ought to be. They call to a man behind, 'Cummon, Alkay'. Approaching Netherton there is a view of bare rugged hills in the Birmingham direction; another break in the urban stereotype. These, too, have a distinctively scruffy quality which mainly comes from the quarries on them.

In Netherton I cannot resist the Old Swan, which advertises 'PURE HOME BREWD ALES' (sic). Nor is it a disappointment, being a dream of a town pub. The tiny public bar has engraved mirrors with carved wooden surrounds and big black handles on the beer pumps. The landlord himself is an elderly man of great dignity with grey hair and a smart suit. He has a friendly smile and sips his beer from a half-pint glass. The ceiling is tiled, with a big swan in the middle. There are big silver cups in cases and a huge and venerable weighing machine. It is all so perfect that I have a mind to write to the Disney organisation and suggest that they copy it for Disneyworld. (Ride No. 47, the English urban pub. Rub shoulders with merry working men. Drink to forget the endless drudgery of your life.)

Except that these aren't working people in the traditional sense. The clientele of the Old Swan are all white, all male and almost all executives. Suits, suntans, ties, moustaches. I order a pint of bitter. It is a very pale gold colour, like lager, but there the resemblance ends, because it is smooth and strong with plenty of body. Behind the bar is a Duncan Fearnley cricket bat with the signatures of all the players, Australian and West Indian, who played in the 1975 World Cup Final. One of the man to my left asks to see it. When he is given it one of his friends says, 'Can we have the ball, please?' in such a deadpan way that the barmaid is worried for a moment.

I order a crisp ham cob and put a lot of nose-tingling English mustard on it and find a place to sit down. To my left the conversation is about a film and its critics, then about the Staffs. Cup, though in what sport I cannot make out. To my right is an elderly man, the boss, with three young executives. They are wondering what will happen to a piece of land which their premises now surround. Nothing, is my guess. Then the boss decides it is time to go. He says, 'Deloightful beer, chaps. Glad you brought me here; oi'm 'avin a blood test this afternoon.' Raucous laughter.

I order another pint of beer and this time, with a simple order rather than a composite, it is clear that the price is *only 42p*. I compliment the landlord on his price and his quality. He seems pleased and says proudly, 'It's ownly just gone up, annall.' Definitely worth a detour, the Old Swan, as Michelin would put it.

On Shaw Road, going on to Dudley, two young black chaps with floppy caps are trying to start a flashy but clapped-out Capri. Such little natural shyness with which I was endowed having been wholly removed by the landlord's ale, I offer to help and we spend about a quarter of an hour heaving the Capri up and down the forecourt of a garage. The pleasure for me, apart from the self-satisfaction of multi-racial altruism, is to hear their rich Black Country accents. After the failure of our fifth attempt, one of them says, 'Eefit run outer petrol carburettor'll be clogged oop, wunnit? Boun norra start.' But on the sixth attempt the Capri roars throatily and they sweep away, waving at me as they go and immediately overtaking a new Metro on a blind hill.

The centre of Dudley is on a hill. My first glimpse is of a huge new Tesco's and office block and, at the bottom of the hill, half a dozen grown men are playing cricket on a piece of waste ground. At the top of the hill, among the shoppers with their bags and baskets, you see a second hill of equal height and half a mile away, but different in every way. It is covered with big, handsome trees and the ruins of Dudley Castle stand on the top. The hill is incongruous; it is like some piece of the deepest shires or Welsh Marches plonked amid the foundries. The eleventh edition of *Britannica* (the classic one) said that from Dudley Castle at night 'the glare of furnaces appears in every direction'. Beyond the castle, to the north, you can see that the Black Country flattens out towards Wolverhampton and the horizon. The castle itself is now a zoo.

Dudley is a multi-racial place with many blacks and Asians. A stone building in the centre is now a mosque and Muslim community centre. There are a number of fine Georgian buildings dotted around the centre. On the other side of the castle hill are big railway marshalling yards, an impressive cricket ground and a strange little field full of fat little horses. Why is there such a field in the middle of a town? The answer is given on a warning notice. Subsidence, constant danger of. As I sit on one of the benches of the cricket field, a man in a boiler suit addresses me, thinking that I am the groundsman. When he finds out that I am not he says, 'Bloody cheek, this, innit? Putting a football pitch on the cricket pitch.' I point out to him that (a) it is a hockey pitch, (b) it is only on the outfield, and (c) the same arrangements obtain at Lord's. But he is not impressed. 'Bloody cheek, even so,' he says, and wanders off to find the groundsman.

Beyond this is the Black Country open-air museum. It is closed now, but I can see that it contains an old pithead. Then Tipton, not a particularly cheerful place, not least because racialist slogans – BM and swastikas – have been written in many places, but in recognisably the same neat, firm hand. There are black paper boys delivering the Wolverhampton *Express and Star* in virtually every street. Such slogans should be removed immediately, regardless of the cost, and the police should put the crime higher on their list of priorities.

In Coseley I am stopped by an old man. His erect bearing and oiled hair, his smart clothes and difficulty in breathing are suggestive of a man who has been in the army and down the mines. He laughs and points at a six-foot chrysanthemum in his minuscule front garden. 'Look at me chrysant,' he says, 'Look at the bloody thing. It just groud un groud'. 'Yer spowse ter toike em in this toimer year, intcher?' (That was me, my voice assuming chameleon qualities as it often does. But he doesn't notice.) 'Ah can't cannae? Rooms is too small.'

Past a hundred foundries, going home time. Men in donkey jackets with khaki lunch bags, riding bicycles and waiting for buses. A sight surprisingly unchanged in generations. The English working class are so unashamedly and confidently working-class at least on their own terrain. That must be counted as one of the good things about our version of class. Through Bilston into Wolverhampton which, overall, is more ordinary than the rest of the Black Country. But even an experienced urban explorer like me is unprepared for the dereliction on the edge of the centre by the Bilston Road. A row of nine shops, not just derelict, but everything, fittings, boards, windows, smashed to smithereens. Then burned-out semis, a black shell of a church and perhaps fifty acres of rolling rubble, as if Verdun had been re-fought in the West Midlands. At least it forms a good big site to operate on. The town centre itself is much more pleasant; the usual mix, some good buildings and more or less to a scale. Finally, Wolverhampton station, which is packed with queues for tickets. How do British Rail lose money?

Incidentally, the Black Country is not particularly black; not nowadays anyway. The little conurbations of Lancashire and Yorkshire are much blacker.

14 *The great white northern mystery tour*

(January 1982)

A nondescript place. A road going gently upwards, a field and a hedge on the left, a brick house and a bit of a hill on the right. A village behind me, the main road up on a bridge ahead of me. But if the landscape lacks distinction, the same cannot be said of the weather, which is the most appalling I have ever experienced. Ten minutes ago it was raining, but now the rain has turned white and is sweeping vertically across my path borne on the east wind. The village behind me is called Birtley. Ahead lie the A1, Gateshead, the Tyne and Newcastle.

After a quarter of a mile or so the thought that I am being extremely silly occurs. I suppose you would call the white stuff 'sleet', but in my mind 'sleet' has a slushy, soggy, not-quite-either, sort of image. This stuff hurts, really hurts. It stings the face and makes the jaw ache, despite my anorak and cap and hood. It is like being whipped so long and hard that the pain of each stroke is only dimly felt through a layer of aching numbness. (At least, I imagine it is like that: despite a varied life. . .)

Approaching the metal signs for the main road I can see that a kind of slimy ice is forming on them and dripping from them only very slowly. The pain is worse in this more exposed place, but something inside my head, the coiled steel loony ME or EGO, tells me that it is unthinkable I should give up. In any case, I have no options: the chauffeuse has disappeared. I struggle painfully along the A1, my right side soaking and numbed. I had vaguely hoped my anorak was waterproof, but it does not pass this test. Wellies do, though: my feet and calves are uniquely warm and dry. Thank God for wellies. I become entirely preoccupied with shelter, welcoming the break in the assault offered even by a passing lorry. In these conditions as a vagrant in the open, a city seems a warm and desirable thing: people, tall buildings, shelter, heated shops.

Gateshead, in these respects, is a disappointment. Modern houses and blocks of flats, no shelter at all. After a few hundred yards there is written on a blue-grey brick wall: 'GEORDIELAND: ENTER AT OWN RISK.' Yeah, of bloody exposure, I think to myself. Moving north towards the Tyne the road turns into one of those strips which often lead into a northern town. Solid stone houses and shops in a ribbon which has run out into the country and then been followed by later development. Below the main street the land rolling away and including low-lying factories and an industrial estate.

For extra shelter I get into a back street behind the main drag. It is very much the old image of a back street, tall dark brick houses, crushed together, with dank little back yards. There was a picture of such a back street with children playing and women hanging out washing in my 1951 Festival of Britain book. It said, if I remember rightly, just 'Tyneside'. Now this one has gone 'up' if anything; a majority of the houses have big modern extensions built into the back yard.

The back streets offers me little shelter. The white stuff seems to swirl, catching me and stinging me whatever I do. The same seems to be true all the way into town, along the main road flanked by big stone houses, hospitals, schools, and so on. The few people about often smile at one another in a humourless, wan sort of way, as if to share the horror and hopelessness of it all. There are some fashionably dressed schoolboys, soaked to the skin. Four apprentices – to judge from their youth and their blue boiler suits – brave it out very impressively, eating and sauntering as if it were a summer day.

The centre of Gateshead seems to consist entirely of new blocks and footbridges and open spaces, subjecting me to the extreme uncosiness of modern architecture. At length, I find the shops and go into Woolworths. Little comfort here; it is not particularly warm and I feel merely wet. There is a church opposite, so I go there to sit down. Here's a funny thing. I open the doors of the church to find myself in what looks like the foyer of a company headquarters. Carpeted space, lounge chairs, electric heaters: paradise for a vagrant. Mine not to reason why. I put cap and gloves on the heater and sit down to try and make some notes in one of the chairs. An old man comes in. He has a leather helmet which covers his ears, but he is shaking all over as he wrings out his woollen gloves and puts them on the heater. 'What a deah. What a deah,' he says, turning his head with much effort to look at me. Then he goes into the interior of the building. When he has gone I note that his blue woollen gloves have holes in them.

Warmer now, but still wet, my curiosity has returned. I find a plaque which satisfies most of it:

TRINITY COMMUNITY ASSOCIATION
TRINITY CHURCH
FORMERLY HOLY TRINITY CHURCH
CONVERSION FUNDED BY THE NEWCASTLE AND GATESHEAD INNER CITY PARTNERSHIP AND GATESHEAD METROPOLITAN BOROUGH COUNCIL 1979-81
OPENED BY THE MAYOR OF GATESHEAD, COUNCILLOR A. C. BRAZENDALE
ON 11TH APRIL 1981

Inside is a place where you can get coffee and tea. Quite a lot of people too: a very varied crowd. There are notices about many activities including a mother-and-toddler group and the opportunity to talk about being raped. As if to answer my remaining question two men, executive types, no local accent, pass me and one of them is saying, 'It seems to be a great success. Always plenty of people in here, anyway.'

Outside again, I walk in the direction which is downhill, on the grounds that downhill lies the river and beyond the river is Newcastle. I am beginning to lose faith in my own logic (it doesn't always work) and am contemplating asking someone the way when I see the great steel bridge which takes the main road over the Tyne. I make my way down a path to the river.

Newcastle, seen from Gateshead. The precipitation is now snow, softer than it was, landing and holding at least on the roofs, if not the roads and pavements. The city is a towering pile of black shapes looming out of the grey-white swirl. The castle and cathedral are identifiable, other, lower, shapes, less so. The old Animals' song comes to my mind:

> In this dreary ole part of the city
> Where the sun don' appear to shine. . .

It is wonderfully real, in the sense that real beer is real. This appraisal will be 'pseudy' to many people, but this morning I awoke in Billingham (which is a badly planned new town) and I have driven through Peterlee and Washington (which are well planned new towns). With their flat, neat, spacious layout and their signs to 'District 15' they have achieved a kind of perfection in the geographical organisation and segregation of human activity. But you only have to come here and look at Newcastle to see that they lack something which it possesses: it is real, it exists in an extra dimension. The chorus of the song was:

> We gotta get outta this place
> If it's the last thing we ever do. . .

But this is the sort of place you would always be drawn back to, from Esher or Milton Keynes or Los Angeles or wherever.

I cross the river by the low, red and white swing bridge. The bridges are the most distinctive feature of Newcastle; there are five of them in close proximity, the other four towering above the swing bridge. To my right is the main road bridge, an elegant and exact parabola of steel. The other way is the straight, double-decker bridge which carries trains and traffic on different levels. The river is a working river with quays and boats. A small gunboat is moored just downstream.

Directly opposite the swing bridge is the Castle Stairs, a steep winding staircase which leads into the city. To enter a city this way gives me a pleasurable excitement even in these conditions and I run up the dark steps. They take me through perpendicular arches and across a cobbled courtyard between the towering brown stone of the castle and an elegant (though apparently unoccupied) eighteenth-century administrative building. As I walk past the cathedral a great bass bell chimes twelve noon. They don't have those in Peterlee, either.

Bigg Market is one of those spaces, part street, part square, which you find in a lot of Yorkshire towns. Except that it is on a vastly bigger scale than anything in Thirsk or Ripon. I admire its architecture as I eat a Doner Kebab in a very smart, neat, Turkish stand-up snackbar. It comes in pitta bread with eight kinds of salad. I have a perverse desire to eat salad in these conditions.

I like Newcastle. It has some qualities I always hope to find in a city: deepness, darkness, cosiness. People tell me that it has been 'ruined' by planners and developers, but it seems to me that they are not making fair comparisons: to me, a stranger, its atmosphere is strong and distinctive. In some ways it is like Edinburgh, with a touch of Manchester. I shelter a while in Handysides Arcade, a steep indoor street, before leaving the city centre. I have a very brief look at Town Moor, Newcastle's great open space, now like a transplanted Siberia, but boggy under the snow, then I go through Jesmond, well-to-do and Edwardian, with tall houses, speckled because made of several different colours of brick. In Gosforth, which is like a Scottish or Yorkshire town with its cool and respectable grey stone buildings, I r/v with the chauffeuse after a brief panic because I cannot see her at first.

The plan is to drive north and then for me to continue walking along one of the most romantic coasts in the world, from Seahouses past the Farne Islands and Bamburgh Castle, round Budle Bay to Lindisfarne. The A1 is still clear and we make reasonable progress to Morpeth despite heavy snow. Radio Metro is giving out frequent weather reports. It is no longer possible to cross the Pennines. Visibility up the Tyne valley is now down to twenty yards. Otterburn is cut off. Outside, the heavy snow is landing, even on the road, and only one lane is now open. There is traffic going north, but nothing to be seen except the occasional wood, its trees heavily laden with snow.

I skid and appear to be going head on into a car coming the other way but I do the correct thing, turning the wheels into the skid and (just) controlling the car in time. As it happens, I have driven in these conditions several times in the last couple of years and am getting used to it. The speed goes down. 50-40-30. Getting down towards twenty we open full negotiations on a new plan. Is it worth it? We turn back. But neither of us likes to give up on anything and most of all I want a warm hotel room. Surely the Great North Road will not be closed? Like Whittington, we turn again. Finally, on a hill we are behind a line of traffic now motionless. The second order problem. With my experience and a couple of tricks (like someone on the bonnet), and front-wheel drive, if I could get a clear run I could get through. But the road is now blocked by vehicles. Turn again.

Back at a garage I hear a lorry driver taking instructions from a phone not to proceed. The A1 is blocked eight miles north, he tells me. I ring the hotel we were going to stay at which is on the A1. Nothing is coming past, says the girl. That means the road is blocked. We turn south, my main intention being to avoid being stuck completely in these wet clothes. Conditions improve slightly as we drive south. I feel frustrated and disappointed, but our decision is justified because now the radio says that the A1 is completely blocked beyond Alnwick. A strange idea begins to form in my mind. We take the A108 which is nearer the coast and goes through the Tyne Tunnel. Conditions are far better and there are even two lanes open.

Thus it is, reader, that I come to visit Sunderland for the first time in my life, though I was born in West Hartlepool and all my family and in-laws come from the North-East. I am not alone in never having been to Sunderland. I have a friend who was elected as a councillor in the first elections to Tyne and Wear Metropolitan County Council. The Council decided, understandably, to hold alternate meetings in Newcastle and Sunderland. My 'source' claims that twelve of the councillors had never been to Sunderland before the first meeting was held there.

Night is falling. I walk from the town centre down to the docks and the sea. There is an air, as there probably is everywhere tonight, of survival being in doubt. But here it has a special maritime quality, given to it by the smell of the docks and the sea and the deep, sinister booming of the foghorn. There are patches of snow, clean and eerie in contrast with the purple sky. Most of the buildings are flats, some tall, but the majority only three storeys, the occasional lighted room looking extraordinarily cheerful and cosy. In the docks I see a lot of Fina oil storage tanks and I make out the name of the Ashington.

I enter the docks, probably illegally, and make my way to the harbour wall. It incorporates a very solid mesh fence. Through this I can see the sea, grey and swelling monstrously with white breakers forming irregularly. Well, I finally made it to Sunderland, even if I came here only for the ignoble and uncomplimentary reason that the roads to everywhere else were blocked.

15 Starting at the end

(April 1982)

First line of the punter's creed: you have to pick a winner one day. This is it. Tower Hamlets in the rain and Sunderland in the snow were very nice in their own way, of course, but Cornwall on a warm and sunny spring day has a more all-embracing charm.

At Land's End sun-bronzed, track-suited young men exact 40p for the car park. Then you go through a (free) turnstile, supervised by sun-bronzed, track-suited young women. They give (free) badges to the children.

'Who owns Lands End, now?' I ask.

'Mr Goldstone. Since March 1st.'

'Who is he?'

'We don't know. We only know his name. His son comes down; he's very nice.'

There are a couple of dozen people pottering around Land's End, mainly pensioners. The sea varies from deep blue to turquoise and there are patches of white which presumably indicate unseen rocks. The sea here can be vicious, but today it is in a benign mood. There are two small boats on the horizon, beyond the visible rocks. Jackdaws go about their business among the cliffs and big black-backed gulls glide more adventurously over the sea. There is an operatic ditty for exactly this place and these conditions, and it runs through my head:

How beautifully blue the sky
The glass is rising very high
Continue fine I hope it may
And yet it rained but yesterday.

I turn back to walk along the coast path towards England. A couple of hundred yards from Land's End a vast armchair has been fashioned from the rocks and a lady in late middle age has sat on it. She calls out to me in a familiar (Lancashire) accent: 'Ah've got meself a good seat 'ere; this'll not wear out.'

It is a beautiful path to walk. The sea crashes gently onto the base of the cliffs. There is a sense of freedom and nature and light breezes which warm the depths of the soul. Rousseau would have loved it here, but I'd rather be on my own. The coast forms fantastic shapes: steep, narrow valleys, bridges of rock, peninsulas which end in arid, rocky mountains which look as if they ought to have Apaches hinding in them. Vast dark caves and beaches that could be reached only by a rock climber or a windsurfer. The names on the map are as exotic as the shapes they denote: Carn Kez, Carn Greeb, Enys Dodnan, Nanjizal, Zawn Kellys.

The path may be beautiful, but it is also difficult. The first difficulty is a physical one: it goes up and down, a hundred feet, two hundred feet, all the time, as it crosses rocky ridges and descends into steep valleys. Sometimes it is not a question of walking, but of scrambling. Although it may look nothing on the map to chaps who regularly shin up several thousand feet, I can assure them it is. Every five miles you will climb about three thousand feet, some of it sheer. Knackering. Assume two miles an hour, maximum, as it looks on the map.

An additional difficulty is that of following the path. The Coast Path is well enough defined, but it is not simply one path. Sometimes there are diversions which lead round, or to the end of, a peninsula. But a traveller who has any kind of destination can't afford to follow all of these, even if he wanted to. Then there are other paths which connect with tracks or roads inland. Sometimes there is a choice of three, the one nearest the sea being marked 'Coast Path'. But the middle one proves an effective short cut. Not always so simple, though. On the second occasion I have a choice of three: I take the middle one and promptly get lost. I am wandering up a rough track flanked by tall banks and find myself in the cobbled yard of a stone farmhouse. The middle-aged farmer and his wife are standing in an upstairs room looking out of the window. They cheerfuly re-direct me to the path in strong Cornish accents. A whole mile wasted.

Cornish people seem very friendly. Do they keep it up for the whole season? I wonder.

There are few walkers on the path, normally only a pair about every mile, though more when you get near any motorised access. At one point you can get a motorbike down near the sea and there are a very young couple, carrying their helmets and with a wonderfully furtive look – you know, looking for somewhere quiet. Shouldn't be too difficult. Most of the people I see are highly professional walkers – expensive boots, thick stockings, beige rucksacks. Without wanting to be foolhardy nor to reveal inverted snobbery, I have a certain amount of contempt for those who wear the full gear. Ordinary clothes seem just as good, and training shoes more comfortable, though I accept that one should carry waterproof things in a rucksack.

At the beginning the land is basically moorland, heather and low gorse. I vaguely assume that this is how it will be all the way, but there is considerable variety. Nearing the most southerly point where I will turn the corner to go east, Gwennap Head, I go through a lush valley with dense thickets of plants. There are a hundred kinds of plants, ninety of which I can't name. Primroses and daffodils and wild white hyacinths give it colour, but the smell is dominated by wild garlic, giving the valley a strange, sweet savoury smell, stronger than any kitchen. It is a purely Cornish combination , a sub-tropical atmosphere in an English countryside.

After that, Porthgwarra in the St Levan valley, the first inhabited place, a tranquil little hamlet of stone houses and warm little gardens. Six tourist cars in the car park and a small golden beach which can be reached by a tunnel which the sea has cut through the cliff. Climbing out of this valley, the density and the aroma of the vegetation are almost overpowering.

In the next valley, at Porth Curno, there is space for a lot of cars. There is an open-air theatre cut into the rock. Men are painting it and oiling the turnstiles. *Godspell* will be the first production. All over Cornwall at this time of year there seems to be the same air of getting ready for the invasion. The emmets are coming. (*Emmet*: old Cornish word, meaning ant. Thus, modern Cornish dialect, meaning tourist.) Here the path goes right down into the bay: a little nerve-wracking because so steep, but mainly debilitating because I know that I will have to climb every step of the way up again. The sea here is a strange pastel turquoise, a vivid colour that I have never seen before. It is not a quiet place, at least not today, because a bulldozer and a digger tractor are noisily shifting all the sand on the beach. Why? I wonder angrily. At the bottom there is a notice which apologises. British Telecom, laying marine cables. That's all right, then. British Telecom and the sea will put it all back. The next highlight is the Treen Cliffs, a peninsula of rocky grandeur jutting out into the sea.

I have lunch on a warm, flat rock a couple of hundred feet above the sea. I have two cans with me and it isn't enough after all that scrambling. I should have brought four. I could have drunk six. An observation on country walkers in England: whereas those over forty usually speak to a passing stranger, the under thirties rarely do. As a trained social scientist I can immediately see two hypotheses, an age relation and a generation effect. Did walkers who are now forty-five speak to strangers when they were twenty? Will the present twenty-year-olds start offering polite gestures when they get to forty? My guess is that it's age that matters and they will, for the most part, stop lowering their eyes and say something polite as time goes on. In Lancashire, when I was a child, you always spoke to everybody in the countryside.

A more local thought: Cornwall is vast. It may be smaller than Lincolnshire and I am sure anyone from the Lone Star State would point out that you could shove it up the arsehole of Texas and not know it was there, like a piece of mislaid bog paper. But these figures of area are merely abstract, not real: it is like comparing a flat, plain piece of paper with something intricate and three-dimensional. I look at the map, at the corner of Cornwall that I have managed to walk. It has been a walk on a vast scale and has taken me through some remote and secluded places. Yet on the map it is tiny. The Tamar and the Devon border are a hundred miles away. At this rate it would take me a full week to get out of Cornwall.

The coast becomes even more varied after lunch. There is a burnt-out area where the gorse has been on fire for hundreds of yards, but ferns are unfolding themselves from the blackened earth. Then the path goes through a *maquis* scrubland of gorse and may, eight feet high and impenetrable, all in bloom. Another part has strong connotations of the Celtic Twilight: there have been small fields bounded by stone walls, but now it is all overgrown with gorse, though the shapes of the fields are clearly visible from a distance. Then, to my surprise, the Celtic Dawn landscape (to borrow from Yeats again): small, walled fields going down to the sea, but immaculately maintained. A Morris Minor van stands near one of them and a man in a blue boiler suit tills it by hand. In this area there is much more evidence than before of a farmer v. walker conflict: barbed wire, pulled down, the path diverting round fields. This may be coincidence, though, because as we approach the more accessible points, the Lamorna valley and Mousehole, there are many more intimidating signs: 'NO CAMPING'; 'NO PICNICKING'; 'THE LAND ON EITHER SIDE OF THIS PATH IS PRIVATE'; 'TRESPASSERS WILL BE PROSECUTED'; 'A BULL CAN CROSS THIS FIELD QUICKER THAN YOU CAN'.

The 'we' is not merely stylistic, because I have entered into a silent and competitive relation with two walkers, both expensively equipped and in their twenties. One is dark with a beard, the other blond and fresh-faced. They overtook me when I had lunch and I passed them as they rested. They were in the Lamorna valley when I was and now they are just behind me. I don't want them to catch me (don't ask me why) and I am late anyway, so I put on speed. As the walking becomes breathless the variety of land increases again. There is the Deep South (the English Dream): detached stone house, with neat lawns and palm trees. (How they must hate all these plebeian boots tramping past.) Then, an undercliff area of thick woods and lush undergrowth. This provides my most difficult moment, balancing on a tree trunk, crossing a bog. Then pine woods with rhododendrons: a sweet smell and surely a Manderley up there in the woods. Across a shore of large round boulders and up yet another cliff. On the edge of the shore is a mass of sea-cabbage, flowering yellow. This is the plant from which all the brassicas were developed – sprouts, caulis, the lot. I pick a leaf and crush it: it smells rancorously of cabbage.

By now I have lost them and I have also reached the inhabited part. A small rocky island (St Clement's Isle) beyond that, through the haze, St Michael's Mount, then Mousehole and Penzance come into view.

Mousehole (pronounced Mousel) used to be a funny name: it is a very sad one now, after the loss of the entire lifeboat crew. It is a beautiful village, grey stone cottages crammed together round the harbour leaving only tiny narrow streets and passages between them. A fishing boat phut-phuts out of the harbour, watched by a couple of dozen people with nothing to do. A fight breaks out between two youths: the pretty blonde girl who is obviously its stimulus stares calmly and contemptuously out to sea. I catch a bus, for no other reason that the bus driver waited for me as I walked towards his bus. It is a good move, though, because the path has become a road at this point and the coast becomes urban and industrial, with a big fishing port and packing stations at Newlyn.

I cannot classify or easily describe Penzance. It has an interesting main street: there are pavements up steps and narrow little step-streets off. A classical town hall (1837) and a statue of Sir Humphrey Davy overlook it. Behind this are terraces of cottages so plain and grey that they are more Scottish than English. A Celtic congress is taking place: the flags of Ireland, Scotland, Wales, Man, Brittany and Cornwall are flying and there are some men in plain black kilts. Where from?

I begin the walk across country to St Ives. Cornish suburbia, many palms and pines, through to the villae of Gulval. Then a rich agricultural land. A field of spring cabbage; a bit of a disaster here, because they are bolting rapidly in the warm, dry weather. Then six fields of cauliflower, most already cut, but some fine fat ones still left. The B3311 goes between those high Cornish banks, which started life as stone walls and gradually turned into low hills with a mass of vegetation and trees growing out of them. There is little traffic, mostly old cars like Oxfords and 1100s as is common in rural areas, but it is hard work after those cliffs. By the time I get to Nancledra, a small stone village, halfway across the peninsula, the land is a great roll of green behind me. Outside the village is one of those ruined tin mines whch are often pictured on the front of books about Cornwall.

It is hard work getting to St Ives, past rocky, barren hills and more old tin mines. I am exhausted. St Ives used to be famous for its artists. Frankly, they can be as artistic as they like. I am thinking about beer.

16 *Lancs. of the setting sun*

(July 1982)

A windmill, white and tall and in splendid condition. It has huge conventional sails on one side and small ones on the other, facing at right angles, like a helicopter. The roof is of wooden tiles, the shape and texture distinctively Dutch. It stands on the flat, sandy grass between Lytham and the Ribble Estuary. It is a reminder that if East Anglia is a smaller version of the North European Plain, then Lancashire's Fylde is an adequate miniature of the same style. Even that strange cricket-pavilion-looking thing next to the windmill could not be in any other part of Lancashire. Round stones set in cement, which turns out to be a not uncommon way of building round here.

There are some family grops sitting on the grass and other people on the promenade benches looking at the two hundred yards of marsh grass and beyond it the water. I sit down. It is warm; the sky is entirely cloudy, but there seems no chance of rain. Raised voices from the next bench. He (30) says, 'It *is* a bloody argument. . . ah'm not yer 'usband, ah'm yer son.' From her angry mutter I can only pick out the words 'You've done nothing for me.'

The main street of Lytham is only three hundred yards away. Clifton Street, built in the hard, glossy, rather garish red brick which is the predominant material of much of west and south Lancashire. It is half-familiar to me; the sight of it recalls days out and away games, but the mood it creates is vastly different from the dark millstone grit of home. Lytham is posh, despite being on an estuary rather than the sea; try accusing a Lancastrian who spends his holidays in Lytham of holidaying in Blackpool! The whole tone of the street confirms this; some nice florists, a shop which has quail, venison and lobster. Those premises which make up the miniature industrial structure of a resort: ear-piercing, cutlery engraving. Outside the Eden Arms, which has three wooden barrels over the door, people are sitting at tables on the pavement, including three of those Lancashire blondes who have an open, uncomplicated sexual attraction which you see nowhere else. Or so I appear to have been conditioned to believe.

Lunch down a side street at The Sandwich Shop. Doing good business, snacks and sandwiches. Much of the food looks good, but my Jumbo Hot Dog contains a peculiarly unpleasant meatless thing, the English sausage at its worst, and my Cheeseburger is a close relation. I regret not having sought out something more traditional, like a meat and potato pie.

Another couple of hundred yards and I am out of downtown Lytham. I pause at the station. The long, straight double line disappears into the trees towards Blackpool and a lone youth jumps and swings on the shelter. The station is both derelict and used, on a bus-stop basis. I follow a footpath sign to the Witch Wood. At first it is a copse of beech and sycamore, fifty to a hundred yards across, between the railway cutting and houses and small factories. A small fat rabbit, sitting on the sandy path, is somewhat less than terrified by my approach and potters off into the ferns. A hundred yards further on, his cousin plays it equally cool. The trees stop, revealing a beautiful cricket field on the other side of the railway, then they broaden out to be a true wood, inhabited by lady dog walkers and a pair of teenage girls, hiding their cigarettes from me with surprising coyness. A romance may be budding between two bulldog owners:
She (Lancs accent): 'She barks, of course, but that is it. She's a real softeh at 'eart.'
He (London accent): 'Maxi's just the same. The only person he ever growls at is me when I play with him.'

At the far end of the wood a notice announces that the wood was opened by Prince Philip for the Lytham Civic Society in 1974. Beyond the wood, I get lost among the huge red villas which stretch to the visible ends of the roads in every direction. Finally getting it sorted out on the map, I decide to strike inland, intrigued by the name 'Lytham Moss' and by the area of little lakes which lie beyond it on Great Marton Moss and Common Edge. I pass Fylde Rugby Club, a surprisingly modest place with no stands or terracing. At last the houses stop and, beyond the neat allotments, is the Moss.

It is a bit of a disappointment and nothing like a moss in east Lancashire. It is arable land, hedgeless and fenceless: carrots, potatoes, wheat and barley with very occasional clumps of tall trees.

That it was a marsh is obvious from the straight, banked road and the drainage ditches. But – here the pulse does quicken – there is the tower, Mammon's spire, in the distance. It beckons me as a mighty symbol of leisure and pleasure, promiscuity and excitement, as it has beckoned four generations of Lancastrians and many others. They would never have built it if Freud had been born in time.

The countryside is very quiet and very distinctively low country. The only intrusive sound comes from occasional small planes which appear from Blackpool, no doubt some containing children having their first flight. The crops are full of wild flowers, including red poppies and the daisy-like camomile. More spectacularly, there is a great glut of the big golden corn marigolds among the wheat and barley. I wish I had a pound for every book and article I've read which has bemoaned the decline of the corn marigold and similar flowers.

Nearer Blackpool, the area of little square lakes. A complete misreading of OS symbols; they turn out to be market gardens with glasshouses. There is an unusual atmosphere to this place, Blackpool's back country. It is like mediaeval Burford or Chipping Campden in that I am walking down a street of houses, the majority of which have a farm behind them, a living being carefully garnered from two or three acres of tomatoes and peppers and flowers. There are three kinds of house along the lane. First, the market gardens. Then, the derelict market gardens, many with glasshouses still intact, but full of towering weeds. Last, the merely residential, with real gardens and paddocks for horses at the back.

A mushroom farm marks the boundary between this area of intensive semi-agriculture and an industrial area. I stop in a garage to buy something to drink. A man is paying for his petrol. He and the lady cashier have a conversation in which every single sentence ends in 'luv'. The style of life in Lancashire gets no less distinctive every time I go back. The cynic might observe that it becomes a caricature of itself, but I am not the cynic, I am somebody else.

A long walk among the red brick factories, shops and houses. No sign of the real Blackpool: I cannot see the sea nor even the tower, and certainly not the sun, so I fear I might have turned back on myself. I ascend a bridge and there it all is: the sea, calm and infinite, a tram clacking along the promenade, putters on putting greens, shrieks from the Pleasure Beach a quarter of a mile away.

Even my confidence baulks at describing the pleasures of the Pleasure Beach. It is as big as Disneyland these days and has the same system of graded rides, a vast funfair with everything from gentle little trains for the kids to 'white knuckle' rides guaranteed to scare you fartless (as the fashionable expression has it). I watch a middle-aged man with tattooed arms being bullied by his wife and a cowboy to go on the bucking bronco (urban cowboy) machine. A crowd quickly gathers, like me keener to watch than to join in.

I watch The Revolution, a form of 'dipper' in which the passengers go completely upside down, saved from a fall which would make them strawberry jam only by the abstract (and wholly counter-intuitive) concept of centrifugal force. Screams of ecstatic terror as brains and stomachs are inverted. No way. No way at all without a spare pair of trousers. I feel the need to go on something, so I ride the monorail which moves gently round for ten minutes and through three stations, giving views of the town and the Pleasure Beach.

I buy half a dozen whelks, 40p, and smother them in salt, pepper and vinegar. I can't be the only person who likes this gastronomic curiosity which tastes like squid 'n vinegar chewing gum, or the market couldn't support them. But I've never found a fellow addict.

What to follow? Ice-cream. I choose a place with Italian-style ice-cream, different flavours in metal canisters.

'Er, I'll have two scoops, please, one. . .'

'Nope,' says large, middle-aged lady.

'Um, sorry, what do you mean?'

'You aren't allowed to 'ave two scoops.'

Flabbergasted, bewildered, silence at the end of which she concedes, disapprovingly, 'You could, ah 'spose, 'ave two separate cones.' I am so humbled that I purchase a single cone with one scoop of chocolate ripple: 25p. Some people, in this great country of ours, haven't quite got into the *spirit* of the market capitalism lark.

Down to the real beach with its vast expanse of ridged, more or less golden, sand. Few people, many seagulls. A group of drunken Scots lads sing their eternal support for Bonny Scotland: one has an England supporters cap and one an England T-shirt! The sea is flat calm, twitching occasionally with a tiny wave, like someone in a deep sleep.

I look back at the great line of the town. Its base is that endless terrace of hotels put up between 1880 and 1930: the Tyldesley, the Manchester, the Glen Ryan and a thousand more. Add three piers and a tower. A twenty-mile length of tramline. A chain of pavilions to shelter people from the wind. Every lamp post decorated with an enormous bauble, due to light up when the sun goes down. Innumerable pubs, cafeterias, joke and souvenir shops, travel agencies offering trips to Wales and the Lakes. The traditional pleasures: donkeys, horses, Punch and Judy, shrimps, rock, candy floss, the view from the Tower. The modern ones: the monorail, restaurants which go up and down, a million electronic amusements, fairly dirty movies. I feel proud; I find myself posing as its PR man and aping an irrelevant advertising slogan: 'What's it got? . . . IT'S GOT THE LOT.' And all very, very competitive. Most rides in the Pleasure Beach only 30p. Hotels with: 'TRADITIONAL SUNDAY LUNCH, ONLY £3 INCLUDING SINGING'. Paul Shane, Dana, the Krankies in the evening. Everybody should come to Blackpool: it is *the* resort and as such it's as significant as Cambridge, as distinctive as Venice, and has more roots than Vegas. It is all still there in Blackpool: the clip-clopping of the horses down the prom, the very silly hats and T-shirts which offer their contents. It embodies the English working class with its hair down, and now its hangers-on and descendants, as nowhere else ever did or ever will.

The truth is, though, that this is a very bad season. The Scots and the Indians seem well represented and there are more than a smattering of curious Swedes, Dutch, Germans and so on, even the odd French family. But these do not make up for all the English who don't come any more, at least not for full-length holidays. At the moment, there are a lot of people in Blackpool standing around waiting to do business; it shouldn't be that way in high summer.

By the Tower and the Central Pier there is a big city atmosphere, aided by the huge Lewis's and the ornate Winter Gardens. I find some shops with the traditional seaside postcards. They are a bit muckier these days, their central preoccupation being female lust and male inadequacy. As a young couple lie in bed he reads the newspaper and announces 'There's been an uprising in Africa.' 'LUCKY BLOODY AFRICANS,' she replies. The husband tries to go into the ironmongers, which advertises 'ALL TOOLS REDUCED'. 'BLIMEY –

DON'T GO IN THERE FRED!!' she says.

The posher hotels are north of the centre, including the château-like Imperial with its American and Canadian flags and brand new, ultra-modern Pembroke, with two hundred beds. It has not yet opened but its existence suggests financial faith in Blackpool. The beach, far below, is vast and clean and empty. I catch a tram to speed things up. It has upholstery of wood, leather and velvet and a conductor and conductress. Pure pleasure, on the top deck with the sun coming out over the sea and streaming through the open window. We pass the Miners Convalescent Home, another brick château high above the beach and I cannot resist a powerfully sentimental vision of clapped-out miners coughing up their guts in sunlit marble halls.

The tram only goes to Cleveleys. It is like Lytham again, perhaps more modest, and I walk north between red-brick houses and neat gardens. Many people are lying on sun-loungers reinforcing their tans in the evening sun. It all fits the image I had of the west Lancashire as a child: a place of peace and prosperity, one's ultimate destination.

Rejoining the coast promenade I walk past Rossall School, reviving schoolboy memories of an afternoon trying to kick goals as the wind howled in from the sea. I didn't last long as a goalkicker. There is no wind today, but the wall and the dyke which guard the western edge of the grounds are evidence of what it is usually like.

On the other side is a new housing estate, part of Fleetwood. It comes as a shock because it is the first predominantly working-class place I have seen: slogans, unkempt gardens, very young married couples, tatoos and a barber offering 'COMPLETE SKINHEAD – ONLY £1'. the older part is very much a port, smelling of boiled crab and estuary mud. I make a rendezvous where the ferries leave for Knott End and the Isle of Man. The day ends with excellent fish and chips and appalling Dutton's beer back in Blackpool.

There is a story about Blackpool which I have heard twice. An Englishman, professional class, had saved all his life to retire to a cottage in Connemara. Shortly before he was due to retire he went to Blackpool for the first time. 'Sod it,' he said (or words to that effect) and retired to Blackpool instead.

17 *In search of Surrey*

(August 1982)

Reverse commuting, leaving Waterloo on the 9.20. The train is empty; it seems to exist for my personal benefit. Opposite, on the seat, is a copy of *The Stage* (incorporating *Television Today*). I divide my time between this paper and the window.

The Stage contains many advertisements for artistes who are available. For the most part I have never heard of them, despite the frequency of the adjectives 'international' and 'unforgettable' (and, more prosaically, 'self-contained'). But there are two acts which have illustrious histories: Lenny the Lion with Terry Hall and Wayne Fontana and the Mindbenders. Still, better to have loved and lost. . .

Glancing occasionally out of the window, as the train moves from inner city to outer suburbs, is like having one of those flick books which give the impression of watching a film. I see the world outside in a detached, abstract way. All that seems to be happening there is that the trees are getting bigger and the buildings smaller, so that by Esher the houses are almost lost among the huge trees.

I bought a ticket to Weybridge because the Beatles once lived there, which makes it a kind of symbol of Surrey. Weybridge station turns out to be one of *those* stations, the ones that aren't in the towns whose name they show. There is a sign to Weybridge along a road through thick woods, which I follow.

I do know what I was expecting in Surrey on a weekday: sleek opulence; elegant upper-middle-class ladies organising fêtes and dinner parties and flirting graciously with the greengrocer. A disappointment: just a busy little country town, with a mixture of buildings and people which distinguishes it only very subtly from a hundred other towns. I get some money from the bank and leave town towards Horsham. It is a bit like going to Venice and not finding any gondolas, or discovering that most people in Barnsley speak with a BBC accent.

Walking on the main road means woods on one side, cars on the other. I soon get bored with this and take the Cobham road, which is very similar, until I see a sign for St George's Hill, private road, no through traffic. The name stirs a memory and the sign is a challenge, so I enter. It is a housing estate. Further down the road there is a map of the estate, an index to house names, and signs to the golf club and the tennis club.

It is a housing estate of very big houses for very rich people. Its opulence cannot be exaggerated. Its eccentricity is considerable: the first house I look at is a grotesquely large thatched cottage called 'Little Rhondda'. Then a château called 'Atlantis', with shutters, sun blinds and ornate fountains. Symphonies on the theme of the mock-Georgian and the mock-Tudor. Predictable names: Pine Close, Pinecroft, Pinedale, Pine Lodge, Pinewood. Humorous ones: Wits End, Toad Hall, Ponderosa, Pop Inn, Rumah Panjai.

Most of these houses were built between 1900 and 1939, but there is still building going on. Generally, they are in about an acre of ground and are shielded by rows of tall trees: pines, oaks, sweet chestnuts and tall laurels with black fruit. The overall impression is marginally between a housing estate with a lot of trees and a forest with a lot of big houses. I watch, impressed, as the electronic gates of a Georgian mansion hum open to allow passage to the Royal Mail van and scurry away as a huge boxer takes exception to my ogling his master's château. Boxer dog, that is.

I am immensely satisfied. As a traveller I have found the real thing, that which fits my image of the place. In Mexico, you want to see dusty villages with chaps crouching down, sombreros pulled over their eyes. In Surrey. . . this. 'Petra' is an exotic house whch would grace Portmeirion. Its name is written in Latin and arabic scripts and it is on the edge of the estate. Beyond it is a steep drop, the first sensation of this being a proper hill. Then a long view of blue-green wooded hills. It occurs to me that these are country estates for people whose only need for land is for defensive and symbolic purposes.

I discover the most eccentric house of all, a thrice life-size model of a windmill with balconies, but no sails. It isn't a house, though, it is the water-tower of the estate, built in 1914. I need to leave, so I ask the way from a Telecom man who is halfway down a hole by a rhododendron bush. 'I dunno,' he says, 'arsk 'im in the bushes over there, 'e's a lowcal.'

It seems odd that a Telecom worker should be local to St George's

Hill, but he means the owner, a tanned man in shorts, who emerges from the bushes. He is about my own age, I would guess, which seems a bit young to be so sodding rich. He explains how to walk through the estate to Cobham with great precision and politeness, laced with a certain enthusiasm. I suppose people round here don't often have to give directions to pedestrians with rucksacks. Bit of a treat for him, really.

I wonder if St George's Hill gets tourists, as such. There are no signs of any today. Architecturally and aesthetically it is rather more impressive than Beverly Hills in my (patriotic) opinion.

The road then crosses the golf course. Instant Scotland, purple heather and pinewoods enclosing the smooth green grass of the fairway. The first time I wait to cross a fairway, a ball pings high over my head and ricochets in among the pine trees. The second time, there is a party of three driving off a tee. One of them takes a very long time to set himself up, is about to hit the ball and then notices that a Telecom van is waiting patiently *behind* the ball. The golfer looks at me and both of us shake with laughter. He says to the driver of the van in a Lancashire accent, 'It's OK, mate, you can go. Thanks very much. . . specially for the compliment.'

Walking to Cobham has me between car and trees again. I sort of bypass the town, walking across a common with playing fields and allotments, but then I cut back into town to find the right directions. Bookshops, estate agents. Detached houses seem to be over £100,000, these days, but the bottom end of the market is less intimidating: flats and even small houses for under £40,000. This seems a fairly logical quirk of the commuter market. An Italian restaurant smells exotically of the Mediterranean, while the swarthy wizened chef draws on his cigarette, leaning on an XJS in the car park.

Lunch time. I am attracted by the Old Bear (and its 'Olde Fayre') which claims to have been dishing out the Watneys since 1430. Everything about it is real, now, as it has been since about 1979, I would guess. It has a range of real beers, none of which existed five years ago. They are expensive. The food is real, too; steak and kidney pie, stuffed marrow, flan with fresh vegetables. Over the bar is a silver salver, presented to the winner of the St George's Day tug of war between them and the Victoria in Oxshott. That doesn't look very old, either.

I have soup of the day, fresh 'crusty' bread and giant sausage: £1.05. All very good. Next to me an elderly couple are decorously nibbling ploughman's lunches. Their conversation is low key:

She: 'I didn't feel hungry until I started eating.' No reply. Pause, nine and a half minutes.

She: 'I see they do sandwiches as well.' Pause, twenty-seven seconds.

He: 'Yes, I noticed that.'

Further along, a blonde American woman, about 30, is explaining to her elderly English relatives how she drank a bottle of champagne to within an inch of the bottom and then fell over. She is the Mark I American, the old image, brash and loud and likeable. Her relatives have obviously taken to her: she is what they expected.

On the benches outside, where I smoke my cigar, there are four perfectly dressed teddy-boys eating bread and cheese. Across the road is the river Mole, meandering gently through a big rich meadow, wih the woods beyond. Such a pastoral English view must be worth many thousands in turnover to the Old Bear.

Along the river, there are detached houses, opulent enough, but almost humble by the standards of St George's Hill. Many of them have a notice outside inviting protests against a developer whose plans will breach the green belt and the Surrey structure plan and add to the insidious process of infilling between Oxshott, Cobham and Stoke D'Abernon. 'Amenity', not employment, is the thing which people most strongly seek to defend here.

Suddenly the valley becomes completely rural: dense woods and rich meadows. I walk towards Bookham and Fetcham which, put together, sound like a police motto. Fetcham turns out to be a poorer sort of place, just ordinary with its little brick houses. Leatherhead is older and more of a town, though smaller. It is early-closing day and most of the shops seem shut. Much of it is traffic-free and it seems very sleepy in the afternoon sun, part of a Surrey which predates commuting.

I fail to find the path I wanted and walk south on the A24. At a garage on a roundabout outside the town, I buy three cans of ice-cold ginger beer and drink one at a single draught. Thirst on a day like this is the most important of all the appetites, its gratification the most sensuous.

The road is now a classic thirties dual carriageway, following the narrow gap cut by the River Mole between steep wooded sides of the north downs. I walk on the cycle path down the middle. The middles of these dual carriageways have become linear nature reserves, with their hawks and great patches of brambles and masses of wild flowers.

I go up a small road through the woods. The village of Mickleham is full of orthodox Jews, with white shirts and black trousers, skull caps and beards. A conference of some sort, I assume. A smaller road again takes me up Juniper Hill into a quiet valley surrounded by woods. Then I take the path on to my own property (in a sense, so to speak, since Box Hill is owned by the National Trust and I am a member).

The path ascends very gently through woods of birch, beech and oak. There are some Brownies coming down and one of them shouts 'There's an Indian', so I hurry on. This is a small valley up the gentle edge of the escarpment, very quiet and with a beautiful variety of trees. On the plateau the woods become big and dark until there, right on the top, is a 'leisure park', a herd of bloody caravans. I'd have them out for a start.

I finish the ginger beer and find a path down the steep slope of Box Hill. There below, are the wooded hills around. Sheep baa-ing on the edge of the downs. Dark green wooded hills and golden flat fields to the horizon.

A middle-age couple are picnicking where the path becomes a road. She asks 'Is it far?' So I say, 'Where to? I've come from London', which is a lie, but delivered with style. She is suitably impressed and says, 'I only mean to the top of the hill, dear.' I give her the welcome news that the best view is half-way up, anyway.

I bypass Dorking in a tedious way along the main road south (lined by woods, needless to say). I make my way into some of the town's southern suburbs, remarkably working-class places which even have tower blocks. There are people mending red cars among the brick houses and speaking in that other Surrey accent, which is London with a touch of the Californian whine about it.

Further south, I follow a bridle path up into the woods through a farm where the family is baling hay in the evening sunshine. Paradoxically, in this most suburban of counties, there is a kind of pioneering atmosphere, because the farm is surrounded by rolling wooded hills which show no sign of any artefact. It is clear that not many peopl visit these woods. And why. The paths are overgrown and there i thick mud.

My path stops completely and I try to continue the directio through dense coniferous woodland until I am stuck in the dark lifeless world of the conifer. Panic: this is the one time of day whe I have no margin of error. I must catch the train. I retrace my steps and find a better path, with grass, through deciduous trees. A bi owl flies silently down the path in front of me.

I am relieved to see a kids' tarzy handing off a branch, a sign c habitation. At the first house back in the valley, I ask a man, mowin grass, where Holmwood station is. He tells me, adding, with pessimism customary on these occasions: 'You won't get a train a this time of night.' I do, though, after a disconcerting wait on deserted platform in an unmanned station.

And so we say farewell. . . (actually the train does go throug Balham on the way back). At the start of the day, Surrey had one c the strongest of county images in my mind, along with Dorset an Cornwall and Yorkshire. I retain the same image but in much sharpe focus. Ruriburbitopia. Old England recreated in the retreat from th city. The natural setting for stories about teddy bears. Quite nice though.

18 *What Manchester does today*

(October 1982)

'Cheshire is posh' (John Lennon, 1964). 'Cheshire is southern' (Lin coln Allison, 1982). The Cheshire plain is a soft and alien place to Lancastrian, a rich parkland into which suburbs have blended t greater and lesser degrees. It has meadows of thick green grass, fa cows, big trees, black and white houses and many sleek and luxurian gardens. Here even the distant Pennines, seen down leafy lanes, seen like a tastefully designed backdrop for suburban windows.

But north of the southern fringes of Stockport lies a precise stylisti frontier. It cannot be more than a hundred or so yards wide an bears no relation to the old Lancashire–Cheshire boundary. Cross that line and you are in the north of England which is, as Tennyson puts it, 'tender, dark and true' (the south being 'bright', 'fickle' and something I can't recall).

I am dropped on the great frontier, a lone pedestrian excursion, Stockport to Turton, calling at Moss Side, Manchester (Central), Ancoats, Boggart Hole Clough and Bolton. The road here is an endless dark brick terrace of shops. A scruffy little yard has a street sign all of its own: 'BIRD IN HAND YARD'. The Pennines are now fulfilling their proper role, which is to complete the ends of terraced streets. They look tougher and more familiar than they did through the trees. Pubs, like the Dog and Partridge which I can see across the road, now lack the polite trimmings of menus and gardens.

Marvelling at the suddenness with which the northern style has crystallised, I go to explore a terraced side street. I find a narrow mossy snicket or ginnel (narrow path between houses) which leads to a cobbled back street flanked by brick-built back yards. Out with the camera and attempt to compose a photograph. A double-take: the film seems to wind on endlessly and there is no longer a click for exposure. Then I remember dropping it as I got out of the car. I did not take the fall seriously because it has suffered so many worse falls in the past. But, this time it is knackered, and my mind's eye searches for a genie to blame.

I take a route through the Great Moor district, ticking off the symptoms of northernness as I go. Cobbled streets. A proper mill chimney. A big dark mill with an Italianate tower. The image is by no means stark, though: there are houses with gardens and leafy little areas, small recurrences of Cheshire. A local speciality, boys in games kit walking back from their Saturday morning game, talking and laughing and kicking the autumn leaves high into the air. What is special about that? These boys are carrying helmets and sticks with nets: not rugby or football, but lacrosse.

I move from well-organised, respectable residential areas to a place with a more chaotic style. Factories and residual car parks at no particular angle. Much litter. An unsurfaced car park where a market is taking place. On a hill not far away there is a big black church surrounded by market stalls. I am entering downtown Stockport. It is downtown in the literal sense; the cobbled street becomes so steep that it turns into steps.

At the bottom of the steps I am in a dark, narrow street, Georgian in scale and thronged with people. High above is a painted iron bridge which it would be natural to assume was a railway bridge, except that pedestrians can be seen walking across it. There are no side streets as such, but several sets of narrow steep steps to climb back out of town. The street is called Little Underbank. I have taken an immediate liking to Stockport: it is cosy and full of life.

These qualities spill over into the new shopping centre. I buy a postcard of the shoppng centre, something I wouldn't have done if the camera was working, and it looks bleak and sterile. But it doesn't feel like that, simply because it is absolutely packed with people. I am desperate for a wee and can only see signs to a disabled toilet. I ask a man carrrying pies where the toilet is. 'Over there behind the bushes,' he says, then adds, 'I don't mean for you to go behind the bushes. There is an entrance to a subterranean toilet behind the bushes. . .'. Now is that his opinion of me? Or his opinion of my likely opinion of the mores of Stockport?

This precinct actually works. As I sit three boys are demonstrating their ball control with a soft, babies' football on the bandstand. Morris dancers arrive and there is the sound of their music and jingling bells, drowned after a few seconds by a jumbo jet on the way into Manchester airport. When it has gone two old women on the seat next to me are discussing a published estimate of the cost of vandalism. 'Terrible,' says the first, 'terrible,' says the second. Then 'terrible' again from the first, intoned with a subtly different emphasis each time.

I look for something to eat. Restaurants take too long and pubs require special knowledge. So I buy a hot pie and a sausage roll. Unfortunately my pie is of the completely collapsing sort. As I sit down and take it out of its little foil container it simply flops and it cannot be eaten with dignity. A pity, because it has a strong, meaty, peppery flavour. I pick some bits up, eat them, lick my fingers and retreat.

I have left the shopping centre on the other side and it is now clear that my impression of Stockport was, at best, partial. Now I am in a great, bleak, formless place, dominated by the dark red railway viaduct and the gashes caused by the river and a road cutting, and of course, dereliction. Like many English industrial towns it looks as if it has been picked up and dropped and then had the contents of an architectural junk shop scattered over it. One of the oddities from the junk shop is the town hall, high up away to my left, a white job with pillars and a dome, part temple and part early cinema.

There is no gap between Stockport and Manchester. The Victorian and Edwardian suburbs of the two places melt indistinguishably into one another. To break the monotony I divert down a track behind some big, turn-of-the-century villas and follow it between them and a deep, well-wooded railway cutting. It is easy to see how so many mammals and birds thrive in our cities. Diverting westwards through Cringle Fields Park I encounter almost simultaneously the formal border of Manchester, heavy rain, and the sentence 'IF HE'S BLACK GIVE HIM A CRACK' in large letters on a wall.

Through Burnage and Withington, getting wet. I always marvel in English cities at the sheer number of big brick houses built between 1875 and 1914. They are sociologically neutral: some of them now form smart, professional areas and others the worst slums.

Slightly lost, I take refuge in the White Swan, a cavernous place built (at a guess) in 1913 and a strange mixture of nouveau and Gothic styles. Like many Lancashire pubs it has a number of different, bar-less, rooms surrounded by leather benches: most of them are completely empty. The beer is good: Robinson's with a strong bitter flavour and, I think, 'real' because it comes from an electric pump. In the main bar are a group of middle-aged men, settled in for the afternoon. There is a large collection of (full) bottles of beer from all over the world resting on ledges around the walls. But every record on the juke box is played loudly in every room; conversation is difficult.

The White Swan does the trick; when I leave the pub it is still a very 'fresh' day, but it has stopped raining. North towards the centre and a complicated sequence of sociological changes: 'down' into an area of council houses with unkempt gardens, graffiti and boarded-up windows. Then 'up' again to council houses of the cottagy, sub-William Morris kind. I realise that I am very close to Maine Road, where Manchester City are just kicking off. I hear the roar and it quickens my pulse. At the William Hulme's Grammar School the chaps are limbering up for rugger.

Just north of the school is Moss Side. It starts with the spectacular symptoms of urban decay: a house burned out, a shop bricked up, a spontaneous people's tip at the end of the street. The back street between two terraces is flooded and full of junk: two dogs are playing in it and I would set up my classic urban decay picture if the camera wasn't bust. What is puzzling about this place is not that the houses are of the same sort as in many a 'posh' area, but that they overlook Alexandra Park, which looks splendid, its tall trees decked in autumn colours and its wet grass shining and clean.

I explore a renewed area of Moss Side, terraced houses built in the last ten or fifteen years. It seems nice, quiet and leafy and children play happily. Only a boarded-up house suggests a 'problem' area. The new pub, the Pepperhill, seems to be still open. I order a pint of (Wilson's) bitter. The landlord says, 'You're only just in time – like it's 3.15.' But he winks and serves me just the same. ''E wouldn't serve me,' says a tattooed white local, but he doesn't mind.

You could not ask for a more friendly, multi-racial, place than the Pepperhill. The landord is white, the barmaids are black. There are groups of white people, groups of black people and mixed groups. It is very smart and good-humoured, cheerful in a way that the White Swan wasn't. I would like more time here.

Beyond the new houses is a plain of grass with a sad cobbled street through the middle of it. Then big old terraces, some of which are in poor condition, but with occasional smartly kept houses among them. I have wandered in a circle and I can still hear the roar of the crowd from Maine Road, a great yell of expectation as (I guess) a scoring chance is created and a groan of release as the chance is missed.

Moss Side to the centre takes me through the University, its great dignified buildings totally silent and deserted, except for a lone security man. All the universities I know would have some life to them on a Saturday in term. But, then, I don't know anything about the English 'civic' universities.

The centre of Manchester: the Polytechnic, the BBC, clubs, theatres, a cinema announcing the imminent arrival of a Koo Stark movie. It has no strong style or distinctive character. Manchester is a con.; Engels and Dickens and that crowd made it famous in the 1840s as a riproaring slum and the front line of modern capitalism. 'If you 'aven't been to Manchester, you 'aven't lived' and 'What

Manchester does today, the world does tomorrow' hark back to those days. But no sooner was the image established than Manchester went respectable, turning its wealth into orchestras and universities and a water supply from the Lake District. It went for heavy dignity which I am looking at now in the shape of its sort-of classical library and its sort-of Gothic town hall. Then it was remade all over again, less distinctive than ever, in the sixties and seventies.

As I sit on a bench in St Peter's Square, surmising that there probably isn't a single thing for miles which Engels and his contemporaries would recognise, about ten youths walk towards me. They are drunk, one of them is wearing an ape's head and they are led by a fat one smoking a cigarette. I have a pen and paper in my hand. The leader shouts angrily at me. 'I know. You're collecting car numbers, you cunt. Get yerself a pair of proper shoes.' (This last a reference to my white training shoes). I very rarely remain silent when addressed, but this seems a good time to exercise the option. They move on, leaving me puzzled about why he thinks it is so wrong to collect car numbers.

I decide to walk from Piccadilly Station to Victoria Station, a journey I often had to make in my youth. I recognise very little; there is a huge Arndale Centre between the two stations now. North of Victoria, up Cheetham Hill Road, big views are opened up. The hills are easily visible from here, almost the centre of town. The high flats of Ancoats and a few remaining mill chimneys are outlined against them. This big view of Manchester looks as if somebody had taken one of Lowry's paintings, thrown mud at it, poked holes in it and then stuck a lot of modern architect's sketches on it: Arndale centres, DIY centres, ASDA superstores, high-rise flats and so on.

By now I am on a pilgrimage to Boggart Hole Clough, drawn by the beauty of its name and the part it plays in Fred Eyre's autobiography. It is an eventful pilgrimage. In Moston a house is on fire; young women stand on the steps of their houses watching the two fire engines and the pall of smoke. 'Oh, cummon,' says on. 'Let's go in. It's only an empty 'ouse.' It must have been set on fire deliberately. In old parts of Manchester like this empty houses seems to be regarded as fair game for anything. Yet sometimes they are next to beautifully kept houses with elaborate ornaments in the windows.

A boy of about twelve, leather jacket, jeans and a slouching hands-in-pocket walk, adopts me. He asks me where I'm going and I tell him. He says, 'Ah know it. Ah'll teck ye.' But his route is clearly about three times as long as is necessary and I make my own way. Boggart Hole Clough. What a name. (Compare it with *Green Park*.) Nor is the place disappointing. I go through big oaks, changing colour, then down a precipitate slope under the trees and among the rhododendrons. Up again onto a wild hillside. On the very top, football pitches surrounded by woods.

This is the end of my walk: an autumn twilight alone in the hills and woods of Boggart Hole Clough. I have cocked up this journey completely, because my destination is Turton on the other side of Bolton, a village where the first Association Football Club in Lancashire was formed. Walking is out of the question. I run to the Rochdale Road, take a bus to Manchester with a most friendly and co-operative driver who makes special arrangements to get me as close to Victoria Station as he can. Then train to Bolton and a taxi driven by an attractive young girl, to. . . where? The cock-up is complete. I had arranged a rendezvous at Turton Station, but there isn't a station at Turton. The problem is solved only by a series of phone calls and a long wait in the Railway Inn at Bromley Cross, reading all thirty-two pages of the Mancester Evening News Special Pink Final, an excellent newspaper.

19 To Hull and back

(January 1983)

In the 1970s, Barton-upon-Humber experienced a double revolution. Formally, it was taken out of Lincolnshire and put into the new county of Humberside. Physically, it was connected with the north bank of the Humber, the old East Riding, by what was, for a short time, the longest suspension bridge in the world. From being a dead-end in Lincolnshire, Barton found itself on a through route in Humberside. As the physical change occurred some six years after the formal, it is intriguing to speculate how local government actually worked for most of the seventies, especially *vis-à-vis* travel expenses.

But Barton seems a wholly unrevolutionised place. The streets in the centre are narrow, formed by terraces of small, old shops and pubs. Most of them have red tiles on the roofs and these are highlighted by the bright sunshine. It is a warm, spring-like Sunday morning after a night of rain. There is a trail of manure down the main street and a very small girl on a very fat pony is moving slowly through. Quite a crowd are chattering outside the Methodist Chapel.

On the hill to the west of the town there is more sign of change. The Georgian manor house now has a big new roundabout next to it and, making a virtue out of necessity, it has become the Humber Bridge Hotel. I plunge down a path just below it to have a good look at the bridge. It is very bright, slim and elegant in the sun and it is difficult to get an idea of its scale. An old man in an adjoining garden strikes up a conversation about the weather; he is very optimistic about 1983.

On the other side of town, by the river, there is the familiar English sense of a town which has outlived the reason for its existence. The canal, which used to connect the railway with the river, is now dried up. A row of pubs, houses and small factories stands opposite its dyke, which glistens green in the morning sun. The 'station' is good for a laugh, or at least a smile: a single line, ending in buffers, a station sign and the platform. The end of the line.

I want to walk across the new bridge and I fear that I may have to walk right across Barton to do so. But the fear is unjustified: a road runs parallel to the river, out of town and under the bridge and there are steps for walkers to get up on to it. I had thought it might be difficult or even impossible to walk across, this bridge being a product of the motor-car age. Nothing could be further from the truth. Pedestrians are numerous and furnished with broad paths on both sides of the bridge. And they travel free. Clearly a walk on the bridge is now well-established as a thing to do on Sundays in these parts.

Once upon the bridge the first vehicle I see is a camper from the Netherlands, heading south. This seems curiously appropriate, because there is something very un-English about the scale of the landscape below. The river is over a mile wide, and getting broader as it goes east. The general effect is of a vast flatness of water and land; the Dutch van seems symbolic because from here the fragility of man's hold on the dry bits is obvious.

The water looks blue in the distance, but a shining chocolate brown immediately below. It is swirling powerfully in complex shapes; ridges, lines and whirlpools. There are beaches on both banks, muddy on the south, but clean and sandy on the north. One of the sandy beaches, just east of the bridge, has an old paddle steamer, a former ferry, beached on it and used as a restaurant. At the far end of the bridge there are leafless brown woods dotted with large detached houses. My eyes naturally pan down the river to Hull which looks flat and clean on the horizon. I can pick out the lights of football grounds, tower blocks, the cranes of the harbour and what is almost certainly a modern flour mill. The bridge itself really appears to be suspended. Every ten yards or so one walks past a pair of huge wires and occasionally the whole structure shakes a little with the passage of a heavy vehicle.

The woods on the far side are part of Hessle. The first of the big houses I see, just below the bridge, is completely derelict. I wonder if the bridge is responsible; you get no compensation in such cases. But I doubt that the bridge was responsible, anyway: the house looks as if it has been falling down for a long time. Other houses look prosperous: very big Victorian mansions and villas, in a distinctive yellow brick. The more I have walked round England, the more fond I have become of this kind of mature suburbia. The charms of the countryside, especially where it has become an intensive food factory, can pale, but the old suburbs grow on you. The great variety of foliage, flowers and berries is the key. And the consequent wildlife: there is an unbroken chorus of birds on this fine morning.

I make my way through Hesslewood and South Field, along smart avenues and unsurfaced back lanes. The houses become smaller. The centre of Hessle is tiny and village-like. Hessle is a place whose centre could be fitted entirely into the grounds of one of its larger houses. Hessle stops, Hull starts, still very green and suburban in character. There are some rows of old people's cottages among great expanses of grass and trees, their arched front doors suggesting a Victorian copy of a Tudor alms house. Then Pickering Park, with its vast wrought-iron gates, painted bright blue.

My appetite is sharply whetted by the sight of a fish and chip shop advertising 'FRESH LANDINGS DAILY.' On closer inspection, it offers six kinds of fish with chips, plus 'crab tastings' and frogs' legs. Frogs' legs!? La Cuisine Hulloise. . . Certainly, fish and chips seem to be a serious and refined business here. A fact I happen to know, because it was published only last week, is that the citizens of Humberside spend more on fish and chips than those of any other county. But I am doomed to frustration. This is Sunday and do you know anywhere were the chip shops open on a Sunday lunchtime?

The road crosses a huge flyover. Boothferry Park, home of Hull City FC, is on my left. On the right there is no building, railway cuttings, woods, even farmland because of its liability to flood. There is an appalling amount of litter. I don't want to pick on Hull in this respect, it is true everywhere, a combination of winter, modern packaging, 'cuts' and the sheer cumulative effect. Past a huge modern Walls and Bird's Eye Plant and we are right in the city. There are certain kinds of building which were only ever built in the middle of cities: a pub whose façade is brown and green glazed tiles, across the road the elaborate front of the Picture Palace, now a bingo hall and freshly painted in bright orange.

The familiar picture of urban decay: as usual, just behind the main road. There are areas of rubble, demolition is still going on and a 'play street' is being created. As if it were the consequence of deliberate irony, there is a big advertising poster of the famous boy and his grandfather saying 'Heinz soup always makes things better' against a background of rubble and abandoned houses.

One of the games I play when travelling is to take songs which include place names (most of them are American) and substitute the names of the places I am travelling through. Hull gets the all-time wooden spoon in this game. It has a name like a dull thump which turns any song into brute prose. 'Hull. Hull. It's a hell of a place.' 'I left my heart in. . . Hull.' 'Twenty, twenty-four hours from Hull.' 'If you're going to Hull, be sure to wear some flowers in your hair.' And so on. Of course, its real name is Kingston-upon-Hull, but there are numerous Kingstons and, over the years, the city came to be known as Hull. In any case, Kingston-upon-Hull is no real improvement as far as the game is concerned.

I decide to eat in the station, as it will be quick and definitely available. A triple sandwich with French onion soup (i.e. Bovril with onions). Generally, only poor people are in station cafeterias on Sunday lunchtimes. The man who sits down opposite me has everything going against him. He is very old and totally blind. His eyes are deep in their sockets, his ears stick out at right angles; his face is long and grey and deeply wrinkled. He looks like the late Lord Wigg. He feels his way carefully into the seat opposite mine and with great difficulty lights a cigarette, the old-fashioned kind, without a filter. Two youths on the next table laugh at him. ('Sod you, sunshine,' I think to myself. 'I hope you stay unemployed for ever.' Such limited compassion as I have is not going to be wasted on the young; they can always hope and generally do.)

I wonder if I can help him. Does he even know I am there? But then he speaks to me and asks me the time. He has half an hour to wait for his bus. A terrible service from East Hull, he says. He comes into the city to buy his cigarettes. (That must mean for something to do, in practice.) I tell him that I am going to spend the afernoon watching Hull Kingston Rovers. 'Good lad. Good lad,' he says. He is really a football fan, Hull City, but he follows all local sport. He is enthusiastic in his praise of the local radio station which is a great boon to his life. He is knowledgeable too, even when we get on to my pet subject, Burnley Football Club. I feel moved by his company because he has trust and enthusiasm based on the smallest resources one can imagine in a 'developed' country. As I leave him, he is keenly reeling off the numbers of the buses which will get me to Craven Park.

I am in a hurry now and rush round the dignified buildings of Hull. They are smaller than in most northern cities and the character of the place is very distinct because of the proximity of the docks to the city centre, a little like Copenhagen, surprisingly enough. Just beyond Queen Victoria Square is the lovely little Prince's Dock basin surrounded by Georgian warehouses and houses of commerce. This is a distinct and stylish part of town; I go down the narrow streets with their high Georgian buildings until I get to the wharf on the River Hull, near where it meets the Humber. There is an attractive contrast between the mud and the working barges of the river and the cloistered gardens of some of the renovated houses by the wharf.

Full speed to the match, luckily catching the bus. The man in front, who seems to be very knowledgeable about Rugby League, briefs his mates on Halifax, Hull KR's opponents. 'Just like Oldham,' he says, 'tackle ye and tackle ye until they wear ye down.' I am quite excited, I have never seen a Rugby League game.

Once inside the ground my immediate impression is of a typically English stadium, a thing that was never envisaged, but just grew. There is a rugby pitch surrounded by a dog track. A stand on one side, a terrace on the other, both covered. A huge results board for the dogs at one end and club houses in two corners. The place is pretty full: in fact, there are about 8,000 people. The atmosphere is what I imagine Jimmy Hill means by 'family': no aggro (no Halifax fans) and a complete cross-section of people. Many women and of all ages.

I happen to stand next to a very beautiful girl, a brunette about twenty years old, with the face and figure of a model, wearing tight jeans and leg warmers and a red jacket in KR's colours. There is a nice, more cuddly, girl on my right.

When play starts, the tackling of Halifax (who wear black and white hoops) turns out to be less impressive than billed. The home backs, especially Gary Prohn, KR's fast New Zealand wing, crash through the visitors three times in the first ten minutes. It is a different excitement from football. Nothing in football matters except the ball hitting the back of the net. It is never certain to do so until it does and the subsequent roar of triumph and relief is the sound of football. Rugby is more cumulative; a good break makes a score increasingly certain and there is a growing chorus of triumph and admiration.

The Hull KR backs are running as if they mean it, flat-out with knees high. The beauty, for all her colour supplement looks, cackles and screeches like a Yorkshire *trictoteuse*, 'Go on. Go on. Cut through 'em. In the middle. Put it in the middle for George.' This last is a reference to Fairbairn, the home full back, who seems to be having the greatest difficulty kicking goals.

Ten minutes gone, 11-0 to Hull KR , Halifax attacking. The cuddly one changes sides and shouts 'C'mon 'alifax, gerra try.' She explains to her relatives, 'Ah like to see a match, norra massacre.' But *la tricoteuse* has no such compassion nor objectivity: 'Kill 'em. Don't lerr'em in. Norra single point.' To a home player who misses a tackle she shouts, 'Yer rubbish. If there were a prat of the match award, ye'd win it every week.'

The hooter goes for half-time with the score at 19-0. I move to the dark, packed covered terrace for the second half. Halifax put on a bit more of a show, hold the visitors for twenty minutes and kick a couple of goals. But then the speed of the home backs begins to tell again: good handling, fast runing and several more tries. This match is not without significance: it is the first of Hull KR's centenary year and by winning it they will go to the top of the Rugby League.

It is also the first game in which the American 'sin bin' system of temporary sending-off is in force. Late in the game, Gary Prohn elbows an opponent in the face and the referee points to the tunnel. The crowd are incensed, so the referee holds up ten fingers to them to indicate this is only a ten-minute sin bin. Half the crowd then explain the working of the sin bin to the other half. In fact there are fewer than ten minutes to go, so the system is off to an odd start. No sooner does Prohn disappear down the tunnel that the tannoy announces he has won the Man of the Match award; he has scored four tries. The crowd content themselves with baiting Ian Van Bellen, the vast and ancient Halifax forward. Incidentally, there is no singing, but there is an impressive sound of boys drumming their heels on the perimeter fence.

Final Score: Hull Kingston Rovers 35, Halifax 4. I still can't think of a song into which Hull fits.

20 *There are, of course, daffodils*

(April 1983)

England in spring. Even more so, Lakeland in spring: incredibly green grass, daffodils waving and yellow catkins trembling in the soft breeze, the air alive with birdsong. Tiny lambs kicking their heels and chasing their mothers among the white limestone and the fresh new grass.

Or: Keswick in the rain under a cover of thick, dirty cloud. There are daffodils along the River Greta, but their leaves and stems are bowed and broken by the overnight hail and there is litter between them, as there is everywhere these days. Much of the town is built in a dark grey slate, almost the colour of charcoal. Different mountains are visible down its narrow streets. In one direction, rounded slopes of dark green merging into thick cloud. On the other side, a crazy variety of pyramids and pinnacles forming a sinister silhouette against a light patch of sky. Straight on, where I am going, a steep 'V' shaped valley disappears upwards into snow and cloud. It may not be like the fantasy, but it is quite exciting if you know you have to walk across it.

The rain is cold and persistent. It seems that I am going to be cold and wet all day and will probably die of pneumonia. The only question is, when to use the change of clothes which I have in plastic bags in my rucksack. I search the sky for any signs of lightening or lifting. It is rational to get oneself in a thoroughly pessimistic mood; I would give anything for just *changeable*, though. I begin to pray:

> Oh, Lord, I who thank You for small mercies,
> Despite not accepting that you exist.
> (At least, not in any serious sense of that word)
> I beg You,
> Please let it be *changeable*.

Of course, tourism predominates in Keswick and accounts for most of the shops: woollens, outdoor equipment, antiques, fancy sweets. The conflicts of interest inherent in the idea of national parks can be easily identified in the town. There are the ideals which informed the creation of national parks: healthy outdoor recreation and the preservation of our rural heritage. These are represented by the booted and waterproofed young walkers who are loitering the streets wondering what to do today. Also, negatively, in the absence of any major expansion in the town and of a vulgarised tourist industry of chair-lifts and water-skis. Then there are the needs of a relatively poor indigenous community: right now, three weatherbeaten old men in suits, talking in strong accents, in the main street and by the cheap looking, almost Scottish, council housing dotted around the town centre. There are also people with a bit put by who retire here; I cannot help overhearing two couples discussing the dinner party for the twenty-sixth wedding anniversary of one of them which they will be having tonight. Finally, and most numerous, are the ordinary holidaymakers, the ones who have rarely, if ever, climbed a mountain or read a poem, but who come here for reasons they do not understand. There aren't many of them on the streets today, but their existence is established by the awful caravan site between the council houses and the tip.

Politicians and administrators involved with national parks nearly always say that their job is to reconcile these conflicting interests. It is the rational kind of thing for elected politicians to say and it requires no clear value judgements. Their job ought to be to further the original ideals of the national parks, to be on the side of the long-term future and of the greatest and deepest satisfactions. This would mean, for instance, that there should not be a single caravan in the whole national park. I leave moderation far behind on the question of caravans. Why on earth people are allowed to block the roads and litter the landscape with these monstrous little tin boxes. . . .

Leaving Keswick, I pass the Rexel pencil factory, a neat little place in twenties style and the source of 'Lakeland' coloured pencils, that favourite gift of concerned aunts. It is still working: cars in the car park and smoke coming out of the chimney. It has stopped raining now and I am on a well-made path which crosses the flat valley between Derwentwater and Bassenthwaite. Several people pass, but nobody speaks or acknowledges, which they would in most places in similar circumstances. Perhaps there are are just too many strangers round here. Alternatively, people in mountain areas are unfriendly: when I hitched everywhere, the Alps were always the most difficult section. Only in Switzerland and the Tyrol did people actually shake fists at hitchers.

In Braithwaite, Cumbria's best-kept (larger) village, the ascent begins. I follow Coledale Beck upstream. It is awful, a tortuous, slippy path of thick mud and wet rocks. It is raining heavily again. Once more, thank God for wellies, for without them this would be virtually impossible. Even with them, it is difficult; I am going to get a long way in a very long time at this rate. In despair I consult the map. I am on the wrong side of the beck. This means retracing my steps, but the path on the other side cannot be as bad as this.

And so it proves. After a steep scramble through wet, dead bracken, I gain the luxury of a virtually metalled track along a ledge. It is there because of the old mine about three miles up the valley. The beck is now just an attractive white bubbling thing a few hundred feet down on the left. The walking is easy and the rain has stopped again. I am able to study the view in front at my leisure. It is formidable:

craggy mountains of black rock and white snow. There is a certain amount of tension. I cannot tell from the map whether the ridge can be easily crossed. And there is the weather. Right now, it is sunny and positively warm; the cloud seems to be lifting, but if it comes down again crossing that precipitous ridge in the ice and snow would become foolhardy in the extreme. Yet I know, as a fateful fact about myself, that I would always try rather than turn back.

The old mineworkings are overshadowed by a scree of dark slate and cliffs of black rock. There is something strangely familiar about them. It is not, in this case, a dream, but an old movie, a wartime one, I think, involving German spies on the run. I have seen nobody so far, except a multicoloured collection of anoraks on the grassy slope, a couple of miles off to the left. As the path gets steeper and rockier, it begins to rain and I pass a party of sixth-form age going the other way. There is no teacher, so far as I can see. The rain turns to sleet and then stops. Just below the snowline I sit down and have lunch. This consists of meltwater and fruit and nut chocolate; there is a satisfying purity about the combination of tastes. I begin to think about that diet, the one where you eat as much as you like of a favourite thing and nothing else. I could have one week on chocolate and fresh water and then a week with nothing to eat but roasted, salted cashew nuts, followed by a week of pickled herrings. . . . Half a dozen Germans come down the slope and pause to look at Underskiddaw in the distance. I wonder if they are impressed; things may be relatively small round here, but that doesn't stop them being spectacular.

Getting over the top is hard work, plodding through a couple of feet of soft snow. But the main thing is that the cloud has lifted and visibility is good. This is a great relief, because the snow has obscured any traceable path there might be. Once on the other side, there is a path, a rugged rocky line on the right bank of a fast-flowing mountain stream in the 'V' est of 'V'-shaped valleys. The path is precipitous and hazardous; it is often best not to look down. There is nothing green in this valley; its side consists mainly of dark brown heather, the rocks are grey, the snow and the stream white. I meet a brace of young couples coming up the valley. They immediately cast me in a certain role. Being alone, and already over the top, and in very old clothes with a flat cap, they treat me as an expert and ask for advice.

I play this role well. Carefully reverting to my Lancashire accent, I advise them that all will be well so long as the cloud stays up and that in my opinion it will stay high for an hour or two. This is what they want to hear.

Suddenly, this steep ravine opens out into pastures above the broad valley which contains Buttermere and Crummock Water. Now that *is* green. Fantastic. The trees and the grass shining green in the sun. Crummock Water deep and still, the snowy mountains beyond. I skip down the grass, the occasional sheep flicking me a glance as it chews. That silly old poem of Wordsworth runs through my mind. When I was young, my mother sent me to elocution lessons to be deLancastrated. The elocution teacher, in turn, put us in for the children's poetry reading section of the local festival. Sometimes there would be the joy of hearing Wordsworth said in a totally unreformed Pennine voice:

> Ah wand'r'd loowenleh as er cleowd
> That floowats on 'igh o' er't vales un 'ills,
> When allat wunce ah sorr er creowd
> An 'ost er goowelden daffohdils;
> Beside the lairk, beneath the trees,
> Fluuterin' an' dancin' in the breeze.

In the valley I walk on soft spongy grass through woods of oak trees covered in thick moss. I pull some of it off and it comes in huge pieces, like a carpet. I quickly fantasise about laying a room with it and then about laying a girl on it. These woods remind me of Beatrix Potter; they must be like some illustrations in her books. I fall over on a wet rock, but no harm done, except a sore arse.

The valley between Crummock Water and Loweswater has a number of little cottages and a chapel. It is all very quiet, windless and empty, and beautiful, the green of the valley contrasting with the dark forests and steep mountains beyond. I wonder what I would grow if I had one of these cottages. Very little of interest seems to grow; just too much rain, I suppose. There are, of course, daffodils.

I walk past Loweswater on its northern bank. It is very quiet; I stand in the lake up to the top of my wellies looking at the woods on the slopes which rise from the far shore. They are fawn, dark green and even purple. When Loweswater ends, so does the Lake District. It just fades out into a rather scruffy, marshy valley broken by copses of trees. The road climbs over a last ridge and from the top I can look north for thirty or even forty miles: Solway Firth, lit by the sun, and the hills of Galloway in Scotland are visible in the damp air.

Down the slope is the village of Mockerkin. I had hoped it might contain a shop, but commerce is far beyond the means of this agricultural hamlet. It is just a collection of farms, with farm equipment parked on the green between them. A single collie, emerging from one of the farms, warily growls at three others which are lying on the road outside the opposite farm. A mile on and down across plain, unpretentious sheep country with a bright, whole rainbow across it, is the village of Ullock. This is a little bigger, but still lacks all the facilities and I am very thirsty. But as my feet are tired from walking on roads I decide to follow the track of the disused railway, which is kinder to the feet but far more challenging. The real problem arises where the railway used to cross a fast-flowing river: the bridge has been removed. I find another disused rail line and follow that, over gaps and barbed wire and through thickets of dense blackthorn. What to do if I cannot get across the river? Fortunately, I find a road and a bridge: by some means which I cannot understand I have arrived at the village which I was aiming, Branthwaite. But this has no shop either and I walk disconsolately on towards Workington, which is still five miles away. Twenty odd miles and no shops; it is time for urbanisation and industrialisation, now visible in the form of a drift mine on the ridge before Workington. Just to remind me that I said changeable would do, there is ice-cold rain again, but only for two minutes or so after which the sun comes out.

It is a dreadfully long haul into Workington, a long road with tired legs. I often look back to the dramatic shapes and colours of the Lake District, now scarcely believable in the context of the plain country of West Cumberland. Past Lilyhall industrial estate, with its flat, brand new factories, partly financed by the EEC Regional Development Fund. Past Workington Golf Club, the car park of which has shabbier and older cars than many a golf club I could name. Yet another ridge before the town. Will I ever see shops and pubs again?

Mathew Brown's 'light' is not a beer I would recommend for prizes or gold medals, but when you are dying of thirst even a fizzy, metallic beer is like nectar. That and a big bag of fish and chips which gives me the energy to look at the town. It is a raw little oasis of urban and industrial England with its mine and steelworks and docks. I look at a ship which is being refitted; there is something greatly satisfying about having reached the coast. Workington is not sitting the recession out comfortably; there are many shops which have closed down and there have been one or two big fires in the centre. But there are nice terraces of tall, painted stone houses. I watch a game of rugby on the big open plain between the football club and the Rugby League club. It has been a very changeable day.

21 *Up the creek*

(June 1983)

London is still a mystery to me, a place where things have different shapes and happen in different ways. Liverpool Street station was crowded and had a sense of people going exciting places. But I have to look for Fenchurch Street, hitherto just a place on the Monopoly board. It is a bright, warm, Saturday morning in the City, which is big and clean and important-looking. A helicopter passes over a nearby office block, shining in the sun. I am accompanied by a little Latin lady, whose comprehensible English is confined to 'Fenchurch Street'.

When we get there, the place is deserted. I have to buy a ticket from the porter, at what seems to be the exorbitant price of £2.30, just to get to Tilbury. The train has compartments and no corridors, the sort of train I associate with sinister events in monochrome movies. I didn't know they still existed. At the last minute I am joined in my compartment by a tiny little elderly couple. If I had to classify them (and I am English, after all), I would place them in the very respectable working classes. He is saying, 'Tomorrow'll be the problem. They'll be waitin' around. They'll 'ave to fill their time some 'ow.'

Beyond the flats and then the houses the train emerges into a great scruffy grassland, grazed by cows and fringed by cranes and pylons and power stations. It is now full, dozens of family groups having got on at Barking. I get off at Tilbury Town, which disconcerts me for a time because it doesn't seem to be much of a town and various names refer to Thurrock, such as Thurrock Irish Social Club. There is a public toilet which is, of course, locked. Painted on it in very large, clear white letters are the words 'ANGELA RIPPONS BUM'. The same phrase is repeated on the end of a terrace. Taken at face value it might be taken to exemplify the motto, 'if you can't have it, write about it'. But is it the name of a pop group? I have no feel for these things: I thought 'Beatles' was a corny name. Tilbury is not a rich place; there are old terraced houses and sixties flats, set in a context of scruffy little business yards. All the people I see are white and it is well decorated with slogans expressing racism, Fascism and football support.

I wander rather aimlessly in the direction I believe the river to be. On my left is a forest of cow parsley and a tin fence; on the right a jungle of small, scruffy businesses: garages, garden centres, welders, hauliers, body repairers. Life is given purpose by the sight of a sign: 'Footpath no. 144. Tilbury Riverside'. It takes me down a muddy ginnel and across the electric railway to a meadow containing an enormous power station. The meadow is vast; buttercups everywhere and skylarks filling the air with song. There are also may and elder, both covered in white blossom, and little flood ponds with white flowering water weeds, cows and horses intermittently in the distance. I have to be careful walking, to find the dry parts.

Towards the river the path converges with a road. A herd of wild horses, a dozen or more, trot down the road followed by a green bus. The horses turn left and spread out into the meadow; they are unaccompained. The bus goes straight on and beyond it I can see the sleek, white shape of a large cruising ship. Such a landscape cannot be typecast. I cross the new concrete flood wall on metal steps and sit down on the river's edge, an unusual surface of stone covered by soft, dry tar. I had a heavy night last night and my mood is one of confused apathy. It is very warm and quiet. The mud by the river makes a soft, singing noise and the river laps gently against it. Gravesend looks quite interesting over the water and my eye is drawn to the square tower and miniature spire of a church, in a style which Inigo Jones favoured. A girl's voice makes a clear, polite announcement in Russian. This adds considerably to the dreamy unreality of the occasion. It comes from the ship, the *Mikhail Lermontov*. I am what they used to call *spaced out*. They may still call it that, for all I know. Or care. A container ship chugs quietly and smoothly up the middle of the river; a ferry sets off. Who cares about anything?

Perhaps I will not bother to do anything today. Who in his right mind would walk down the Thames estuary, just to see what it is like? But the path along the river is curiously easy and inviting, pristine white concrete alongside the river wall. An open invitation, of course, to the wall writer. Approaching the power station I can see one of the least meritorious examples of this form of self-expression which I have ever read. It says: 'WOGS R CUNTS' (sic). But the next one is: 'LISA RADLEY I PLEDGED MYSELF TO YOU ALONE'.

This may be one of the world's most expensive footpaths as it consists of thousands of tons of concrete with steel steps to take it across obstacles. It goes past a wooden clapboard pub and then through the power station in a series of steps and tunnels. It has to do this because the station stretches down to a loading quay on the river. On the other side of the power station I am on East Tilbury marshes. I imagine marshes to be dark, dank places covered in reeds and rushes. But this is a meadow wilderness, lush and dense with plants. There are flowers of many colours, but yellow clearly predominates. Bushes of hawthorn and elder punctuate the landscape and the foliage is made even more dense by a plant which seems to be a kind of wild spinach. There are larks and butterflies and snails. It seems strange that here, in one of Europe's greatest concentrations of oil refineries and power stations, there should be a far richer mixture of plants and creatures than you will ever find on modern farmland. But it is perfectly logical; in ordinary circumstances, catastrophes apart, these industries are clean and are compatible with a much richer ecology than is modern arable farming.

On my right is the river and rolling wooded hills on the Kent side. The mudbanks around the river are huge here and there are the hulks of a couple of big ships rusting and rotting away in the mud very close to the bank. As always, I am re-planning the world. This is to be a wetlands park, flanked by tall trees to separate it visually from its industrial context. People will be able to see many varieties of plants, birds and insects which they would no longer see in the normal course of things. ('Ah, but where's the money coming from?'

We must all face the Thatcherite question now.) It wouldn't require much, mainly tidying up and a certain amount of policing to ensure that people did not have a deleterious effect on it. And some more building up of dykes, so that people could walk through the wetter bits.

No sooner have I formulated these plans than I find them come to fruition, albeit on a small scale. Thurrock Council have constructed a park with trees, lakes and meadows around the great gaunt building of the Coalhouse Fort and there are a handful of strollers and picnickers, the first people, barring a couple of distant fishermen, that I have seen for a while. I decide to cut inland to East Tilbury as, according to the map, continued progress along the river is likely to be difficult. Beyond the Coalhouse Fort is a little village, a strip of suburban brick houses and a pub. Curiously, the pub has no name. It used to have a name, for there are marks where the letters were attached to the brick and a gap at the top of the part where an inn sign would go. Inside the pub it is surprisingly bare and most people are outside in the sun. While eating my crab sandwiches and drinking my beer, it occurs to me that the village has no name either, being just a twentieth-century strip down by the river. This is very worrying; in my present mood of sleepy unreality the idea of being in a nameless pub in a nameless village could send me over the top.

It seems to be a very close place. Everyone who comes in is greeted with some loveable Cockney sparrowism like 'Eow are yer, boy' and 'Nah then, gel'. Three men are talking about the building trade; one says, obviously of a mutual acquaintance: 'Is ahse is werf nuffink; 'is garden's worf abaht sixty farsand quid.' At the bar a Scotsman is lecturing with great precision on the question of which is the most economical 'reg' of car to own. (There's an interesting effect of bureaucracy on language: 'age' is now 'reg'.)

The inland countryside is strange in some ways. Often it is very dense: thick hedges and tall trees, meadows of long grass and flowers, fields of peas, potatoes, wheat, rape and beets, lakes where gravel has once been extracted. But half the time it is backed in the middle distance by the vast range of oil containers and installations by the river at Coryton and Shellhaven. The tallest and most frequently visible thing is a silver chimney, burning off gases. This collection of installations is just about the biggest there is, many times bigger than that on Canvey Island proper.

For many miles there is this incongruity of foreground and backdrop, through East Tilbury and Muckingford, Linford and Stanton-le-Hope, suburbia varying from Victorian (in the case of Stanford-le-Hope) to modern and from A to C, as the Registrar General might see it. At Corringham, just past the Shell Sports Club, I have reached the great mass of tanks and chimneys itself and can hear the burning of the gas. But turning left I enter the old village; there is a stone church which looks French because it has a small, spired roof on the tower, white wooden clapboard houses in the style of Essex (or New England) and a dense mass of tall chestnut trees. By peering carefully through the leaves I can just see the gas burning at the top of the chimney.

I go through a prosperous suburbia to Fobbing. It is a day for naked pottering, a day of shorts and the exposure of hairy white paunches to the sun. It is surprisingly hilly, for I had thought that Essex was flat. Finally, at Fobbing, I leave the houses behind me and am back on the open marsh. It is a remarkable place, a vast open prairie of a dozen or more square miles completely dominated in aspect by the oil installations at this southern end. The two things seem unconnected. More than ever, the marsh is a wilderness where man grazes his animals, but otherwise has little effect on the birds and the insects. I set off along a path; it runs along a dyke, perhaps ten feet high, and there is the exhilarating feeling of walking above the landscape. I rest and drink my last can of Coke, a cuckoo the loudest sound, distant but distinct. Surely millions of people would come here for the sense of wilderness and space, if it were not for the view? But the view destroys nothing, except itself.

Musing on these minor philosophical nuances and whether they will finally win me a place in Pseud's Corner, I am unaware that I am on the brink of disaster. It is another mile or so along the dyke before I realise that I am not on the footpath at all. Instead of going north-east across the marsh to Basildon, I have walked due east to Vange Creek which is an obstacle to any further progress. However, the map shows a dyke running north by the creek and I should be able to get round the creek by following that.

It is a struggle. Obviously nobody comes here because the grass and flowers are waist high. The creek is a dank stretch of water, perhaps fifty feet across, between mudbanks. Ugly little crabs scuttle among the litter on the mud. The tide has covered the place with largish floating items, including many plastic bottles and a lot of polystyrene.

I have to make my way round little off-creeks. If they are small I jump them. I am very hot and parched, the vegetation is long and thick, the air smells and is full of flies. To my horror I realise that there is another broad creek flowing into Vange Creek and trapping me inside a 'U'-shaped marsh. I turn back along it, but little creeks, usually about six feet deep and eight across, block my way constantly. I become increasingly brave and careless as to how I cross them, throwing my rucksack across and leaping after it. After a dozen or more jumps, I fail and fall back, sinking eighteen inches and more into the mud. Fortunately, I am still upright. But the mud, which is pale brown on the surface, is black and oily underneath. It stinks, a fishy farty smell of methane and rotted fish, giving a new and horribly accurate meaning to the phrase 'the bowels of the earth'.

For another two hours or so I struggle along creekside dykes and through long grass. The birds and insects provide some consolation: unfamiliar coloured butterflies and dragonflies, shelducks and herons. Finally, in full view of Basildon New Town and obstructed by the high fence of a woodyard, I face a man, robust and tanned and in his twenties, across a creek.

'You're trespassing.'

'There isn't a criminal law of trespass in England.'

(Sullen mutter.) 'I can have you thrown off, though. . .'

'Nothing would give me greater pleasure.'

'. . . and fined a hundred pounds.'

'I doubt it.'

'How much do you want to argue?'

'Not a lot.'

Positions established, I cross the creek on a little plank bridge and we negotiate on a friendly basis. It is obvious that I am in the wrong, but by mistake. He has a management agreement with the Nature Conservancy, which means he has to keep people off his land. He is impressed by the distance I have walked. His farm, he tells me, has to remain a kind of ranch, semi-wild bullocks on wild meadows, because there is soft mud everywhere, twelve inches below the surface. He shows me a path in the direction I want to go.

After several miles of pretty, surprisingly hilly, country, I reach prosperous and wooded Benfleet where I sit in a pub near the station, looking over at Canvey Island and drinking ginger beer shandy. I am a broken man; hot, knackered, cross and smelly. I had meant to get right down to Canvey Point, but I didn't get close. The man who had conquered everything, beaten by bloody Essex.

22 ***Costa Inglese***

(July 1983)

I walk down the main street of Teignmouth asking the way to the quay. The day is cloudless, becoming hot; the street is unspoiled Georgian with places that sell fudge and Devon Cream Teas. The people are helpful, giving detailed instructions in their strong Devon accents.

I join the queue for the ferry across the river; most of the people are old. The black, flat-bottomed boat glides up onto the beach and we are assisted up a wobbly plank to board it. I take my seat alongside a brace of elderly couples as an old man comes round to collect the 25p. One of the husbands is saying to the other, ''Course, the seasons was more seasonal in them days. August and September it was always fine.' (Absolute crap. Guaranteed to meet with assent.) The young man who drives the boat (steers it? sails it?) is blond and suntanned. He wears a black vest and a little black cap, a medallion round his neck and an elaborate earring in his left ear. A definite image: poofy salt? Salty poof. Billy Budd.

A spit cuts right across the mouth of the river, so that it is less than fifty yards from sand to sand and the estuary of the Teign is enclosed into something very much like a lagoon. A very busy little lagoon, full of boats, enclosed by quays and houses and well-populated beaches. Beyond the buildings is the Devon countryside, cosy with its small fields and thick hedges, dotted with occasional squares of red ploughed earth.

The black boat runs up the beach at Shaldon. There is much

content at Shaldon: girls in bikinis loll on the beach, people sit on yachts watching the activity of the estuary. Shorts and little peaked caps are much in evidence. As I walk up the hill between the palm trees and guest houses and putting greens, I decide that there is still time to arrange a late family holiday in Devon. The place I like to spend my holidays is very exotic, but quintessentially English. It has a predominately Italian atmosphere, but with middle-eastern souks and French hotels. The inhabitants pride themselves on their bacon and eggs, real beer and perpetual sunshine. They spend their time playing cricket and sitting in pubs. Of course, the place is very fashionable, but quiet, and the wrong sort are conspicuous only by their absence. . . ('Have you thought about Gibraltar, sir?')

By now, I am on the Devon South Coast Path and have left the people behind. The path climbs up a steep little ravine, lush with huge cow parsley and wild mustard plants and out along meadows full of daisies and buttercups. The sea is flat calm, an opaque pale blue. I climb a steep hill, past a couple gazing out to sea and through a herd of sleek brown cows.

The path alternates, being sometimes across open meadow and then narrowly enclosed by tall hedgerows. These are superlative in the density and variety of their plants. Of course, there are the predictable tough guys of the plant world: nettles, brambles, gorse, bracken and cow parsley. But there are as well wild irises, dog-roses, cornflowers, ox-eye daisies, honeysuckle and buddleia, a Chinese import gone native. The smell is usually rank, but occasionally a more delicate scent, such as honeysuckle, predominates. It is extremely hard work, up and down hills the whole time. I can hear someone speaking German in the fields on my right.

At the top of the steepest hill I met a fellow walker, a red-haired man in his twenties. Both of us are pouring sweat and we stop and exchange remarks which are a mixture of condolence, encouragement and self-congratulation. 'It gets easier beyond Maidencombe,' he says, and strides on. Out at sea I can see a water-skier zipping along behind a speed-boat and I feel an intense, almost bitter envy of the motion and of the cool spray flicking against his body. I have a disreputable desire for a pint of lager shandy. Or five, or six.

The path plunges back into thick hedgerows. Quite often, these hedges produce sharp cracking noises. I cannot imagine what these are but I surmise that they have something to do with snakes. But, on reflection, this is only because I know nothing of snakes nor of the noise. The going is very difficult at times, the tunnel between the hedges being almost eradicated by plants and I am constantly attacked by nettles and brambles. A bee gets into my shirt, mistaking me for a flower (No way, sunshine!), but we part by mutual consent. But then it does get easier: first a thick track, moved down between the hedges and then a broad path through thick woods which brings me out at Maidencombe, a valley and a beach.

The valley is on the verge of being suburban, dotted with modern homes in unusual styles. I wonder about how and when they got planning permission. In general, there is something slightly naughty about Maidencombe; the young English, lying in the sun, all but naked, totally motionless, listening to rock music.

The woods beyond Maidencombe are tall and thick so that the ground had no vegetation. Occasionally the sun comes through a gap, illuminating the leaves into a patch of brilliant yellow-green. I pass a man who says 'Eow do', reminding me that it is Nelson holidays.

At Watcombe, by the ETU convalescent home, I move inland in search of Torquay. It proves difficult to find: there are houses, new estates, then old terraces, but not a town. Much of the time I am walking past terraces of houses in gorges of wooded cliffs. It is more like being in a miniature Welsh valley than in a town. My image of Torquay was of Basil Fawlty saying: 'This window is in Torquay, madam. The view you see through it is, therefore, a view of Torquay. . .', coupled with images of nut-brown pensioners and some crime and gambling. But now I begin to think of it as an anarchy of self-governing gardeners, boat-owners and landladies which has no need for a centre because it has no need of commerical or administrative centralisation. There are many nice gardens with their palm trees and multicoloured flowers and small conservatories full of tomato plants.

Of course, Torquay does have a centre, pale grey civic buildings and Victorian Romanesque brick shopping streets leading down to the harbour. It is very quiet on this sweltering day, though there are many youths hanging about the square outside the Library. They are all French, when I come to listen to them. Presumably, they are learning English at a language school. Why do the French send their offspring to the English *costa geriatrica?* Hypothesis 1: it confirms them in their belief that we are past it. Hypothesis 2: it is nearer to, and more like, France than any other parts of England. Hypothesis 3: 1 plus 2. Is it not true that Nopoleon first saw England at Torquay and said, 'Enfin, la belle patrie'?

Down in the harbour, I look back up around the town. It is not at all like the other English resorts that I know. There is no 'front' in the sense of a terrace of buildings facing the sea. The overwhelming impression is of white buildings, palaces and châteaux and pavilions, set in rolling wooded hills of dark green. The claim to be a 'riviera', visible in the vast lettering of the Riviera Hotel, seems reasonable in that it looks a lot more like Provence than it does like Blackpool or even Brighton. It is also much busier than most resorts, packed with people wandering round the harbour, lying on the grass and the beaches or sitting in deckchairs on the promenade.

The normal commerce of a resort is in full swing. There seem to be relatively few amusement arcades, but many places offering deep-sea fishing trips and, more modestly, mackerel fishing. There are coach trips to Dartmoor on offer or a tour of Devon Inns or a mystery tour. And boat trips to Alderney and Guernsey or round the bay or to a dozen other places. You can be photographed and have the picture glazed into a plate within three hours. A deckchair on the promenade costs 30p for the whole day and there are thousands of them filled by brown old ladies and gentlemen doing absolutely nothing. I think back to the time when I thought that life beyond thirty was aesthetically distasteful and should be discouraged. Now I rather like the idea of being old and sitting in the warm sun in a deckchair doing absolutely nothing except, perhaps, running over a few memories in the mind.

If the promenade is elderly and English, the beach is young and laced with foreigners. There is much respectable flesh on view, firm and golden. The young foreigners are mainly male: Italian and Spaniards with roving eyes and fat Germans with beer cans. There are many Scandinavian girls, one revealing all of her plump prettiness through a wet white dress. Most adults seem to be lying very still; many of the children are in the water in rubber dinghies or on airbeds.

Beyond the beach, I make my way south through the palmurbia

on the edge of Torquay until I rest in a park at Hollicombe. Opposite the park is a notice put up by Torbay District Council for the attention of drivers. It shows half a woman in a bikini and says 'WATCH THE ROAD NOT THE BEACH.' The park was part of the gasworks until 1979, an attractive piece of de-industrialisation with its ponds and exotic grasses.

By the time I leave the park I am in Paignton. The mood is very different here, highly traditional and a bit vulgar. There are raunchy litle hotels behind the promenade and on it there is a row of white beach huts as far as the eye can see. These are all occupied and deckchairs and sunbeds are laid out in front of them. The English extended family is alive and well and soaking up the sun in Paignton: grannies and aunties and teenage daughters with the straps of their bikini tops naughtily undone as they lie face downwards on sunbeds and dads standing and talking with their bellies hanging out. At first, the predominant accent seems to be Brum, but then the familiar tones of E. Lancs./W. Yorks. predominates, with London a poor third.

The far end of Paignton is very attractive. There is an elegant little terrace of hotels overlooking an exotic formal garden. Some black people, the first I have seen all day, are sitting in the shelter out of the sun. Curiously, the Black and White Minstrels are on at the theatre. In the old village part of the town, around the harbour, there are thatched cottages and views round the bay to the little island known as Thatcher Rock. (It always has been known as Thatcher Rock.)

Goodrington Sands, beyond Paignton, revives the great chain of beach huts. It offers ample evidence of the English love of industrial antiquity. A powerful little black steam engine hauls four coaches into the station behind the beach while on the promenade there is a rally of veteran cars, old Austins and Morrises and Rolls and Jaguars, with their running boards and mysterious controls, being inspected by men and boys. Beyond Goodrington Sands I can no longer follow the coast, but have to make my way inland to the A379 and south along that. There is fennel growing in abundance by the side of the road. Since I was quite pleased at getting it to grow in my garden, I am confirmed in my belief that South Devon must be a very easy place to grow things.

There is an unpleasant couple of miles along the main road until I find a path through the technicoloured gardens and bungalows of Churston Ferrers down to the sea. It is going home time, weary red and brown legs hauling picnic baskets and dinghies and hot children back for supper. This is a most attractive part of the coast, its rocky coves alternating with thick woods. I cross a beach of pale grey, disc-shaped stones where water-skiers are setting off from the shallows. Many people are leaving, but a few familes are chopping up driftwood, making fires and pulling out frying pans to make supper.

The rest of the path to Brixham is on a broad track through thick woods. Brixham is a fishing port. This is clear from the size and sophistication of the fishing boats in the harbour, as well as from the smell of fish and the car parks for fishing captains only. More subtly, it is evidenced in the age of the white terraces of houses which crowd the steep hills round the harbour. Even so, Brixham is full of holidaymakers, wandering the narrow streets, visiting the life-size replica of the *Golden Hind* and waiting for boats in the harbour. One of them is a big fat man whose T-shirt says 'SEX IS LIKE HOUSEWORK IT NEVER SEEMS TO BE FINISHED'. The theatre is showing Agatha Christie's *The Hollow* all summer; Mrs Christie used to live only four miles away.

I make my way round the harbour and along the coast to Berry Head. Little groups of boys from Ulster are following a treasure hunt and reading out clues like so many mimics doing John Cole. At the head is a big grey hotel. Next to that is a most peculiar edifice: it is a circular brick wall, perhaps thirty feet high with an arched entrance, now overgrown with ivy and surrounded by woods. It is like the bottom part of the world's biggest mill chimney. Now it has some jumps for horses in the amphitheatre which it forms; but the map does not show it.

Beyond it is a path through the woods to Berry Head where I can see the whole bay in the clear evening light. I have a great sense of triumph, because this time I have made it to my destination on the hottest day on which I have ever walked. The heat of a day can be measured by the number of lager shandies you have to drink before you can appreciate real beer. This has been a 5.2/5.3 day.

23 *Dear auld Glasgie toun*

(August 1983)

The high road to Scotland must be one of the most beautiful drives in the world. Since there may be some ambiguity, I mean the route which is mainly on the A68, which goes by Crook, Consett and Corbridge over Carter Bar to Jedburgh, Melrose and Peebles.

We drove it yesterday, on a beautifully clear evening. The land becomes increasngly wild as you approach the border. There are range after range of hills, varying in shape from the plateaux of Northumberland and the domes of the Cheviots to the strange, spiky ridge of the Eildons. There are woodlands of every description, baronial manor houses, rivers flowing sometimes through broad meadows and then past steep red cliffs. There are rich parklands where fat sheep graze under the trees and solid old border towns. All this is deep and green after a summer which has left most of Europe parched and bare.

And then, somewhere alongside Carluke, we saw the mass of tower blocks and industrial shapes which is Glasgow, a certain cure for any boredom or complacency which might have resulted from three hours of sleek landscape. Now, on a fine morning, I am walking towards Glasgow. It is a pleasant rural scene in some ways: cows grazing in meadows to my left, birch woods full of mauve willowherb on my right. But behind is the roar of the M73 and ahead is the vast grey mass of a housing estate. As there are no walls to paint just here, a considerable amount of writing has been done on the road: 'BROONY', 'C.Y.T.O.', 'U.V.F., 'FUCK TRUCKERS 10.4.' These expressions are repeated frequently.

The housing estate is Easterhouse. On entering it my emotions react with a special thud which is reserved for Scottish housing. Grey and dull yellow, breeze-block and pebbledash, three-storey tenements with dingy little balconies, giving a closed-in feel to the street. Why is it so depressing? I know the conventional explanations: there is a firmly rooted tradition of low rents; the size of the public sector and of the housing problem has always been enormous; these combine to explain why Scottish housing has always been built on the cheap. But surely there must be something they could do to stop the houses looking like punishment cells?

Affiliation has changed. On the pavement is written 'NO QUEEN HERE. I.R.A. I.N.L.A. GOD BLESS THE POPE 1982.' There is litter everywhere and the overwhelming majority of gardens are just masses of weed with the odd rusting domestic equipment and occasional children playing. There are a few minor exceptions and one spectacular case: a front garden laid out with tiny gravel paths and flowers and shrubs.

I feel very alien here; I have a sense of trespassing where I do not belong, more so than if I was wandering round a poor area in Naples or Warsaw. Listening to the women and children speak I have the utmost difficulty in picking up anything they say. 'Scotland is an accent', an SNP candidate once told me; the accent seems to get stronger rather than weaker over the years. It can turn, for instance, Kirkintilloch, the name of a town just up the road, into four rapid clucks.

On the recreation grounds there are seven red shale football pitches and numerous boys heading and shooting into goal. The reasoning behind the red shale is impeccable; the Scots play football all year and Scottish boys play it all day. Fifteen acres of red shale can support a great deal more football than fifteen acres of grass. But in England football is still mainly played on grass and walking across this red shale in the sun reinforces my sense of foreignness, as if this was part of some Mediterranean port which had lost its way.

There are relatively few cars in Easterhouse. Not only is there the negative evidence for this, very few cars on the streets, but there are many examples of what is, to my mind, the old-fashioned phenomenon of the mobile grocers' and greengrocers' shops. Correspondingly, public transport is much in evidence. Apart from the green and orange Glasgow buses, there is a fierce competition going on between Strathclyde's micro-buses and the black, London-style taxis. The taxis have neat advertisements on their sides, favourably comparing their own rates to those of the 'micros'.

Another red recreation ground I arrive at the 'EASTERHOUSE TOWNSHIP CENTRE'. Outside there are large billboards advertising day trips to Blackpool, one pound down. It is only a shopping centre. The main doors tell you that there are 'NO DOGS. NO LITTER. NO CYCLING. NO CONSUMING ALCOHOL. NO LOITERING', by order of Donaldson's Property Management.

I leave Easterhouse across a hilly field bordered by trees in a ravine. A boy in his early teens is in front of me. He looks nervously back as I catch him up, then quickens his pace and then finally runs away and eyes me watchfully from among the trees, much as an animal would. I follow the Wardie Road and the Hallhill Road, past Glenduffhill (Hebrew) Cemetery and Sandymount Cemetery, whose graves, visible from the road, are all Pakistani. There are long views from here and I stop to look. It is clear that much of Glasgow, if not most, is essentially like Easterhouse; there are line after line, cluster after cluster, of three and four-storey tenements, spread across the rolling hills, all of them built since the war. It is as if the whole thing is stuck in a rut, each generation of builders, planners and architects having no option but to build tenement slums parallel to those of its predecessors. There is one important change, though: whereas Glasgow in 1914 was said to be the most densely populated city in Europe, with fifteen thousand people to the square mile, the modern tenements are now spread out among the woods and fields. Glasgow is now partly inside-out; it is like a French or Italian city, and unlike most cities in England or America, in that the poor live on the outside.

No sooner have I formed this image than I am down in a very different Glasgow, older and more attractive. At the bottom of the hill, by Shettleston Station, there is a large square made up by three terraces and the railway line. The terraces are tall and built of rust-red granite. The space between them is large and has lawns, trees and flower beds. There are smart young women pushing prams.

This turns out to be typical architecturally, but perhaps not in other ways, of the older Glasgow I see walking down the Shettleston Road toward Parkhead. The street is flanked by tall, dark, stone temements. It is derelict, but lively: there are plenty of people going about their business, but much that has closed down, shops that are boarded up, tenements entirely deserted, some with the ground floor deserted and the upper floors inhabited and pubs that will never open again. These are the real tenements, the kind one associates with Glasgow and Dublin before 1914. The communal halls of those which are inhabited are dark and scruffy and somehow these qualities are made much worse by the shiny Victorian tiling which lines them. These tenements are obviously doomed. I still have my doubts about this doom; they look so much more strongly built than the modern tenements of Easterhouse. Those were generally in much better condition, but occasionally the pebbledash had fallen off, revealing the poor quality of the brick inside.

All the shops have steel shutters and grilles along the Shettleston Road and all the slogans are Catholic (or nationalist, or Celtic, or what you will). I go through the big gates of the Eastern Necropolis. This is a very grand name for a grandish cemetery, a well-kept place of granite and marble graves surmounted by urns and columns. As a kind of spontaneous visual joke the necropolis backs onto Celtic Park, the huge stadia and lighting pylons of which dominate views over the tombs, surely a rich source of sportswriters' clichés.

I walk south-west, through Camlachie and Bridgeton, pausing to read a notice inviting people to a public meeting to discuss the propositions that Sunday is not the true Sabbath and that the Christian churches have made a serious error in considering it to be so. There is a little row of tiny one-storey crofts by the road; looming behind it is a new block of flats, thirty odd storeys high. I have come across these little rustic crofts in other Scottish cities and can only assume that people moved into the city from the country and continued to build in the only way they knew, though it was a highly inefficient use of urban space.

There is an exciting sense of a city like a phoenix rising again in this part of Glasgow. There are areas of rubble, old factories and tenements falling down or boarded up. But there are also many new things: flats which look much smarter than anything in Easterhouse, new schools, neat gardens and shrubberies. There are little breeze-block workshops where welding is going on, a smart new hotel and futuristic new factories, including a radiator factory with a duck pond and geese roaming its grounds. This is all what enterprise zones are supposed to be like, though this isn't actually part of an enterprise zone.

I stop at a bar called the 222. It is definitely a bar, not a pub, like most Glasgow drinking establishments, and it is an extreme case, being no more than a shack with booze in it. I have given Scottish beer a lot of stick in the past, but the pint of Alloa Diamond Heavy which I drink here has a refreshing and distinctive taste and it goes well with the whisky. That is the trick, of course, and it is aided by the sale of whisky in Glasgow on the narrow profit margin of 50p for a quarter of a gill, as compared with something like 70p for a sixth in much of England. Turnover is much higher in Scotland. I watch the men play pool for a while; the convention that the winner stays on the table now seems to be universal.

Overlooking Glasgow Green there are some attractive new yellow brick town houses. Standing on the Green, I can feel the underground trains below. I enter the dark ornamental building which is now called the People's Palace. It contains a permanent exhibition devoted to the history and people of Glasgow, with strong emphasis on socialist politics and the *Glasgow Herald*, though there are sections on the early origins and on different industries and on football. The *Glasgow Herald* claims to be the oldest newspaper in the English language. By the time I have left the People's Palace I have developed an affection for Glasgow and am wrestling with the problem of whether it makes sense to wonder if I would have been a Socialist if I came from Glasgow; this embryo of affection faintly echoes the enthusiasm of most of the Englishmen I know who have lived here, who all extol the virtues of the city.

I cross the river and visit the site of the Gorbals. It is all changed now, a great rolling lawn covered in huge blocks of flats and some small town houses. There is little evidence of what it used to be like: the odd rotting and deserted tenement on the edge, a black little workshop called Gorbals Metals under the railway bridge, and I can just make out where some of the streets were.

This area is just across the river from downtown Glasgow. I follow the main shopping streets, Argyll Street and Buchanan Street in to George Square. Much of Buchanan Street is now free of traffic. In the Square, the city still seems to retain all its mighty wealth and grandeur. It is absolutely packed today, with people sitting or lying on the grass and benches. I join them, drinking chicken soup and eating one of those strangely satisfying amalgams of pepper and greasy mutton which the Scots call a pie. I can pick out the accents and languages of French, Italians, Spaniards, Americans and Canadians and I realise that I am not the only tourist in Glasgow.

My next stop is, just for a moment, in the cool Gothic gloom of St Mungo's Cathedral and then behind that, over a bridge and up a hill to the main necropolis. This is my fourth cemetery today. (Still, if it's what you enjoy doing. . .) 'Cemetery', though, undersells this necropolis. Here lie the chief Glasgow merchants of the nineteenth century under dark columns, in classical mausoleums and in miniature Romanesque cathedrals. It is a marvellous place even if you don't like cemeteries, having extensive views in all directions, over the city, down to the Uplands and up to the Highlands. At the very top of the hill, on a tall black column, is John Knox, 'incorruptible guardian of our best interests', as his inscription has it. This necropolis is a work of art, a heavy-handed but beautifully vivid expression of the spirit of Scottish mercantile Protestantism.

Away down Sauchiehall Street, where the revival of the city seems to owe much to Strathclyde University, aided by the Clydesdale Bank and others. Beyond the shops and restaurants Glasgow suddenly turns 'naice'. I go up into the brown Gerogian terraces and circuses of Kelvingrove Park. This is a very different Glasgow, one where smart young men are leaving architects' and accountants' offices and getting into sports cars. I descend the steep ravine of the park itself and climb up again to the dark Gothic castle which is Glasgow University: the architectural range of universities must be as broad as the whole range of architecture. In parliamentary terms, I am now in Hillhead, held by Roy Jenkins as the only non-Labour MP in Glasgow.

I do not feel alien here, among the apple trees and the chaps going out for their evening run and peering into the spacious front rooms with their pot plants and bookshelves. It is partly a question of class and partly of nationality, though the two are twisted into a complex compendium of images. In Kelvinside there are even cricket pitches, though surrounded by enormously high fences. Here I feel only a passing envy of urban life as I have felt in Kensington or Edinburgh New Town, watching smart young women coming home to their apartments and thinking how much more fraught with possibility their lives must be than my own.

I follow the evening sun through Anniesland, Knightswood and Drumchapel to the edge of Bearsden and eventually to Clydebank and Dalmuir. I am walking towards the Kilpatrick Hills which appear clearer and higher every time I glimpse them. They mark, in effect, the edge of the Highlands: the Antonine Wall runs along their foot and thus forms a satisfying destination.

Incidentally, during the whole walk, right across Glasgow, I must have seen many thousands of people. Barely half a dozen of them were manifestly drunk, whch is surely an improvement on Glasgow's reputation and may say something for the new liberal licensing regime in Scotland.

24 *Dwy Dref Cymraig*

(November 1983)

The Milton Hotel, Llanwern, was built, I guess, in the sixties; its gable end owes something to Switzerland and its white clapboards would be more at home in Essex or New England. It lies at the head of a shallow valley, surrounded by modern bungalows. The rest of the valley consists of pleasantly rich fields full of sheep and there are woods on the slightly higher ground.

A miniature rusticity invades all parts of the village. In a field between two houses a young man is whistling. His sounds, shrill and abrupt, are directing a collie which is itself marshalling five fat sheep with brutal precision. A little livestock allotment, defined by corrugated metal fences, has been carved out from the field on the opposite side. There are hens and ducks and a brown goat who is stretching his neck to get his tongue around some forbidden leaves. There is a tiny triangular field, scarcely an acre, freshly ploughed and bounded by the railway.

But this place cannot reasonably be described as a rural village. At the bottom of the valley, through the fuzzy visibility of this dank morning, is a vast cylindrical building inscribed with huge letters: 'LLANWERN'. As I walk through the village it reveals an anarchic collection of towers, chimneys, pylons and girders, seen over the fields and the bungalow gardens with their little plots of leeks and sprouts. It is an exciting sight, but it poses the problem of adjusting to its scale. British Steel's Llanwern plant is over three miles long, a mile wide and much of it towers hundreds of feet into the air.

The noises are as strange as the view. The works always drones, sometimes it roars, occasionally it squeaks. From time to time there is a clattering, as of goods trucks being battered together in a chain reaction. Most spectacularly of all, it sometimes gasps as it gives off a puff of white steam. As if this were not enough, a 125 Paddington to Cardiff hurtles through the foreground: 'NEEEEEEEE-ouououou oughbudumbudumbudumbudum.' It makes me think of a monstrous giant, lying in its death throes, being tormented by a beserk snake.

I leave the village by the path which runs across the golf course. There are many men, all middle-aged, playing golf on this cold, damp midweek morning. I stop while one of them takes a shot off the path and turn to look at the vast steelworks which I can now see as a whole.

Leaving the golf course, I am on the playing fields of Hartridge Comprehensive School, a glass box construction of the sixties. A game of football is in progress on the all-weather pitch. It is impossible to follow the play because the boys are all wearing different coloured shirts and following the ball around like a herd of sheep, as twelve-year-olds usually do. There is no teacher, so far as I can see, but the herd is pursued by a fat black dog. It is a bad-tempered game. A boy called Billy misses a reasonable chance at goal and they all shout at him, 'Bloody 'ell, Billy. You're bloody useless, that's what you are.' Billy gesticulates and makes it clear that in his opinion it was their fault anyway.

The grounds of Hartridge Comprehensive School break all known records for litter. The place is awash in bags and wrappers. I have seen town centres on a Saturday teatime cleaner than this; it ought, as a school, to have its own free labour force. It may be a conditioned reflex on my part, but I find it hard to imagine minds being disciplined or elevated in Hartridge Comprehensive School.

Large parts of Newport are now visible: Coldra, Ringway, Bishpool and Alway. They consist entirely of very plain modern houses and small blocks of flats, but the aspect is made more pleasant and interesting by the hills and valleys on which they are spread which set them at odd angles and break them up with grass and wooded valleys. As I walk on, Liswerry (or is it Alway?) seems rather pleasantly planned, built around its little becks, the houses having dark clapboards and brick back yards. After a couple of miles I conclude that Newport is very new, at least in terms of the average age of its buildings, as everything I have seen is post-war.

As I approach the river Usk the buildings become much older, tall Edwardian shops and houses. I go up on to the bridge which takes the A48 over the river and look at the town centre as a whole. There is no point in pretending that Newport is ever going to experience any kind of boom in tourism: what I can see is the mud of the river, a lot of dereliction, roads cutting right through the town and a number of modern 'blocks' in the centre which are too small and mediocre to give the place any look of importance.

My guidebook says, coolly, '. . . the town is not very distinguished in architecture, being a rapid and utilitarian growth in the nineteenth century'. Walking up Corporation Street on the east bank of the river, I am inclined to agree. It is not a nice town; it is an industrial town. For some time, I have held the theory that much of the English attitude to cities (and, therefore, to much else) can be explained by the industrial revolution having taken place virtually on virgin sites and not in the established centres of culture and power. Newport, though Welsh, seems to be a paradigm case; it was not much more than a village (it had a thousand inhabitants) in 1800; it has never been a focus for pride, but only a place to make money. South Wales seems more extreme than northern England in these respects: industrialisation here was later, faster, bigger and brasher than it was in Lancashire and Yorkshire.

I am musing on my theory and concluding that Newport is, after all, the extreme example, when I pass the gates of the rugby club on Rodney Road. Someone has painted 'NCFC' (i.e. a reference to the football club) in blue on the green gate. Since the bridge I have been walking level with a dark-haired man in his forties who is wearing a blue club blazer and tie, a combination which is superficially smart, but which is rather tattered on closer inspection. I imagine him to be unemployed and proud. There is another man in a shabby suit eating chips on a bench. Even as a traveller, tired and alone, it would be difficult to feel sorry for yourself here: there are too many other people to feel sorry for.

I am beginning to think that Newport has taken this business of being utilitarian so seriously that it has no grand or symbolic buildings at all when I reach the war memorial, a very big one in white stone.

I cross the river, passing the ruins of the castle and an attractive mosaic illustrating the industrial history of the town. Commercial Street and the area round it turn out to be Newport's best feature, the Edwardian buildings and the absence of traffic giving the street a surprising combination of grandeur and intimacy.

Even the most unlikely places (and Newport is just about the most unlikely) can now offer a selection of international culinary styles. I pass Chinese restaurants, two which claim to be American, a Greek restaurant, a Spanish one and a number of Indian restaurants. In the window of the Greek restaurant it says, 'WE HAVE *NEVER* HAD ANY CONNECTION WITH VANS SELLING DONER KEBABS AROUND THE TOWN'. Even more intriguing, though, is the spick and span Tandoori restaurant which advertises 'AIR CONDITIONING'. I imagine a woman's voice, not unlike that of the actress Ruth Madoc, saying in the harsh, sing-song, Newport accent: 'Owen an' I wouldn't even considah eatin' in a restaurant if it didn't 'ave air conditionin.' I eat cod, chips and jumbo sausage on a bench: 93p.

The west side of Newport is older than the east, a more settled place of inter-war semis. After a mile and a half the town peters out. Even here, in this most southerly and densely populated part of the country, Wales is not urbane; the brown grassy hills at the back of Tredegar Park have a wild look about them. On the other side of the main road is a shiny steel INGLOS plant which looks like something out of a giant's kitchen and reminds me that, as purely 'industrial' towns go, Newport is said to be surviving the recession relatively well.

I decide to walk by the A48, at least for the time being. There is a pavement, but a lot of traffic. After another mile there is the interchange with the M4 and the 'A' road becomes much quieter as it bends around the gloomily impressive park which surrounds Tredegar House. For three miles, the M4 is up on a ridge to my right and there are attractively rich pastures with big trees sloping away to the left. Then the village of Castleton, which is itself a humble place of plain old cottages. But its status as being just outside Newport and Cardiff has made it a place where executives eat lunch and put each other up. There is a large Beefeater steak house and an even larger 'Ladbroke's hotel. The sign outside the chapel says 'LIFE IS FRAGILE. HANDLE WITH PRAYER.'

I hang a left and head for the Bristol Channel, through the straggling village of Marshfield with its Ansells brewery and Unigate dairy. Before Marshfield the road is sloping down through unexceptional countryside. But aferwards, I am in a strange Welsh fenland, which is totally flat. It was a marsh and is now sliced into a grid by stagnant green ditches. A heron rises off one of them and a coot flaps across another. There is a huge field of winter wheat to my left, but most of the land is pasture. It all seems much bigger than it looks on the map. I hurry on down; the road turns into a muddy track and this finally joins the earth dyke which is here called a 'wharf' and which runs along by the channel.

Inland are flat fields with black hedgerows. On the other side are marsh grass, driftwood, mud and water. I pass two men, setting up a camera with a telescopic lens. They ignore me. Thereafter nobody: wild ducks, seabirds, domestic animals in the fields. A foghorn booms constantly from the channel. In part I am cursing myself for having chosen such an obscure route, but I am also deeply glad to be on this great, flat, muddy place on a wintry afternoon. It occurs to me that perhaps its sense of loneliness is dependent on the conditions: if the day were clear and brash, instead of still and misty, it might seem a less remote place.

I walk the dyke for several miles. The church of Peterstone Wentlooge looms out of the mist and I pass a caravan surrounded by goats and ducks, then jog a while to make up time. I have no watch and this murky day gives little clue to the time. Finally, industrial shapes can be seen across the estuary. There is a notice which says 'ARMED TRESPASSERS WILL BE PROSECUTED' and many horses.

These horses vary enormously: there are fat little ponies scarcely two feet high and big brown jobs indistinguishable from what one sees on the racecourse. I pass very close to one of the strangest, a sturdy creature of medium height with the spotted decor of a dalmatian. As I do so he lifts his head and neighs dramatically. There is a drubbing of hooves as horses gallop towards us from all over the marsh, joining together into a stampede. I panic, but cannot think of anything to do, so I walk onward as if calm. Some yards behind me the stampede halts with much panting and snorting and breaking off in different directions.

Cardiff begins very inauspiciously with the tip and three teenage boys sitting by three fires. This is followed by mudflats, an unfinished overpass, waste land, a big new night-club, the Freightliner terminal and some bitty little allotments with jet black soil. But after half a mile or so of this fringe existence I am in the city proper and it is immediately clear that Cardiff is a lot fancier a place than Newport. The predominant style is of tall grey villas, faced in white and magnolia. There are many medium-sized hotels (*gwesty* is Welsh for hotel and I determine to add it to my vocabulary) and several Welsh headquarters of organisations: the Theosophical Society and the RAC are the first two I see. As I move from the villas into the city centre, it feels like a really big city: it has large, very modern buildings and dozens of insurance companies and banks. Queen Street is now a pedestrian precinct in which I hear Arabic, French and a Scandinavian language being spoken. I pass the enormous castle and, accidentally, I find myself at Cardiff Arms Park. A security man give me that kind of friendly greeting which says, 'I've 'ad a good look at you boyo.' I walk into the stadium where Cardiff play rugby. It is an impressive stadium in its way, but now entirely dwarfed by the huge bowl of the National Stadium. I stand and breathe in the atmosphere in the dusk, reviving memories of smart young men with blazers and moustaches and intense Welsh voices whose lifetime ambitions were focused on this place.

The car park of the stadium is used daily as a commercial car park, though part of it says 'WRU OFFICIALS ONLY'. I talk to the old man who takes the money and he explains that the Cardiff ground, still called the Arms Park, and the international stadium are now entirely separate and that there will not be a game in the National Stadium for another seven weeks. 'I was last here in 1964,' I tell him, and he says, 'Oh, it's all been changed since then. That was the old days.'

After several cream cakes and six cups of tea I walk down towards Butetown and the docks in the dark. This was Grandpa's Toxteth, where they rioted and held the police at bay for three days in 1912. Respectability seems now to have spread southwards down Bute Street: I pass the Welsh National Opera (funded by the EEC). Like many ex-slums it seems now to consist of relatively smart flats and terraced houses. I go under the railway along Schooner Street. Here there are sininster derelict warehouses and boarding houses looming out of the misty night, but mostly the area is still active and prosperous. There are no lascars looming in dark alleys, but I pass a secretary and her boss leaving a brightly-lit company headquarters.

Down by the docks is the old area of Georgian buildings and a medium-sized sailing ship is visible on the water. I go into the Mount Stuart, a near-derelict pub, half hoping that it will be full of swarthy lascars with eye patches. Instead there are about a dozen men, drinking quietly. It is rare, though, that life is entirely disappointing and the barman *is* a lascar, so far as I can see, having Chinese features, African hair, a Mediterranean complexion and a Welsh accent. And a nice smile. I drink Brain's 'dark' as everyone else seems to, an unusual beer, something like a mixture of stout and mild.

25 *Shredded Wheat country*

(December 1983)

It is bitterly cold, stinging my cheeks. The sun is rising and lighting up the high, brown-grey cloud and making stripes of a weak, shiny yellow across the sky. The Chilterns above Berkhamsted are plateaux of winter wheat, frosted white, interspersed with black woods. Yet somehow the countryside has a bluish look to it, despite the absence of anything which is actually blue. Days like this are frightening to any rational creature; they bring us so much closer to the ancient problems of survival; so many more things can go wrong.

Berkhamsted straggles along the A41 and, presumably, prays for the M41 to be extended. On the edge of the town are AA notices which warn of long delays due to road works. The main street has a style formed in the coaching era: small Georgian shops and hotels, set back from the road. Little lanes of cottages run off the main street and behind them are Edwardian villas and then woods. It is Sunday morning and I can hear singing from the church. A man walks past me carrying a Bible and does not smile. I leave the town, going east, past a garage and a caravan sales yard.

I am walking down a valley which contains, as well as the A41, the main London-Milton Keynes railway on my left and the Grand Union Canal below it. Much of the rest of the bottom of the valley is taken up with timber yards, pony stables, and hay barns. There are places advertising hay, manure and livery. Among the litter on the verge, I spot a big, heavy-duty workman's torch. Out of curiosity I pick it up and switch it on. It works, so I hide it in the long grass behind the bus stop, to be retrieved later.

At the sewage works just outside Bourne End things are beginning to go wrong. A big pipe is gushing water into a tank, but the water in the tank is frozen so the water from the pipe bounces out on to the grass where it freezes and looks like a crashed chandelier. Bourne End caters extensively for the modern traveller: it has a Little Chef, a modernised inn and a large Moat House. At the bus stop there is a notice which says that Green Line buses accept US dollars on certain routes, at a rate 'slightly below that offered by the banks'. A family in an Astra stop and ask me the way to Bovingdon and I am able to show them on the map.

I find a lane which takes me under the railway and over the canal into the outskirts of Hemel Hempstead. It is getting warmer by the minute as the sun rises; the day is going to be very pleasant, at least for a time. There is a cress farm on the other side of the canal and it consists of compartments of water (now ice), about ten yards by ten, with a stream flowing past the end. I don't think I have ever seen a cress farm before and it looks quite exotic, like a frozen paddy field. In the distance a game of football is beginning, even though the ground is completely frozen.

Hemel Hempstead is something of a surprise. As new towns go, it does not seem very new. Even the houses and flats which were put up by the Development Corporation are well established and traditional: there are yellow brick terraces and small blocks of flats and flintstone semis, all with conventional gable ends. And there are a lot of genuinely old buildings, some most impressive detached houses and several Victorian terraces. There is a most attractive pink pub, dated 1720, overlooking the park and the black wooded hills beyond. In the distance I can see a tall modern block and I make a bet with an imaginary companion that it is *not* a block of flats. The ideas of the Town and Country Planning Association held sway in the new towns more than anywhere else and they were never persuaded of the virtues of high-rise living.

In making my way towards the high building I pass the Dacorum Sports Centre, Home of Ovaltine Basketball Club. There's a good quiz question: 'In which county would you find a local authority called Dacorum District Council?' The high building is the Kodak Building; on the lawn in front of it is Rodin's Monument to Balzac. I strain to think of a connection, but none is forthcoming. Access to the town centre seems very difficult: there is a six-storey curving office block surrounded by scaffolding and high wooden fences between me and it. This turns out to be the BP building and it is falling down (which, surely, is a reasonable interpretation of 'DANGEROUS STRUCTURE'). But it is possible to get round the BP building by following a series of arrows and into Marlowes, the main shopping street of Hemel Hempstead.

Marlowes is unusual for a new town in that the focus or centre is a street with traffic. At first glance, I dislike it intensely: there is a vast mock-Tudor steakhouse and two or three hundred yards of the nastiest possible fifties/sixties tat, buildings made of glass and coloured panels which make me want to kick them down and sweep up the pieces. Under the pedestrian access to the car park there is a complete disaster of a pond garden, surrounded by graffiti and full of soggy litter. It is a planners' gesture, 'landscaping', a watered-down, compromised descendant of what might once have been a good idea on paper.

But, further along the street, there is much more solid and traditional building and a broad pavement high above the street which seems to provide the best of both worlds, a street and a precinct. Then there is an attractive market square, the striped colours of the stalls' covers backed by thickly wooded rolling suburbs. It is now a beautiful day, warm and fresh, the air with that total clarity which is only fully achieved in winter. There are plenty of people about, just strolling. I make my way into Gade Park which, in the style of new towns and garden cities, is a vast river valley of parkland leading out into open country. There is a walled flower garden beneath an old church. I sit for a while, watching the park and a bold robin joins me, his chest puffed out. He perches very close to my shoulder and on my shoe and, at one point flies so close that his wings flap in my hair.

I still have very ambiguous opinions about new towns. Many of the ideas which went into their planning seem admirable: here, the sense of space and cleanliness is astonishing in a town centre and only a few of the most elegant cities could rival it. But there remains something odd to my mind about the idea of planning a town from scratch, and new towns often give me a strange sense of there being something missing.

I have no ambiguous feelings about the English Sunday, though. At this time of the year and in weather like this there are something like twenty hours per day of a desperate, unpleasant coldness and about four hours of exhilarating beauty. Yet a large proportion of the population spends these hours in pubs and clubs and /or putting away a huge meal. By the time the sun goes down, nothing is open. Quite mad.

Above Gade Park, on the top of the hill, is the old centre of Hemel Hempstead, an early nineteenth-century provincial town of narrow streets. Behind it is an old residential area, with steep streets, bright colours and jaunty little terraces. I pass the hospital, which is old and small, and walk out of town through the Adeyfield district. In the planning of Hemel Hempstead there was unusually little attempt at originality in house design. The vast majority are traditional brick houses, unexceptional and more or less identical. I don't suppose that Hemel Hempstead can compete with Stevenage's hundred varieties of house (even though they don't seem very different), or the eclectic approach to style in Milton Keynes. But then there are virtues to the solid, vernacular method: I feel equally confident that Hemel will not suffer from five thousand leaking (flat) roofs as Peterlee did. Curiously, given that I passed the hospital, one of the few large wall writings, on the out-building of a school, says 'HEMEL NEEDS A NEW HOSPITAL NOW'.

As I leave the town there is a sign saying four miles to St Albans. I have no desire to linger on such a short day nor to walk by the main road, so I try to hitch, but nobody takes any notice. Or, if they do, it is to be aggressive, roaring past within a foot of me or turning in the back seat to give me curious, contemptuous glances. I give up and jog instead. An Indian stops and asks how he can get onto the M1. With the help of my map I explain that you have to go into Hemel, but this is, of course, the wrong direction for me.

The M1 itself is only another two hundred yards. Road works are in active progress on the bridge, the final stages of widening the motorway from two lanes to four. All four lanes are now open and full in both directions. There is a thick wood, called Prae Wood, on the left after this, but I spot a footpath sign saying St Albans 1, away to the right. Sick of the road and its humiliations I set off, running past a line of oak trees, through a field of rape leaves and into a pine wood. Hundreds of pigeons take off as I crash through the wood; I am making excellent progress and this is a pleasant change. But then the path veers within a few feet of the M10 and back towards St Albans and I am left among the pines and the bracken facing a barbed-wire fence. I cross the wire and run through fields of winter wheat, now softening to mud, until I reach a lane on the edge of the town.

At first sight, St Albans looks newer than Hemel Hempstead as what I can see is a new estate called St Stephen's. But first sight is extremely misleading and soon I am in a grassy valley, about a mile wide. This is the site of the Roman city of Verulamium and there are bits of ancient wall cropping up among the trees and football pitches. My eyes are drawn to the enormous, squat cathedral on the hill on the other side.

I make my way round a frozen pond at the bottom of the valley and dash for the pub which is by the old mill on the stream which runs out of the pond. It is a very olde worlde pub full of beams and dark smoky corners and has that atmosphere peculiar to the home counties on a Sunday lunchtime, of prosperous and complacent young people taking their leisure. But, unfortunately, it has stopped serving and I am unable to try a pint of Benskins.

On the hill going up to the cathedral there are a trio of young couples looking at a row of tiny cottages. One of the men quotes the most recent price: £62,000. I like visiting cathedrals, but I am unprepared for the exotic qualities of St Albans. It is a partly brick cathedral, largely using second-hand brick and stone from the Roman site. On entering it through the smart new (1982) brick chapter house, there is a strong smell of incense. The brown and white round arches are 'Romanesque' rather than 'Norman': they produce an atmosphere very different from the sense of northerness in, say, Durham cathedral. Beyond the screen there sound to be hundreds of people and, indeed, there are, old men with moustaches and medals moving into their places for the British Legion carol service. There is still almost an hour before it begins. The choir, in red gowns, rehearses one of those old English, multi-part carols which always make me think of an old peasant gathering firewood in a thick forest with a castle in the distance. I listen for a while and then begin to feel self-conscious about how scruffy I am compared to the growing audience and I move out.

St Albans is impressive, its hilly centre having buildings of every period, a place comparable to York or Chester. I suppose I had dismissed it because I thought of it as Outer London. But it wasn't, historically, and it isn't, architecturally. I have a pressing need to make up some time and I decided to take a bus. I ask directions of an Irishman and then an Englishman, both of whom have been drinking and are extremely friendly and I just manage to catch the Green Line 340 as it is leaving for Welwyn Garden City. There are only two passengers, the other being an old lady. The countryside is undistinguished; much of the way we are passing the flat expanse of Hatfield Aerodrome. Then the bus seems to spend an interminable time getting on and off motorways and dual carriageways as we go through Hatfield.

I get off the bus on a bridge over the railway in Welwyn Garden City. Across the lines is the only building in the City which I knew to be here, the only reason I had heard of Welwyn for the first twenty years of my life: the Nabisco Shredded Wheat factory. When I was a child, the factory was always pictured on the box, looking clean and smart, surrounded by lawns. The real factory is not so ideal, being now a dirty off-white and rather unshapely, though I can see it would have looked superbly modern in the thirties.

The town is very impressive, though. It looks like nowhere else on earth, except Letchworth, and it is more impressive than Letchworth because, though inspired by the same set of ideas, influenced by William Morris and conceived by Ebenezer Howard, it has kept more closely to a symmetrical plan, the centre being a great 'T' of gardens flanked by shops and offices. In the gardens there is a large memorial plaque to Louis de Soissons (1890-1962) who 'built the town'.

It may only be like Letchworth in real life, but it is very much like the towns which are pictured in children's books, an unexpected combination of Englishness and order. The railway station is a neat little neo-classical building at the bottom of the 'T' and it looks as if you ought to be able to move the porters about and wind the trains up. On one side of the gardens are the factories, but on the other are the houses, Everybody here lives in a cottage, a brick or whitewashed building surrounded by trees and gardens.

As I walk among these cottages I try to analyse why the atmosphere of the two garden cities is so different from the new towns which they helped to inspire. It seems to come down to three things. First, the architecture: there are no concessions to grandiosity or modernism. The town centre is built in red brick, in a neat thirties Georgian style, and the cottages are folksy and proudly old-fashioned. Second, the trees are now mature so that a suburban backcloth is like a woodland in style and ecology: the place is full of birdsong even on a winter afternoon. Third, space and nature were not just a duty or a fashion, but the end in themselves, so that the formal gardens, the cottage gardens and the great swathes of parkland and woods give the place its atmosphere.

My walk has taken me alongside an open valley and into the dark thickness of Sherrardspark Wood. It is beginning to be really cold again as I plod through the leafmould and reflect on the significance of Hertfordshire. In 1900 it was a sparsely inhabited area. Now it has towns strung across it in a sort of conurbation. But this urbanisation has not merely happened as it did in Middlesex; it has been inspired and ordered by the Garden City movement and the Town and Country Planning Association and their followers. This whole conurbation has grown as a kind of antithesis to London, but it is not a historical backwater. It is part of the mainstream of the twentieth century, leading the way in its emphasis on space, ecology, recreation and the home. The style of life in much of the rest of the developed world has followed it, but has generally been less impressive than the original.

I have got this sorted out in my mind when, in the gathering gloom, I come across an old man and two granddaughters struggling with a bike through the mud. They show me the path out of the wood. It is now dark and very cold. I cannot help feeling anthropomorphic about the night, imagining it as a creature pinching me and threatening me and dancing round me as he reclaims his territory.

I retrace the day's steps in a creaking taxi to Berkhamsted. The driver is a talker, a dark, passably handsome man in his thirties whose transcendant attitude to life is that people get too het up about it, whether it is kids at discos or wives or men with ambition. For two and a half years he played every night in a rock band all sorts of stuff, whatever pleased the punter. His wife left him. Then two members of the group wanted to develop a much more distinctive style and go for the big time. There were rows and here he is, driving a taxi, not bitter, but philosophical. Welwyn is an excellent place to live, he says, though a bit short on pubs. The story ends as we reach Berkhamsted and it starts to snow. The workman's lamp is still there, where I hid it.

26 *Scott-ish walk*

(January 1984)

Wellies today. Following the thaw and the rain, the land is bright and damp, the road glistening in the sun. I ask myself the parachute question: if landed here, on a mystery drop, how accurately would I know where I was? The rolling hills, verging on mountains, and their patches of coniferous forest could well be in central Germany. But then there is a rugby ground with a fair-sized stand, by the river. Either Scotland or Wales. But turning the other way, there are buildings: plain little cottages; light, shoddy council terraces, stolid, grand, self-consciously romantic stone houses. This is Scotland: Selkirk, to be precise.

I cross Ettrick Water which is wide, shallow and white, and go into the town. After some zig-zagging among the grey houses, trying to go upwards all the time, I find a narrow lane of hundreds of steps and it takes me up into the town centre, facing a stone building which is, according to the large painted letters across its upper storeys, the 'HOME OF THE SELKIRK BANNOCK'. Below that is a large statue of Sir Walter Scott, Sheriff of Selkirkshire 1800-1832. Not one of your garret writers, Sir Walter.

It is true that in the remote country areas the pace of life is slower. In the main street of Selkirk there are a number of groups standing and talking and some pairs of men walking very slowly with empty shopping bags. There is a plain greyness about the street, which reminds me of Ireland, but also a decorative quality to the gable ends and mock towers which is more Flemish. Either way, you would have to be very ignorant to mistake it for an English town. I pass the offices of the *Southern Reporter* and the *Saturday Advertiser* and the local travel agent, which is advertising its fortieth anniversary tour of the Normandy beaches. At the other end of the main street is a statue of the explorer, Mungo Park, equal in size to that of Sir Walter and also on a large plinth, in battleship grey.

Beyond the centre, walking east through the town, I pass through some very nice houses and flats: solid, varied and compact, but undeniably in the local tradition of the Borders. After all the rude things I have said about modern Scottish housing, this has to be remarked. Out on the main road above the town the theme of *The Big Country* surges irresistibly into my mind as the vast prospect of hills and forests open up. There is nowhere bigger than Hawick within a radius of forty miles; by English standards this is a huge and remote place.

Over to the left I can see the narrow lane which I think I should be on. There are two fields between me and it which raises problems of farmers, animals and Scotish law on trespassing, about which I know nothing except that it is different from English law. But taking my courage in both hands I plod stolidly across the fields and up the lane which has a hedge on one side and a dry-stone wall on the other. It peters out on an area of rough ground and becomes a track which descends into a valley of conifers and winter cereals. The track consists of mud, ice and water and my decision with respect to footwear is now entirely vindicated: wearing anything other than wellies I would be spending half the day trying to pick a route to tiptoe through the countryside and the other half bearing the consequences of icy, wet feet.

The track goes up to a farm, its surface now largely ice so that the farm is cut off except to a Land Rover with an experienced driver. The farm itself is big and solid, its vehicles, stores and outhouses spreading over several acres. I briefly wonder, as I often have in similar circumstances, what it *feels* like to live in such isolation and relative self-sufficiency. I follow a track which climbs up into the hills above the farm, though I am now beginning to have some doubts about my direction, since nothing has quite fitted its appearance on the map. These doubts deepen when I get up on a plateau and there is no sign of the Eildon hills! This is like losing the Mont Blanc in the Chamonix Valley, or the Malverns in Worcestershire, or Pendle, where I come from, and it gives me a fearful sense of frustration and disorientation. I set off south, towards the sun, where at least I will find the main road. I am following a line of snow, preserved in the shadow of a dry-stone wall, when my eye is attracted by the brilliant blue of a lake and there, beyond it, are the Eildons, steep and black. Not seeing them has been a trick of the slope; I had been looking upwards instead of straight ahead.

I vault a fence and follow a path round the lake. Two herons rise off the lake and then three ducks, while a pair of swans paddle serenely. A nature reserve: am I being naughty to enter it? There is a notice facing outwards which says 'THIS IS A NATURE RESERVE. PLEASE *WALK* YOUR HORSES'. The lake is much larger than I expected, the best part of a mile long. At the end is a road and, most useful, a notice announcing Lindean Nature Reserve, which enables me to place myself exactly.

My path now lies along a farm road between black hedges and green fields of winter wheat. The land slopes gently away to the south, my right. There are bullfinches, chaffinches and a yellowhammer in the hedges and several million rooks in the fields. I have now formed a clear idea of the character of the Borders; it is not wild and romantic, like the Highlands or parts of Wales and the Pennines. Not deep and intimate, like the Cotswolds, but bright and big and clean, the sun shining on pale grass chomped fine by sheep, more like the Downs of southern England.

My route has become easy now, heading for the Eildons across sheep fields and between obvious and easy landmarks like farms and woodland plantations. I talk to a farm worker who is throwing out bales of hay for the sheep. He directs me through the woods and the best way up the Eildons and wishes me good luck with the weather. His accent is Northumbrian, not local. I follow a muddy track between sheep up the Eildons. Several of the sheep are coughing badly, like me. At a height of six or seven hundred feet the vegetation changes to brown heather, punctuated by occasional stunted trees. A red grouse flaps away to my right. The wind is bitter; it is incredible to think that there was a Roman army camp right on the top of these hills and that the evidence suggests that most of the troops came from Dalmatia. That is, volunteers having been recruited and trained, the poor sods were dragged all the way from the nice, warm Adriatic to freeze on top of a mountain at what was literally the end of the world.

There seems to be no path up to the top, so I begin the steep scramble through the heather and scree. It makes me feel very bad, limbs leaden and aching, confirming what I have suspected since early morning, that I am ill with 'flu or bronchitis or something. Half way up I desire only to be transported to bed, where I will be served ice-cold ginger ale and thin toast by my female relatives.

At the top the wind is cruel, but the view is stupendous. We are on a pinnacle in the middle of a bowl which is perhaps seventy or eighty miles across, ringed by snowy mountains and filled with lakes and woods and rolling hills. It is surprising how much of the land is now arable: the red-brown of ploughed earth and the bright green of winter cereals. I say 'we' because I have been joined by a family. There are paths, of course, but not from the side from which I made my approach and the family have come up one of them. He is slim and bearded and has carried the baby (eighteen months, a stone and a half); she is chunky with a face bright red in the savage wind. They look the sort of family who never go indoors if they can help it and I am pleased to see that they are wearing wellies.

I go down the hill toward Melrose slipping and sliding on the nasty red mud and cross the golf course. Out on the road I fancy that I see David Steel in a Ford Escort, but this seems unlikely. I fall to thinking about the image of the borders: farming and weaving; golf clubs and rugby clubs: Liberalism; vast, stable, dependable, uneventful. Melrose is a sort of home from home within the Borders for me as I have stayed there and been to the famous seven-a-side rugby tournament held there in April.

I go straight into the bar of the Station Hotel and order a pint of Tartan shandy. On the television the singer Anita Harris is lying naked, face down, her buttocks covered by a towel, surrounded by bunches of flowers, being massaged by a blonde girl. She explains that she has been using 'aromatherapy' for two years now. The barman says, 'Is that no the cheekiest thing ye ivver saw?' and switches it down by remote control. In the corner is an old woman, drunk and miserable, verging on tears, talking to a slightly younger man. She looks pitiful, just about all-in. It must be a medical problem: she says, 'There's only been two other cases, ivver.' Two old gentlemen drink up saying to each other, 'This'll nae pay the rent', and I follow them out.

I wander through Melrose, vaguely hoping to find something to eat. It is a very small town (population 2,000) which caters for golfers, riders, fishermen and rugby players and has more than its share of retired colonels. I pass mill shops and wool shops which have nice things, but higher prices than my local main street. Down at the Abbey the price of admission has just been raised to 70p, 'not haf an oor sin', as I am told apologetically. The much destroyed, much rebuilt pink stone ruin is being actively restored, but only as a safe ruin. Here at last is a hint that the Borders have not always been a solidly respectable place where the greatest excitement is to play round in par or catch a salmon. There were a thousand years of wars and feuds which made the contemporary struggles between Guelphs and Ghibbellines in Italy seem a polite game by comparison. Family against family; English against Scots; supporters of the English King against supporters of the Scottish King (not necessarily the same as the above). Last (and nastiest), the Covenanters against Montrose. In each case, no holds barred: massacre, genocide, kidnap, rape, sacking, burning, looting, torture. A local custom which caught on like wildfire in the late Middle Ages was the seizure of one's opponent's wife or daughter, placing her in a box and suspending the box by a rope from the ramparts or over a gorge. And now it is a place where the rules of golf are observed as if they were self-evident truths. Beirut and Belfast should take heart from the Borders.

Out on the lane which runs across the plain by the Tweed an old lady is shuffling slowly down the pavement. On the other side of the road an ancient black dog is snuffling in the hedge. It turns to face the road and a beige Cortina screeches to a halt. The Cortina draws past us and stops violently again just as I pass the woman. The driver gets out and walks towards us. He shouts, 'Is that your fuckin' dog? Ye've hurt ma bairn' (there is a woman and a child in the car).

I have no time for dogs at all, but I don't like his tone of voice. In any case he has pink-tinted spectacles and a moustache and I dislike his type. With my dander up I always overact, go for the throat.

'As a matter of fact it has nothing to do with me. But I saw what happened. It was an appalling piece of driving. Ridiculous over-reaction. Totally stupid.'

He was shaken at this and at a loss for words.

'Go home, you ignorant pillock,' I add.

'Ignorant what?' he says, angry and frightened and not, I think, having heard the word before.

He retreats to his Cortina, from the safety of which he angrily waves two fingers. I respond with a much ruder gesture, which might roughly be descrived as an act of mime loosely based on a Barbary ape indulging in onanism, though I do it behind the old lady's back so that she does not see. Finally, he drives off.

The old lady has taken no notice of all this, being mainly concerned with wiping her eyes, made tearful by the cold wind.

'Is it no yoor dog?' she asks. '. . . It's no mae dog, either.'

The path by the Tweed is easy and pleasant, meadows and wooded banks, with rolling hills on the other side. I reflect that I am the stuff of which fights are made because I would always trade a certain amount of pain and discomfort for the chance of inflicting some. But not disfigurement or disablement. So I tend to be as rude as I can and see what happens. I consider all the ways one might deal with such situations in a cool, laid-back manner, taking numbers, mentioning lawyers, and so on. Where's the satisfaction in that, though? Even so, I do wish I'd asked him whether the child was properly strapped in.

After a couple of miles the path leaves the river and enters the Tweedbank industrial estate with its low new factories, including that of DYNAMIT NOBEL (UK) LTD. I am quite close to Abbotsford now on the fringe of Galashiels and in the most controversial part of the Borders. Between 1966 and 1973 there was a great political wrangle between those who supported the plans of Willie Ross, the Scottish Development Agency and (among others) the Duke of Roxburgh, to bring new people and new industry into the Borders and those, including Lord Dacre, as he is now, and most local people, who liked living in a backwater. It added insult to injury in many minds that the whole thing was planned as being within a few hundred yards of Scott's home at Abbotsford.

Well, it is all here, now, including ten thousand new people. The first houses I see, in Neidpath Close, seem nice enough, solid and very Scottish with walled gardens, but on the old footbridge over the Tweed which leads into Langlee, the higher and larger part of the new development, there are numerous graffiti and a lot of litter. I wonder what the colonels make of that.

Langlee is essentially a piece of outer Glasgow transferred to the Borders. Its blocks and terraces and tenements are discordant in both style and scale, though it is cleaner and better kept than Glasgow estates and its high-heeled teenage mothers have a slightly less pinched look. On the main road which runs through Langlee is a plaque which says

AT THIS SPOT
ON HIS PATHETIC JOURNEY
FROM ITALY
HOME TO ABBOTSFORD
AND
HIS BELOVED BORDERLAND
SIR WALTER SCOTT
GAZING ON THIS SCENE FOR THE LAST TIME
SPRANG UP WITH A CRY OF DELIGHT

As I am reading it I am aware, for the briefest instant, of somebody giving me vigorous 'V' signs from a beige Cortina. I am not at all surprised to find him here. He drives on without slackening his pace.

The town (and its rugby club) are often called Gala, both 'a's being short, as in 'hat'. BBC sports announcers often make the place sound like a charity evening at Glyndebourne, which is quite wrong. Galashiels itself reminds me of Halifax. It is a solid mill town with some nice old buildings and some modern rubbish, including an enormous cinema. I am overwhelmed with curiosity as to what people think about Langlee and I wander into John Menzies with the vague idea of finding out where the local newspaper offices are. But the first person I see is my wife, so I get her to drive me out to Abbotsford while it is still light, through droves of kids, most of them smoking, coming out of the local comprehensive. The house is hidden away in a hollow by the river. It is closed for the winter, but the gate is open and we sneak in to look. The style is grand baronial, as I would have expected, and it is shielded from sight of all the new development by a thick belt of conifers. Smoke is rising from some of the chimneys. I have no strong feelings, caring little for Sir Walter and his works, but a curiousity satisfied because never have I seen an area which has, to this extent, tied its image to one man.

Back in Galashiels I try two local newspapers but there are no news nor editorial staff about and they say only the Editor can give me an opinion. I buy shortcake and a Selkirk Bannock (which turns out to be a rich, alcoholic teacake) and six haggises. I ask the butcher what local people think of the new development.

'Up Langlee? Ah'll nae speak oot of turn. . . when ah tell ye that, in th' opinion of most people. . . Rubbish! Rubbish! The people who live there, they're the scum iv the earth.'

There is a pause. Perhaps I look a little shocked, because he adds, 'Mind ye, we've some grand customers from up there. . . but trade isnae everything.'

It is interesting to note that the street price of haggis (90p per pound) is currently twice that of frozen turkey.

27 *Walking home*

(July 1984)

'Bacup? *Bacup*. It's that rough, nettles won't grow in Bacup.' So said the man from Nelson and when I put it to a man from Bacup, he said, 'Do you know he could be right? I always associate nettles with holidays.' And, unlikely as it may seem, I can't find any nettles in Bacup: there don't seem to be any on the road verges or round the garages. But 'rough' is misleading, an image belied by the solidity of the stone terraces and villas and the many-coloured opulence of the rhododendrons and azaleas which do grow superbly on this acid soil and hang from the gardens and the edges of the woods.

I walk north from Bacup, passing the Deerplay pub. I had always thought of this as very wild, poor land, which it is. But my strongest impression now is of how old-fashioned it is. The fields are small, carpeted with wild flowers and bounded by tumbledown stone walls. Larks sing abundantly, staking out their claims on this early summer morning. There are cattle, sheep and horses looking for grass among the reeds and not an arable crop in sight. Up by the war memorial to the men of Weir I can see the land for many miles around. This is not the 'English countryside' as normally conceived; it is the hinterland of Lancashire, big, rough, scruffy, disordered, thrown down by the God of the Book of Job who said, 'Se if thi can mek sommat out'er that.' On the map it appears as the forest of Rossendale, but this is a Norman–French misconception as there is scarcely a tree in sight: it is an open grassland hunting area with no trees, a place for which Norman–French did not have an accurate word.

Over the top, on the unclassified road. Rougher country than ever, a pale brown in colour: reeds, sheep, skylarks, broken stone walls. Very occasionally a car passes, usually an ancient Mini or Minor, but once an 'ober-rep' Granada; then coming much earlier than I expected to see it, the familiar broken-backed massif of Pendle is hazily visible in the distance. It will be with me, on and off, all day. This is not going to be a walk through strange or unknown places, but through the place which I still regard as home.

I always have a memory of Burnley as a dark place of cosy terraces and Gothic mills. But there it is below me, spreading around its valley like cake mix in a basin and it is not black or grey at all, if it ever was. It is a pale beige in colour. There is a small patch of nettles by the road, shortly before it starts going downwards.

Much of the descent is on a sunken lane between banks and stone walls. Both sides are part of the golf course. Bilberries grow prolifically along the banks, reminding me of the soft fruit we used to pick as children: brambles and wild raspberries and hips from the pink dog-roses to sell to Andrews at 4d per pound. The long downhill stretch, taxing for the backs of the legs, takes me into a part of Burnley I do not recognise with semis and a pub called the Scarecrow. Then I divert into a hilly rural area of paddocks and copses and big stone houses; the amount of walking down you can do, without getting to the bottom, seems far greater than I would have thought possible. At last, the terraced houses. In this part they are solid and prosperous, the stone façades painted magnolia, yellow, brown, grey, pale blue. It seems to me that they are much more brightly painted than they used to be, probably because of the abolition of that pollution which used to turn the snow grey overnight.

The bright colours and the angles of the terraces remind me of San Francisco. Having thought that, I cannot restrain a smile because I can so easily imagine various of my friends saying, 'There he goes.

He only does it to draw attention to himself. Burnley like San Francisco, indeed. Whatever next?' To which I can only reply, 'Go and look at both.' A lorry driver asks me where Towneley Park is, so I tell him and he says, 'Aye, but 'ow do ah get there?' So I tell him that as well.

I make my way to Turf Moor and the bottom of the basin. Many terraces have been demolished to create greens and play areas. There are new houses opposite the football ground. My relationship with this town consists of two things: I have often falsely told people that this is where I come from, because they are likely to have heard of it and I have watched its football team and wanted it to win with unswerving faith and hope for the last thirty years. If I expected, on standing opposite the entrances to the Bob Lord Stand and the Burnley Building Society stand, both smart and modern, that the triumphs and tragedies of those thirty years would come flooding back to me like the roar of a great crowd, that there would be some throat-filling Proustian moment, then I have over-estimated my own imagination. A football stadium on a summer day is nothing in particular. The cricket club, next door, is more interesting. The groundsman, clad only in shorts, is preparing a wicket. I admire the size and smooth quality of the outfield and remember that there has always been a certain amount of local resentment that Lancashire never play on any of these Lancashire League grounds.

The centre of Burnley is only a quarter of a mile away. It is an undistinguished place: its scale is not much above a country town. There are some nice old pubs, but most of the buildings represent the full variety of twentieth century ordinary: a twenties' Burtons, a sixties' precinct and hotel and so on. MacDonalds have moved in and Sainsbury's are building a large supermarket in what should turn out to be an attractive style, here in the heart of ASDA territory. In general, the town centre is lively and full of people. I buy a potato pie and a steak pie and take them to Thompson Park. I eat the pies watching the children play cricket. They shout, 'Steh' when they don't intend to take another run, just as we did. It is a lovely park, formal lawns and gardens and a lake in a circle of trees, made all the better because dogs are completely banned from it. I note that the chief executive responsible for implementing this policy is an official of the Old Boys of the school I went to. A black 'recreation security' vehicle patrols the park: good old Burnley, realistic and ahead of the times as usual.

I go up Hebrew Street and into Hebrew Square: more terraces with greens, gardens and playgrounds where the surgical removal of buildings has taken place. There are a lot of Pakistanis now living in this area and the children playing in Hebrew Square are about half-and-half, ethnically. This area is not so smart as Burnley Wood, where I entered the town, but it is lively and respectable. There is no high-rise in Burnley; its 'inner city', based on a policy of small-scale demolition, seems to work well. It is a more spacious and cleaner place than a generation ago, whatever else has gone wrong.

I cross the 'Prairie' where the town thins out and there are many millowners' houses, both the traditional grand stone ones and some post-war modernist, including a house called *Domus* which seems to be on stilts over a pond. I note that the Labour Club is now called the Socialist Club and that some of the millowners' houses are changing use, to a squash club and a conference centre, for instance.

The village of Brierfield is between Burnley and Nelson. Its purpose-built UNIT 4 Cinema, an early example of its kind, is still going strong and there is a queue outside. The ex-England footballer John Connelly still has his chip shop on the edge of Brierfield, called *Connelly's Plaice*. It now overlooks a junction on our very own local motorway, the M65, which follows the canal route to the north-west side of the towns. Often on the way into Nelson I can glance down the side street and see the familiar view: stone terraces, wooded hills and the high, grey-brown ridge of Pendle beyond.

Nelson centre used to consist of a row of shops on either side of the Burnley Road. But the south side has all gone now, replaced by a colourful Arndale centre, modern buildings, fountains and such. I take a pint in the Lord Nelson, the pub after which the town was called. Even ten years ago, it consisted of little rooms with old people drinking mild by open fires. Now it is all knocked together into one big area and has lost its distinctive atmosphere. There are a dozen customers and a noisy fruit machine.

Back outside, I seek out Every Street, for the sake of the old joke ('Ah'm fair worn out. . . ah must have walked down Every Street in Nelson.') It has not changed, except that is is now inhabited by Pakistanis and the Labour Councillor is called Iqbal. But Scotland Road, the main street which runs north out of Nelson, has disappeared! Acres of close, dark stone buidings replaced by a great emptiness of roads, car parks, saplings and 'landscaping'. All of these towns have suffered great losses of population – they were at their peak in 1911 – and have simply knocked down the spare buildings and used the space as space. This seems fair enough; they were hideously crowded and I didn't care much for Nelson, anyway. But are there to be no dark, congested old towns? Must they all look like parks?

I am keen to get to Colne now. It is my home and the place in which my daydreams are most often set. The town fascinates me far more than if I were a native: we moved there when I was five and stayed till I was twenty. So I walk quickly down the thin line of urban straggle between the two towns towards Colne, which is piled up on its hillside ahead. Once across the Boundary, as it is known, the first person I see is a girl who was at our primary school. Now she is a well-stacked, rather sexy mother, but she does not notice me.

I go under the railway viaduct into Colne. My first port of call is the gasworks, where I used to report for work every morning. It is physically unchanged, but no longer used by local government and the yard and surrounding buildings contain a junk store and a garage. Then I go up the steep street which leads to Tum Hill to the south of the town. There you can see the town spread on its hill, less than a mile away across the valley. 'Bonny Colne upon the hill', as it was traditionally called: famous, if for anything, for Luddite riots and Hovis advertisements and for producing Wallace Hartley, the brave bandmaster of the Titanic.

Unlike Burnley, Colne *is* dark. It straddles a sausage-shaped ridge, eight hundred feet high and in a bowl of higher hills. The sun has gone and purple cloud is banked over the moors beyond the town. In this town, I reflect, I had my first kiss, first job and first game of football. It takes me some time to realise that the town has contracted; some of the rows of stone houses on the lower slopes have disappeared; the grass has regained its territory.

I follow the valley to the south of the town. This is called Waterside and I know of no other place quite like it. Ramshackle rows of houses are oddly distributed on rich, flowered, meadows. Horses and goats wander between the houses and the mills. The main mill, which is now called John Cotton (Colne) Ltd, and makes felt, is still in full operation, much to my surprise. It was largely to this part of town that the great hippy migration of the late sixties and early seventies came, the establishment of 'alternative Colne', the Kathmandu of the north. Some of it remains, a much-resented village-in-a-town of some two hundred people.

I climb the steep streets into the town. They are full of children, but the shopping area is deserted as it is half-day closing. Market Street in Colne is like Burnley Road in Nelson used to be, but has changed earlier and less. I have a good look at an estate agents. Phenomenally cheap property is what brought the alternative society to Colne. It is slowly disappearing now. True, a house has just been sold for £4,000, but many of the terraced houses are now in the teens, and some, in good condition and 'rural locations', are over £25,000. Local farmhouses, once relatively cheap, now command up to six figures.

I wander east, though this is the wrong direction, with no conscious aim. But in the back of my mind is a desire to see if the confectioners on Keighley Road still exists and whether the meadows overlooking Colne Cricket Club are still full of buttercups. Both are unchanged and I enjoy the middle-aged delight of an unchanging home town, eating Slater's home made ice-cream and watching them put up the nets for an evening practice.

I cut across the ginnel by the cricket club which is too narrow to take a genuinely fat man and set off towards Pendle along the North Valley where I used to walk home from school. My childhood was full of talk about closures and redundancies as the cotton industry collapsed. But now Colne's industry seems to be holding its own: Smith and Nephew are fully operative and I have also noticed a pine factory, a bakers, an oil blenders and a textile machinery factory which are new. But at the end of the North Valley there is a great sadness: Vivary Bridge Mill, a strange dark little building which used to overlook its gloomy little pond, has gone. It was one of the first buildings I was really fond of, when I passed it on my way home from school. It has only just gone: the bulldozer is still there.

My last pilgrimage is to our house. Little has changed in the area generally, but Priestfield Avenue has changed quite a lot. It consisted of blocks of four grey terraced houses, encircling a rough field where we made dens in summer and bonfires in winter. It was a wonderful place to grow up, surrounded by parks and woods and where a child could walk into any house. But now the field has gone, replaced by neat bungalows. The road is surfaced and there are more trees and extensions and car ports. To my astonishment, Mr Pearson is there in his garden, looking more or less exactly as he did thirty years ago. He used to take me to watch Burnley sometimes. I think about walking on, but he looks up, sees me and says, 'Lincoln.' I talk for a while to him and his wife about their children and the old days. Colne is getting by, they say, and seems busier than ever before when the market is on at the top of the town. They are involved in a campaign to save the old grammar school by the parish church. I feel extraordinarily pleased that they are still there.

Beyond Priestfield Avenue I am really on my home ground, in Alkincoats Park and the country beyond where we used to roam as children. This is quite different from my other walks: I do not need to consult a map here. Remarkably, almost nothing has changed. Woods, farmhouses, hedges, walls, stiles – all are where they were. The Cross Gaits Inn still says 'Good Ales Tomorrow for Nothing (1736)'. Where there were lapwings, there still are: the same goes for sheep, cows, buttercups, bluebells, ducks, curlews. Where else could people say this? This only changes I can see are connected with leisure: the park has a golf course, the quarry has been used for scrambling, and there are many more boats on the Leeds–Liverpool canal.

North of Alkincoats Park in Colne there is open country right through to the North Pole. For many miles I walk across meadows, alongside becks and up wooded ravines. There are flowers of every colour. This was always a beautiful countryside, but now, having stayed the same, untouched by the cereal boom or by Dutch Elm disease, it seems more wonderful than ever.

I am late, I note by reference to a clock in the village of Barley, at the foot of Pendle. The old Communist rambler who first showed me the way up warned that 'It'll tek breath out on thee' and this time I have walked more than twenty miles already. The final thousand feet are agony, an aching chug up the black–brown peat, through the ferns and screes and bilberries and onto the huge plateau at the top. The Pennines and the Forest of Bowland, misty purple ridges, stretch away in all directions.

This is a sort of holy place which inspired much belief in witchcraft and where Fox had the vision which started the Quaker religion. When I was young, I was furious with my cousin for suggesting that a hydrogen bomb could level it: as if anything invented by mortals could affect old Pendle.

I had hoped to have a kind of reflective experience up here on the occasion of my last walk for *New Society*. Curiously, it is five years to the day since I did my first. Now I am more than half-way through my allotted span, my reproductive cycle complete, and I should take stock of myself and the world. But I am late and tired and knackered and desperately thirsty and probably not the stock-taking sort in any case.

So I make my way down into the vast, opulent limestone country to the north of Pendle, reflecting only that it would be nice to buy a bit of property here, before prices go through the roof.

Last seen, heading for the pub. . .

28 *On the levels*

(March 1985)

A very ordinary place on a damp morning: a row of grey cottages and a small factory. Below them, box-shaped red brick houses. But there is something extraordinary above the street. It is a green volcano, surmounted by a church tower without a church.

Glastonbury Tor has been associated with almost every conceivable kind of mythology. This seems entirely understandable. It rises from the land below so dramatically that ordinary explanations of its existence seem inadequate: in short, it looks as though it was put here for a purpose and that the purpose must have been supernatural. Even as I walk towards it a certain vulgar association with magic emerges. On Hill Top Lane a 'strictly private' parking bay has dragons elaborately painted on it and a bungalow advertises astrological services by a garish sign, stars on a midnight-blue sky.

At the top I am alone with the tower and an all-round view of Somerset. And no wonder: although the hills to the north are clear and bright, a storm is rolling across the flat plain to the south and west, dark purple clouds giving off grey rain. Two minutes later, it hits me, steeply angled and bitter cold. The tower has no roof, but affords me some shelter because of the angle of the rain. Incidentally, it is mercifully free from vandalism and graffiti.

They say that head-banging is nice when it stops. The same is true of vicious little showers, so it is in a singularly cheerful mood that I stride down the Tor, its path now blue, damply reflecting the sky. I follow the signs for the Somerset Museum of Rural Life. The museum concentrates on the parish of Butleigh in the nineteeth century and on the life of a labourer called John Hodges. Although it has a great range of exhibits from corn dollies and butter stamps to carts and ploughs, the thing which most impresses itself on me is a village child's schoolbook. On one side of the page he had been made to write repeatedly, 'Youth is the season for forming good habits' while on the other, in much bigger letters, he repeats, 'Death is inevitable'.

I leave Glastonbury on a minor road, striking across the plain. The land is like a lake, flat calm in a circle of hills, Glastonbury, the Isle of Avalon, being an island in the lake. It was probably rather less accessible than islands on real lakes when it was all marsh. Drained lands like this have a particular atmosphere. They seem artificial with their vast fields and symmetrical drainage ditches, but remote, too, because there are no buildings. Some of it is now arable, but most remains pasture, a flat green surface punctuated by groups of cattle and clumps of willows.

I cross the River Brue, which looks like a canal, and walk down to Candlebridge Farm where there is a sprawling conurbation of farm buildings, though the traditional sight of ducks and a vegetable plot alongside the drainage ditch. I am uncertain where the path goes next, so I ask the farmer, who is shovelling slurry with his tractor. A cheerful young man in a deerstalker, he explains that one of the bridges is down, but he plots me a course to Ashcott. As I cross the meadows a big hare bolts for the cut and a heron rises off it.

Here a mystery begins. The earth, black as coal dust, is being cut into turves. It is only ten acres at first, but a little later hundreds of acres of this open-cast farming and thirty-foot heaps of black earth. What for? To satisfy my curiosity I enter the premises of the Torrex Peat Company. In the yard there are large bags of peat from Ireland

and Denmark. I ask a tall dark man in the warehouse what this is all about. It is sold as compost for gardening and the foreign peat is: 'Corse wuy mux ut wi this stuff. Whoy? You wanna buy some?' 'I couldn't carry it.' 'You go' a baarg on yer baarck. You're a strong laard.' We both laugh, being about the same age.

I head south across the Polden Hills, just slopes really, but high enough to be above the bogs and to be English countryside in the accepted sense. After a pint in Ashcott I descend the steeper and prettier side of the Poldens and the long haul across the King's Sedge Moor begins. This is not, of course, a moor in the conventional sense, but a fen, just as there are 'forests' in the Pennines with no trees. It is the same kind of remote grassland as before, but bigger. There are curiosities in the unfamiliar landscape: pollarded willows with stout brambles growing out of the tree itself, rotting piles of mangle-wurzels, black molehills like slag heaps in a minature coal-field. Pairs of mallards rise frequently from the ditches: there are very few cars, but occasional tractors. Something very close to silence: this place is a world of its own, ringed by hills, farmed from the outside in.

I turn west along the King's Sedgemoor Drain. There are swans standing in the fields, pale green duck mussel shells left on the grass by the oystercatchers which now live inland in thousands. The walking would be easy if it were not for the fences which cover the gap between the small drain and the main drain which I have to cross every furlong. Stopping for a snack on a fallen willow I note that there is no sound except for the breeze in the trees. As a youth I had a studied contempt for lowlands, but now I have acquired the taste. I seriously doubt whether anybody else has walked this way this year; there are no footprints in the molehills or on the path. A sheep has met a horrible death, stuck in the mud by the cut, a swan a much quicker end; it looks as if it has been taken by a fox and later picked clean by the crows.

Beyond the A361 the atmosphere of the Moor is less remote and more workaday; the hills and villages are closer and there are tractors working in the fields. There is a network of unsurfaced lanes here, their peaty surfaces showing hoofmarks and wheel ruts. I imagine they looked more or less the same in the eighteenth century. To my pleasure and surprise I successfully work my way on them to the battlefield of Sedgemoor.

The battle was a pathetic affair in which the remnants of Monmouth's forces, mainly local Nonconformists afraid of popery, were routed in the night. It has left no great mark on the landscape: no earthworks, no artillery scars. Even the crucial landmark of the battle, the old Bussex Rhine, has long since been filled in. All that remains is a stone between two tall trees, commemorating all those who died doing right as they saw it and whose bones lie under the fields around. More people were killed in the reprisals: it was said that this part of Somerset stank of quartered bodies for many months. But it is difficult to imagine this on a pleasant spring evening three hundred years later, as a farm worker fills a sheep trough nearby and a young woman gallops her horse across the pasture.

Westonzoyland, the village by the battlefield, has an impressive Gothic church with a tall tower, but is otherwise a place of modern suburban homes, with large orchards and gardens. I make my way across country to Bridgewater, the land becoming more ordinary as I get to the edge of the moor and noisier close to the M5. The most interesting place is Fowler's Plot, a hamlet of the old style, consisting of a number of farms clustered together on the high ground. Three farm workers in blue boiler suits are chatting in the lane.

I am a great believer in the principle that when in Rome one should do as the Romans would do if they were sincere about being Roman. So when I finally make it to a pub for a hard-earned rest I order a pint of (Williams) scrumpy. It tastes very fruity and much better than the last time I drank scrumpy, but it costs 54p, as opposed to 10p on the previous occasion.

29 *Rockingham game pie*

(May 1985)

I set out to find a piece of ordinary Midlands countryside, but Rockingham is ordinary only by the standards of English Tourist Board posters and American dreams. The village stretches up the road to the castle and church among the tall trees at the top of the hill. The houses are orange-gold; limestone, laced with iron. Many of them are thatched and most of them have orchards and vegetable gardens. It is hard to believe that Corby is on the other side of the hill.

There is no sign of the path leading north-east from the village. The postmistress tells me that it was moved when they knocked the cottages down to make the gardens bigger; a man in a Range Rover tells me that it now skirts the woods up on the ridge. I head for the woods across a meadow which has some very ancient oak trees. Walking is not going to be easy; after the heavy rain there is thick mud where the cows have congregated and waterlogged patches in the clay. I pick my way between a mesh fence, bounding the wood on my right, and a wheatfield on my left. For a time, I have a companion, a cock pheasant who scurries along in front of me and occasionally throws himself, bewildered and cross, at the fence. Eventually he manages to scramble over a gate into the wood.

They are attractive woods. I count a dozen species of tree within seconds and there is thick undergrowth and a carpet of flowers. I zig-zag my way across country, following the edge of the woods. This would be an easy place to live off the land, pheasants and fat woodpigeons in profusion, partridge and squirrels. Eventually the woods break and I am out on a kind of downland, with rough grass, sheep and rocky outcrops. A ewe is laid on her back in a dip, vainly waving her legs in the air. Three times I try to roll her over, but she staggers weakly and falls back. Finally I get her up and she walks, off with growing confidence; this is achieved at the cost of a slimy mixure of mud and sheep droppings on my hands and clothes.

Puffed up by this rustic good deed, I now make a big mistake. I try to return to the path as it is on the map, running across the fields in the valley. These fields are a mixture of meadow and wheat. I have at least a target, the tall tower of Gretton church, which is mistily visible on a hill a couple of miles away. But there is no obvious way of getting there; I have to scramble through hedges, jump ditches and make a careful deviating progress around muddy patches. To make matters worse, I can see that if I had stuck to the ridge walking would have been a doddle. But there is the consolation of feeling that I am in the very depths of the countryside. There are butterflies, yellowhammers and a cuckoo. The list of edible material is augmented by many rabbits, a pair of mallard on a pond and a big hare.

Eventually I am tempted by the railway: anything dry and visible which is known to lead somewhere would have an immense attraction at this stage. The distance between the sleepers is all wrong for walking, but it is better than mud, and I get to Gretton at a brisk pace through the scrubby woodland. The station is now a small factory of some sort and there is a Rolls Royce parked outside it. The centre of the village is the top of the hill, a green surrounded by stone buildings, including the church. Behind the altar in the church is a perpendicular window of four arches which lurches crazily outwards and sideways. A middle-aged woman, who cleans the church on Thursdays with her friend, shows me round it enthusiastically but she doesn't know that much about it, she says, as she has only been here seven years. Strangely that is *exactly* what the postmistress at Rockingham said.

Leaving Gretton I am struck by its extreme prosperity and, in particular, the amount of renovation of stone houses which is taking place. I stick to the road this time. It is quiet, but rather dull, the valley of the Welland down to the left seems very empty, vast fields of wheat and rape punctuated by low hedges and small trees. There is one spectacular feature, however; the Welland viaduct carries the railway across the valley on eighty-two arches. Much of the old red brick is in poor condition; it seems a spectacular piece of engineering for such a relatively shallow valley.

Haringworth is very quiet. There is no sound in the little stone village except for a distant tractor and a dog barking at me. In the White Swan I order a pint of Ruddles, which costs 94p (!!). The only other customers are the sort of well-to-do retired couple who can be found in every English country pub. They are talking about accents in a desultory way. He remarks, 'You can hear more broad Scots in Corby than you can in Aberdeen.' When they leave it is to see if the grass is dry; he says it won't be, she says it will. A line from an old Who song is going through my mind: 'Ah hope ah die before ah get old', though I don't share the sentiments.

On the plateau above the village a huge crane-like thing is quarrying. My attention is attracted by a war memorial which commemorates the American airman who flew from Spanhoe aerodrome, in 1944-45. A block of limestone bars the entrance to vehicles; a windsock is still visible. I go in; the buildings are overgrown, but the runways remain in good condition. The space between them is now wheat. I am walking down the runway; there is forest to the left and right and in front of me, a huge bank of purple cloud has built up. It is a moment of vivid and eerie unreality. Something very strange ought to happen now; perhaps an aircraft will arrive and take me off to another life altogether.

But, of course, nothing does happen and I enter the forest. There are some ancient trees but many new plantations. I follow the tracks which are marked on the map. There is always a cuckoo to be heard and a pair of jays flies across the path. There are rabbits about and at one point there are a pair of muntjac deer on the path which turn away with nervous elegance and bolt into the trees. Later the forest becomes more tourist-oriented with neat little notices explaining that the dips in the land are old ironstone pits and that the beech trees are of poor quality.

The A43 (Corby to Stamford) cuts through half a mile of farmland between two large stretches of forest. Its noise comes as a rude shock after the quiet places I have been and it is with some relief that I get back into the forest. Top Lodge, where the Forestry Commission have their Northamptonshire headquarters, is a very elegant stone building, though there is a Caravan Club site on one side of it. At first this stretch of forest, perhaps the largest in the country, is disappointing because a lot of it has been cleared and replanted, leaving the land looking like the Somme in 1916. It is difficult to make progress after a while because huge Swedish tree extractors (machines, not men) have turned the track into a quagmire. To make matters worse, it begins to rain.

The rest of the way is largely along the fringes of ancient woodlands in fields alternating sheep and wheat. Pheasants constantly start up in front of me and my feet and legs get very wet. For a time I have to walk on the A47, past a deep quarry and by a minor road across to Collyweston, another attractive stone village where the roofs are made of unusual stone tiles.

Collyweston is the end of my journey. Was it an ordinary piece of Midland countryside? I'm not sure. My predominant impression is of the quantity of game to be found in Northamptonshire.

30 *The rambler's heartland*

(August 1985)

Until today, I never visited the Peak District National Park. This is not strictly true, because I have many times driven the Ashbourne–Buxton road as a neo-Luddite alternative to the motorway. But I have never come here for the sake of it, nor walked anywhere in it.

In honour of my belated visit, the village of Bradwell has put bunting out in the streets. It is a grey village, almost big enough to call a town, surrounded by grey hills and under a layer of grey cloud. All morning, as I drove, there have been persistent showers of cold, heavy rain. As I apprehensively tighten the string of my hood, it stops and I gratefully remove the hood: the small miracle of Bradwell.

This is limestone country; walking on the hills above the village the dominant colours are of pale stone and bright green grass. There is a great variety of flowers on the banks beneath the stone walls: clovers, harebells, parsleys, dog-roses and the mauve-blue scabious in profusion. Pure white goats are scrambling among a large patch of wild raspberries just above the village. For all the omniverous reputation of the goat, they are not touching the raspberry plants. There are still small fruits on the plants, so I eat some; they always seem tastier than the cultivated variety, but this may be my fancy. I smile to myself, remembering an incident in which I proved to an American friend that raspberries grow wild in the North of England, a proposition he was very reluctant to accept.

The only sound, the only traffic and the only eyesore in this particular area concern quarrying which has given a scruffy, battered look to the land. Going over the top towards Castleton there is a colossal quarry works, then the road leaves it behind and pursues an attractive tree-lined ledge which slopes down into the village. It is similar to Bradwell, perhaps more prosperous, and it certainly has more tourists, though they are predominantly local, with their boots and anoraks and northern accents. In the all-purpose shop where I buy a film for one of my cameras the girl behind the counter is simultaneously conducting negotiations with her boyfriend about a holiday in Greece: £240, setting off tomorrow. Everybody wants to escape the summer with its endless series of Icelandic depressions.

Castleton has an excellent and unusual fish and chip shop, a stone cottage with no signs but solid wooden benches and tables built on to the building at the front. It also has two things which Bradwell does not have. The first is Peveril Castle, a Norman ruin perched on an impregnably steep ridge above the town. It is not a particularly interesting place, having had neither inhabitants nor military significance for the last six centuries. Most people who pay 60p and trek up the steep concrete path to the castle find it worthwhile for the views. But I have already seen the same views coming over the hills, so I am slightly disappointed.

The other unusual thing about Castleton is a large number of jewellery shops. I count three and then enter the fourth and demand of the young lady in charge, 'Why are there so many jewellery shops in Castleton?' 'That is because of the Blue John,' she replies. 'Let me show you some.' Blue John, she explains, is an unusual form of fluorspar mined uniquely at the top of the Hope Valley. Its colours are formed by the oil in the stone and they are predominantly blue and yellow. It was discovered by a Frenchman, thus its name ('bleu–jaune').

Twenty minutes later I am heading for the ridge which divides Hope Valley from the Vale of Edale. The sun is shining and I have a silver Blue John ring in my pocket, admittedly bought at half-price: life is good. There aren't many other walkers, despite this being the height of the holiday season, though I catch occasional glimpses of large groups up on the ridge and the paths are excessively well-worn. I cross the ridge by Back Tor, diverting to ascend its steep rocky summit, which commands views in all directions. The next ridge to the north is The Peak itself, very dark and rather forbidding.

Halfway down into Edale I become aware that there has been a profound change in the land. This is no longer limestone country, but millstone grit and acid peat with its dark rock and soil, rushes and sparse brown grass. I follow the path to Edale, along the road and under the railway, then through the village where there are many tents in the narrow fields by the beck.

Now comes the serious part, climbing up onto The Peak. A few hundred feet up as the path crosses a stone wall there is a distinct break in the country. The grass stops, heather begins and a notice announces: 'Boundary of Open Country'. There is free access to this land by agreement with the owner, says the notice, except on occasional days in the grouse season, though guns, fires and camping are forbidden.

Beyond this point the vegetation is very simple, heather and bilberries with bare patches of black peat and brown rock. The first grouse whirrs explosively away from under my feet with heart-stopping suddenness. Then there are a pair and a group of five. It occurs to me that this is the height of the grouse season, though there is going to be no shooting on this particular moor today. There *seem* to be plenty of grouse, despite reports of a paucity in recent years.

On the plateau at the top the land has dual personality typical of the Pennines. Depending on the clouds and the lie of the land, it is sometimes a rolling, craggy wilderness with the minimum of features. But then, near the edge, when the cloud lifts it becomes the high part of a much larger world which contains distant ridges, railway lines, towns and mill chimneys.

I work my way down on the other side among ferns and hawthorn trees, drinking from the fast-flowing stream at the bottom. Exhaustingly, I have to climb again, a modest ridge where still-green hay is being rolled by three tractors. Then down into the woods, dark and boggy and difficult. These are Forestry Commission woods, not without a certain sinister charm, but containing the sad shells of old barns and farmhouses, now overgrown with ferns and trees.

At the bottom of the woods, completing this artificial wilderness, is the Ladybower Reservoir. The Highlands of Scotland have been imported to Derbyshire; across the apparent Loch are brown, craggy mountains above the thick coniferous woods. Here I meet the only person I have seen since Edale, a young fisherman arranging his tackle. It is an excellent place for trout, he tells me, probably the best of the upland reservoirs.

The walking is easy now for several miles along the side of the reservoir, with its elegant modern white bridges, and down to Bamford. In the pub there a family of gentry are eating a substantial meal, telling tales of Uncle's Bugatti and making claims like, 'D'ye know, I probably shot my first grouse when I was ten?'

The question is, does the National Park work? It was the first to be designated (in 1951) and has received numerous European conservation awards. It is certainly a remarkable place, because on a large-scale map it seems to be almost an urban park, a gap between Manchester and Sheffield. But is it what Sir Patrick Abercrombie and his Victorian intellectual mentors wanted? For the most part, I think it is. It is a wilderness, albeit one within an hour's journey for twenty million people. It is fortunate to be less fashionable than the Lake District (perhaps an advantage of its urban proximity); there are few signs of the more destructive leisure activities, though walking causes enough problems. It does offer, even in August, that precious commodity which John Stuart Mill thought might be lost long before our times: 'solitary contemplation in the presence of natural grandeur'. It is, and must remain, the home of the stout boot and the reliable waterproof, the rambler's heartland.

31 *The small world of Jersey*

(October 1985)

Jersey has had several agricultural revolutions. In the eighteenth century it was known for its sheep, and its name went into the language, meaning a woollen garment. By the mid-nineteenth century cider was the main product, and Jersey provided the original stock of trees for most of the English cider industry. For a long period until 1939 the island's name was associated with its famous breed of cattle which were exported to many countries of the world, a trade partly maintained by the belief that the stock deteriorated after generations off the island. After that, 'Jersey' primarily meant potatoes, the early delicacies known as 'Kidneys' and 'Royals'.

I am standing in the ruins of a castle on Gros Nez point, the north-western tip of the island, wondering what Jersey produces now and how its agriculture is standing up to fierce international competition. I am also intrigued to know whether the island has been completely anglicised or whether any real French influences remain. I intend to walk across the island at the maximum distance, from Gros Nez to La Rocque, the south-eastern corner.

It is a beautiful day; the turquoise sea is two hundred feet below me and the pale jagged rocks are bright in the sun. I walk east along the cliff path, across a heath of gorse, heather and bracken. The only buildings visible on this part of the coast are some of Hitler's follies, the elaborate fortifications which the Germans put on Jersey because of the Fuhrer's belief that Britain would be emotionally committed to regaining the Channel Islands before invading Europe; the allies simply ignored them. There are an unusual collection of birds: a robin, a kestrel, larks, tits, yellowhammers and, I think, a raven, inland, gulls and oyster catchers on the seaward side.

At La Grève au Lanchon there is a perfect beach, flat and clean beige sand beneath high walls of pink and pale grey rock. Unfortunately, above that is a very imperfect Pontin's holiday village. The cliff path proves slow, as they usually do; it winds its way down into wooded ravines and around small peninsulas. At La Grève de Lecq I move inland. The countryside is one of giant allotments. Grey stone farmhouses, often clad with ivy, are rarely more than a few hundred yard apart. The small fields are surrounded by banks out of which trees grow, like those of Brittany and Cornwall, so that they seem like colossal seed trays. The crops grown are leeks, parsley, calabrese and, most of all, cauliflowers, alternating with rectangles of rich grass on which ruminate tethered Jersey cows.

M. Frank Avrill is out in the sun, supervising the autumn tidying of his enormous hedge. He is a fit-looking, bespectacled man of uncertain middle age, dressed in a trilby hat and overalls; he says he would be happy to answer any questions I might have. He began farming at the end of the war with thirteen *vergées* (about six acres) of land, his only capital equipment being a fork and two crates. He had four cows, but potatoes were his main concern. Everything depended on the potato, but they never failed and they fetched a good price. He expanded, rented land in addition to his own and also bought some. When he stopped active farming in 1983 he was still growing potatoes, though cauliflowers had become more important. Now he rents out thirty *vergées* of land to younger men and takes in guests at his Eagle Lecq farmhouse.

He tells me all this in perfect English, though in an un-English accent. Nor is the accent French; in fact, if I met M. Avrill without knowing anything about his background, I would guess he was an English-speaking South African. Does he speak the patois, I ask? Yes, of course, he says. It is his first language as well as his usual language. This is true of the great majority of the country people of Jersey who are over thirty-five, he tells me.

Farming in Jersey is still doing well, he says, but only because it is heavily subsidised by the States. Cauliflowers have expanded enormously and some new crops, like courgettes, have come in. Flowers have become even bigger trade. He himself was disillusioned by the time he finished; farming has become too mechanised and too subsidised for his taste.

'I suppose you must remember the war?' I suggest. He turns his head away for a second and glances back with one of those looks which people give you when you ask them about a subject on which they feel deeply. 'Of course,' he replies, 'everyone who *stayed* remembers the war.' The other man joins us. The Germans were inhuman, they assure me; they buried Russians alive in the Atlantic Wall. They were reasonable to the natives, provided you kept your head down, but tensions grew towards the end when the island was short of food. M. Avrill remembers the Germans coming to his father's farm demanding eggs. His father refused outright, saying there were only enough for the children. The Germans went away, but next morning the chicken coops were staved in and the hens had disappeared. He does not care whether I think him mean, he says, but if a German couple come to the farmhouse there are no vacancies. As I leave, the two are talking guttural French, like that of Normandy and very difficult to follow.

Walking across inland Jersey is not easy. There are very few footpaths, the 'A' and 'B' roads are narrow and crowded and the 'C' roads are an unsigned maze of high banks. I travel on the latter, much helped by the bright sun: so long as I am going south or east or somewhere between the two, I am going in roughly the right direction.

The countryside is much more French than English, though I really mean specifically Norman or Breton. This impression is created by the architecture, but also by the intimate, enclosed small fields, the banks overgrown with bramble and ivy, the ancient tractors and the lines of skinny trees along the roads. The same is true of the people, who look more like Breton peasants than English farmers. The villages, St Mary, St John, Le Coin Tourgis, are more like concentrations of smallholdings than suburbanised English villages.

I stop at Carrefour Selous for lunch. Two pints of Randall's 'ordinary' (which turns out to be mild), a large bowl of vegetable soup, bread, a large cheese and tomato roll and a cigar, all for well under two pounds. In the bar, they are discussing the merits and demerits of dogs, as everywhere these days. The discussion is in English, in the same accent in which M. Avrill speaks.

On the other side of a rolling, hilly stretch of country, is Trinity, the agricultural capital of Jersey. Here is the Jersey Agriculture and Horticulture Training Centre. On the lawn, three lads are being taught about irrigation and inside two girls are doing something connected with seedlings. There are many kinds of tomato plant, all neatly labelled, and a pear tree with pears which must weigh half a pound. (Jersey's next attack on world food markets?)

Next door is the Howard Davis Farm, an experimental farm and headquarters of the Jersey Agriculture and Fisheries Division since 1984. Here they are able to satisfy all my curiosity about Jersey's curious agricultural economy. There are 739 farms on the island; the number is decreasing by about twenty-five each year. Half of these farms are under twenty-five *vergées* (not much more than ten acres) and sixty per cent of farmland is rented. The value of vegetable exports has expanded by ten per cent per year (to a total of £22 million) during the eighties and that of flowers by ten times (to £2 million). Cattle have remained constant, pigs have expanded, poultry has declined sharply.

I am particularly interested in the relative success of the vegetables. The area of potatoes had contracted slightly, that for tomatoes has halved. Cauliflower is the second biggest crop after potatoes. Calabrese has tripled. The range of crops is enormous.

Much of the rest of the day is spent confirming what government statistics say with my own eyes. There are flowers, mustard, beets and asparagus. There are whole fields of parsley and tomatoes, the latter rotting away in heaps. What I haven't seen is equally interesting. Only two sheep, and those on a farm open to visitors. Not much area under glass. Scarcely a dozen apple trees all day, although I have seen two of the old cider presses, now used as outdoor ornaments. So the earlier stages of Jersey's remarkable agricultural history have been left well behind. Away from the coast there is nothing remotely wild; it is a cosy, clustered, intimate landscape.

I reach La Roque at dusk, the sun going down big and red over the sea and the western half of the island. I have come to regard my trip to Jersey as a kind of miniature experience. I drove down to a very small airport, got on a very small aeroplane, flew (a short flight) to a very small country. I have now walked across it entirely and have seen its small fields and very small farms. If small is beautiful, Jersey is the best, though it has stayed small and successful by being adaptable.

32 *Area of outstanding natural controversy*

(February 1986)

The Vale of Clwyd looks very pastoral today; the sun is shining brightly on grass whch is fawn-green after the cold, dry spell. Ewes are feeding lambs in the small, tree-lined fields and in the background is the long line of the Clwydian Hills with every possible shape of peak picked out in clean white snow. This is spring and winter together, not in some mediocre mixture, but on a day which has the intense flavour of both.

Ruthin is a country town in every sense. It used to be the administrative centre of Denbighshire. The loudest sound in town is the bellowing of the cattle in the market and the second loudest is the bleating of the sheep. There is much grey stone in the town, some medieval building, some Georgian and many Victorian imitations of both. The town is full of farmers, green-clad, red-faced, Welsh-speaking, standing out as if they wore a uniform. The building of the National Farmers's Union is prominent, in Well Street, alongside the Conservative Club. I have an appointment with Dick Hughes, the Denbigh and Flint NFU Secretary.

He is a lively man of mature years who smokes cigarettes and wears a tie which says 'LAMB THE FLAVOUR OF WALES'. He speaks Welsh to his secretary and, of course, English to me. Like other people I have heard in the town, he speaks English not with a strong 'sing-song' Welsh accent, but with a more local variety which sounds to my ears as if it contains intonations of Lancashire and Merseyside.

I am particularly curious to hear about the farmers' attitudes to the designation of the Clwydian Range as an Area of Outstanding Natural Beauty; the area in question is sixty-two square miles in a narrow 'U' shape with Prestatyn on the North Coast of Wales at its mouth. The farmers do not like this for two reasons, he says. Although not a form of recreational development as such (unlike National Parks and Country Parks), farmers do fear that designation will greatly add to the number of visitors. They can cope with the increase which is occurring anyway, especially since the M56 was built, but they see no reason for the Countryside Commission to encourage a further boost in numbers. They are also very worried about the strict planning controls which will apply; farmers get very worried about what they can and can't do to their land and buildings and the public are quick to report anything which they consider untoward. In particular, the NFU's view is that the designated area is too big; it comes right off the hill-tops, some of which is rough grazing of the lowest quality, and into the Vale which contains some of the best land in Wales.

In any case, says Dick Hughes, for the farmers the whole issue has become laced with suspicion and uncertainty. The proposals was first raised in 1974, but there was a lull of seven years until Michael Heseltine, at the Department of Environment, started to take an interest in AONB proposals for such places as this, the North Pennines and the High Weald.

The Countryside Commission has always made soothing noises to the farmers and told them that their interests will not be adversely affected. But the day-to-day running of an AONB is entirely in the hands of the County Council and the farmers have found Clwyd unsympathetic and even hostile in the past. Talking about more general matters, before I leave, Dick tells me that local farmers are doing no worse than the average at the moment: quite an admission, for a farmer.

I leave Ruthin on the A494, going east. Normally I do not like walking by main roads, but here there is a pavement and little traffic and I am walking straight towards the hills. At Llanbedr Dyffryn-Clwyd I follow a tiny road up a steep 'V' shaped valley. It is very pretty, suburbanised by white-painted Victorian villas perched on the slopes. One has a vast bank of snowdrops in front of it and there is also a beech copse with a rookery. Two Liverpudlians stop and offer me a lift and seem offended by my determination to walk.

The road becomes a mountain track, Z-bending upwards among pasture and moorland and the bold white domes of the hills. I had thought that I would be alone up here, but I had neglected the winter sports potential of the conditions. On the edge of the Moel Famau forest there is a car park and a couple of dozen people sledging down the lower slope of a nearby hill. The snow is hard and dry, having melted and re-frozen, and the pace is terrifyingly fast. One boy takes off about three feet into the air on his plastic sledge and another totals his wooden sledge after a lurch and a leap into the air. He lands safely, but his sledge is in three pieces. As I leave to enter the forest, two men are talking in Lancashire accents; one is saying, 'Do you know, I was dreadfully disappointed with Switzerland. You get up a mountain and there's half a city on top. No mystique.'

I do not recommend walking in this kind of forest in these conditions. I follow what I take to be a path to the top, but it peters out. I have to struggle through the trees, trying to make sure I go upwards all the time. There is the visual pleasure of the sun and the trees making patterns on the snow. But getting anywhere is an exhausting struggle through thick snow, doubled-up to avoid the branches and with twigs whipping my face. There is the occasional hazard of a stream, around which the snow hides thick mud; the water is delicious, however. For a time I am completely lost and entertain my usual calmy morose vision of blundering about here till nightfall and dying of exposure.

Eventually, I do struggle out onto open country, grateful, as ever, to my wellies. At the top of the hill is the Jubilee Tower, a heavy, rather ugly building which looks like a pill-box with no roof. It does, though, afford dry stones on which to sit and eat a belated picnic lunch and look at the view.

The Clwydian Hills have the same particular charm which is possessed also by the Malverns in England and the Eildons in Scotland: they are steep and narrow and the land curves away in both directions, giving the sensation of being on a white path which is suspended far above a green world. Both going up and going down have their disadvantages on this terrain; one is hard work and the other is extremely slippy.

The path I am walking on is Offa's Dyke path. Offa, being no fool, appears to have used the natural barrier of the range rather than dig something for himself. It takes me through the Moel Famau Country Park, an area of domes of black heather and white snow. A dozen years ago the property rights governing the area were divided: the manorial rights belonged to the Lord of the Manor of Ruthin and the grazing rights to the commoners, neighbouring local farmers. A Leeds property company bought the manorial rights for very little; the commoners did not compete because they believed their interests would not be affected. In the very last days of its existence Denbighshire County Council bought the rights and handed them over to Clwyd for use as a country park. Clwyd has since acted (whether rightly or wrongly only the most sophisticated property lawyer could tell you; I certainly couldn't) as if they own the freehold and have excluded grazing, so that the lower slopes are reverting to foxgloves and bracken. Curiously, on my reading, this situation is very much parallel to that of the Wyoming ranchers in the early days of Yellowstone National Park. It does not look worth a range war in the condition it is today.

I make a very steep descent into the narrow valley that passes under Moel Arthur. The snow is a couple of inches deep in some places and many feet in others. At one point it is so well crusted and re-frozen that I am able to slide down it in an exhilarating way, crouching down with my feet together. There is a young man skiing. He says he wishes the hills were bigger. I can see his point; the snow may be right, but you would be just going beautifully when you hit a stone wall at the bottom.

Walking down the narrow lane towards Denbigh I am passed by three cars, which all stop and offer me a lift; nobody could call this an unfriendly place. It is beautiful country, varying from rough moorland to lush pasture and well-treed on the lower slopes. In what is, for a walker, a very gradual transition, the steep hills become a flat valley. The vale of Clwyd at this point is much more spectacularly a lowland than it was further south, an open grassland whose features are rivers and ditches, willow trees and copses. This is the most beautiful time of the day, among herons and hares and geese, looking back at the hills which are now pink in the gathering gloom. I pass through plain grey villages with smoke pouring from their cottage chimneys and along a long muddy path between two huge hedges, eventually reaching Denbigh at nightfall.

I am very clear in my own mind that, ultimately, the aesthetic and recreational value of this place is far more important than its material product. But, of course, in our tradition, the two go together and everybody would want that, so long as it remains possible.

33 *On the blossom trail*

(May 1986)

On my right, a wood full of a million bluebells; on my left, a field of green wheat and a distant glimpse of Bredon Hill. The sun shines from a cloudless sky; a lemon-coloured brimstone butterfly flutters around may and crab-apple blossom. I can hear thrushes, wood-pigeons, skylarks and a cuckoo.

Yesterday, I sat in my study, reviewing a long book on the effects of modern agriculture on the ecology and beauty of the countryside. The rain slanted against my window from a dark grey sky as I read about pricing under the Common Agricultural Policy, the loss of herb-rich lowland meadows and similar issues of the contemporary countryside.

Today, by Wheethley Wood, on the border of Warwickshire and Worcestershire, seems like a miracle. It is customary (for male writers, at least) to compare one's native land to a woman. In this case, she seems to be an actress of unknown age and mixed reputation. She has had seven husbands and an unknown number of lovers; it's been a hard life and many say she's an alcoholic. She's been beaten about a bit, so they say. But catch her on a good day, fully made-up, and you can't get over how good she looks. . .

I cross the wood into Worcestershire. On the far side there are many pheasants in a small wheatfield surrounded by woods and I can hear distant shooting. Re-entering the wood I have the problem of thick mud and the shooting is getting closer, so I try to cross the wood again but lose myself in mud and brambles, finally struggling out into a new plantation of trees, spindly and arranged in parade-ground lines. By easy walking down the lines I reach Morton Spirt, a hamlet of idyllically expensive black and white houses where two alsatian dogs are thwarted in their manifest desire to tear me to pieces by the fence which surrounds their orchard.

South of Morton Spirt the land is thoroughly modernised and I follow first a line of newly implanted pylons and then a hedge and ditch which skirt huge wheatfields. For a time I rest under an oak tree by a ditch. I have now to cross a field of wheat which must be the best part of a hundred acres in size and slopes upwards with thick woods on three sides. There are rights of way on the map, but no visible paths. I am no longer intimidated by this problem. Modern arable farmers spend the spring taking wheeled vehicles over their fields to spray and fertilise. All you need do is find a tyre track going in roughly the right direction and follow it. Any damage you do will be infinitesimal in comparison to that done by the wheels.

This field has beautiful fine, pale brown soil, reminding me of Cobbett's claim that the land visible from Bredon Hill is the world's richest, though it is doubtful whether his travels adequately qualified him to make this judgement. At the top of the field, I meet the farmer on his tractor. He is a bald man of middle years with the remains of blond hair on his red–brown head. He tells me the way to Church Lench and I follow a track between wheat and plum trees in flower. Some new plum trees have just been planted and some old ones chopped up and heaped into a neat pile of wood. Now I really feel

I am in the Vale of Evesham.

At the bottom of the hill, the farmer is filling his tank with liquid manure and I get chatting to him. He grows wheat and plums; business is hard and most farmers in the Vale need the wheat subsidy to survive. Commercial apple-growing has gone from the Vale and two-thirds of the plum trees have been ripped up during the eighties. Land stays on the market for a long time and the Italians are moving out. The Italians? Yes, there are Italians in the Vale, growing onions and leeks for their home market. This seems historically apposite since it is supposed that a Genoese ambassador, Count Francis Banardi, introduced market-gardening to Evesham in the seventeenth century. There's no market for plums, says my farmer; they are a gamble, anyway. I am reminded of a passage by the local writer, John Moore, a horrific description of a farmer running round his orchards on a May morning, discovering in panic that sixteen degrees of frost have wiped out his newly-set plums. This year, the blossom is so late that at least it should be safe from that fate. I point out to the farmer that he has just put plum trees in. 'Yes, a few,' he concedes. I suspect farmers are always overtly pessimistic, but secretly optimistic.

Church Lench is a very traditional village in two ways. It has many black and white houses of an almost incredible quaintness and every house, old or new, is surrounded by orchards and gardens, many of them selling lettuces and eggs. The Lenches are a group of villages in the 'Lench' hills on the north side of the Vale – Ab Lench, Rous Lench and others. I follow the minor roads to Atch Lench and over Hipton Hill to Lenchwick. The country us mainly wheat, but with extensive plum orchards. AA notices direct motorists along 'the blossom trail'; I seem to be leaving it and re-joining it regularly. In a field on Hipton Hill a little owl is standing doing nothing; it only bothers to fly away as I approach within a few yards.

Towards Evesham itself there is a variety of crops: gooseberries, currants, onions and spring cabbage. Much of the cabbage is bolting; men are cutting it and boxing it and a small rabbit is furtively chomping one just by the road. The fruit here is largely on a pick-your-own basis, as I approach the main A435 which goes south into the town: the garage at the junction sells asparagus as well as petrol. On the way into the town there are many large Victorian houses, a high proportion of which are now guest houses and one of them a school, for girls 3–18. Several times small pick-ups pass me with cargoes of spring onions.

I will not dwell on the attractions of the town, except to say it is a nice town and that the National Westminster Bank must be just about the most impressive black and white building in the Midlands. I am more intrigued by the many greengrocers. Most of them have local asparagus at £1.50 to £1.80 a pound, but one is selling *Spanish* asparagus at 85p a pound: Evesham growers live in a difficult world.

South of the town my OS map seems to have taken leave of its senses. Instead of a quiet footpath by the River Isbourne I follow a track through a housing estate to a generator factory. Beyond this is a strip of mud across the land; they are building an Evesham by-pass. The Lancastrian foreman shows me the route on the map. I am not where I thought I was, having crossed the Severn too far east. This allows me to do something new; I have followed many kinds of line across country before, but never an embryonic road. A further benefit is that the road has enclosed part of a field of leeks. I pick several pounds and put them in my rucksack; I am a true scavenger and these will give me far more pleasure to eat than bought leeks.

On the far side of the Cheltenham road the land is like one of the great continental valleys or deltas. The flat brown earth is divided into a patchwork of strips, growing peas, beans, parsley, spinach, rhubarb, onions and so on. At length I do find the River Isbourne and follow it through wheatfields to Hinton-on-the-Green. This seems one of the most boring villages I have ever seen. It has no shop, no pub and no architectural merit, apparently consisting entirely of twentieth-century brick houses. But I am hardly a fair judge, being hot and tired. In any case, a red-faced old man on a bicycle gives me a 'We don't want your sort here' look of such extreme grumpiness that I would be prejudiced against the village anyway.

But there is a straight track out of the village, leading towards the wooded slopes of Bredon Hill, from where you can see the opulent valley below. And Ashton-under-Hill *does* have a pub, mercifully open at 6.15 pm (a rarity, these days, among country pubs). On a day like this, the first two don't touch the sides.

34 *Fat land*

(August 1986)

As I recall it, Orenz, sitting cross-legged in the Bedouin tent, was asked where he came from. 'Oxfordshire,' he replied. 'Is that a desert?' asked the sheikh. 'No,' said Orenz, 'it is a fat, fat land.' He may have said only one 'fat', if so, it was said with great emphasis. 'A fat land' has been my abiding image of Oxfordshire.

There is nothing here in Adderbury on a fine summer morning to contradict this image. The land, O sheikh, is fatter than ever. The people do not work on it; they merely return from the city to rest and cultivate their gardens, leaving the farming to the machines. They amuse themselves with their games: look at the large signpost to the squash and tennis club. The very stone of the houses is gold. The brightly coloured flowers fight each other for a place in the ground.

Adderbury looks as if it was always rich. There are more than half a dozen Georgian mansions in rust-gold ironstone, any of which looks as if it could be good enough for the squire or the Lord of the Manor in most villages.

The road to Milton is 'unclassified', but could almost be an 'A' road because it is wide and there is plenty of traffic. The land is bleak, in a fat sort of way: fields of wheat, barley and maize with a crop-spraying helicopter clattering overhead. There is no sign of the cross-country path which I intended to follow, so I walk all the way to Milton on the road. The verges are broad and herb-rich, as they say these days. They are jungles, forty feet broad, with every colour of flower, including scarlet poppies and blue cornflowers, with a dozen kinds of grass, half a dozen of wild parsley, two sorts of bindweed, with elderberry and bramble, camomile and horseradish.

Milton is a modest village: plain council houses with well cultivated vegetable gardens instead of Adderbury's stone palaces. On the map, the road south from the village is a yellow line identical to the one I am already on. But in reality it is a narrow track whose surface is breaking up and which seems barely to survive between wild verges and thick hedges. There are no helicopters nor cars now, and the main sound is of sheep, which are grazing on the Ministry of Defence listening station on my right amid tall, slim metal towers and complex patterns of wires.

Suddenly there is a great deal of litter and a single caravan parked by an old van. There are blankets hanging on a line and a swarthy, dark-haired man fiddling with his tow-bar. On the other side of the road a grey-haired woman is heating an iron pot of water over a wooden fire. They neither acknowledge me nor look at me, from which I infer that they are real gypsies or, possibly, good 'method' actors playing the part of gypsies. The two of them and me and the wind in the MOD wires, all reminds me of how quickly the English countryside can change from drearily urbane to strangely threatening.

The map shows a 'road used as a footpath' which makes its way around in the MOD property. I determine to follow it, not knowing what it means. I was right not to know what it means. It changes from a military-style concrete road which has seen better days to an overgrown track by fields of wheat and oats to a strip of meadow between fences and finally to an ordinary track which leads me into Barford St John. If I had thought that Barford St John would be the sort of place where the first thing I would see would be an old man in a linen jacket tending a well-ordered vegetable garden which surrounds a stone house, then I would have been right.

Between Barford St John and Barford St Michael are the meadows of the River Swere, whose valley I am roughly following. The Swere itself is two yards wide, its banks rich with flowers. On the hill outside Barford St Michael I walk for a mile between horse-chestnut trees whose leaves have many holes in them. (These seem to be difficult days for trees.) In South Newington there is an untended stall with vegetables for sale and a sign advertising 'gardening services', the smallest of small businesses.

By Wigginton the Swere is only a yard wide and has almost disappeared between the foliage on its banks. In five quiet, gold-coloured villages I have seen perhaps seven people working on the land, five manhandling sheep and two driving tractors. There have been twice that number renovating houses and perhaps twice that pottering around gardens, cutting sweet peas or feeding chickens. Remind me to bore you with my thesis on the post-industrial peasantry some time. . .

From Wigginton I strike across country. It is deep old country with thick hedges and large trees and meadows, but the path on the map is impossible to follow. The Swere is merely a streak of damp grass across the land. Even so I penetrate the impenetrable and reach Hook Norton. The sign on the edge of the village has a hole blown through the n-o-r with a shotgun at short range: there must be a story there. It is clear that Hook Norton is different from the other villages, it has almost become a town. It has six pubs, a pottery, an iron-cladding works and a swimming pool firm, quite apart from its famous brewery.

In The Sun I have a pint of Old Hookey, which is fizzy and strong like a German beer. But there is no food in the pub and the only other customers are a dozen old men in flat hats playing dominoes. So I try The Bell. When I ask for a pint of Hook Norton, the landlady gives me a strange look which combines resignation and iron self-control. They don't sell Hook Norton, she says. They are a free house and the brewery won't let them have any. Pilgrimages come to the village and often they are the only pub open, certainly the only one selling food. So every day people come in and order a pint of Hook Norton and she has to explain that they haven't got any. She does have six real beers, though, of which I choose John Liddington's. She and The Customer, a man of thirty-five or so, assure me that this is the best pub in the village and the best village in the area because it still has adequate shops and 'plenty going on'. The Customer is interesting; he works in Vanuatu, teaching English, and comes fourteen thousand miles home for his holidays.

After a good lunch I walk down to the end of the village where the brewery is. As a place of pilgrimage – and it is a pilgrimage for many – it is not a disappointment. The sickly smell of fermenting cereal. A towering Gothic building, straight out of Citizen Kane. The thump-thump-thump of the great steam engine. Men shovelling malt and rolling barrels. Soon I am inside among the dark-panelled Victorian offices, looking at the Managing Director chatting with his door open, learning that the firm dates from 1849 and the building and plant from 1900. The firm has had its ups and downs, with the arrival of the railway and the closing of the ironstone quarry in the twenties, but it has thrived, especially since its product became a cult in the seventies.

Outside the weather has slowly, but very steadily, deteriorated. I don an anorak to make my way westwards over the hills, walking under a dark sky and against a fresh breeze. Near the Rollright Stones it begins to rain and the pace of the rain gets steadily harder. Below Whichford Wood I am forced to walk through chest-high bracken and become thoroughly soaked.

As I shelter in Whichford's (ironstone) bus shelter waiting for the pub to open, I excite the interest of the local bobby. 'Lorst or stolen or strayed?' he demands and determinedly engages me in conversation, in the friendliest possible way, to find out the maximum of information about the stranger who arrived over the ridge and through the woods. His determination confirms my growing belief that there is something odd about walking in this fat land. I had great difficulty in finding the paths I walked on today. When I could find them, I never saw a soul on them, nor evidence that they had been used recently.

35 *The last train from Skegness*

(October 1986)

High pressure brings clear air, which means heat in summer and cold in winter. In autumn it can bring both at the same time. Driving across eastern England I am experiencing a strange and inconvenient beauty which defies all expectations. The heavily frosted white fields of winter, shrouded in mist, suddenly give way to a late summer landscape: trees in leaf, cows in field, fruit on bough. Winter and summer alternating crazily as the sun's efficacity varies with altitude, longitude and time. Until the battle is over and I am on a featureless plain which basks in clear sunlight.

Boston, Lincolnshire, is dominated by the Stump, the tower, 272 feet high, of St Botolph's Church. It looks very exotic, bringing to mind Bruges rather than an English parish church. Indeed it was built in a period (the thirteenth century) when the sea was rather easier to cross than the Fens and Boston had more connection with Flanders and the Hanseatic ports than it did with London.

In the porch of the church are two notice boards, labelled 'HER MAJESTY'S GOVERNMENT' and 'THE DIOCESE OF LINCOLN'. Both are empty. It seems impossible to go up the Stump, because it is hollow inside. My attempt to study the stone carvings a hundred feet above my head cause concern to the small committee (one gentleman, several ladies) which guards this, as every prominent English church. They point out that a mirror can be used for looking at the ceiling. I point out that it's a pity one can't go up the tower. Not true, they say. If I cross the man's palm with 30p, the door to a narrow staircase will be opened. I am torn between the strong temptation of a church tower on a clear day and the thought that I have an awfully long way to go. So I ascend, to see the town on four different sides blending into a haze of flat fen and distant mist.

Back downstairs, the town seems a very relaxed place. It is the usual English mixture of the scruffy and the interesting; I am particularly intrigued by the sculpted mudbanks of the drains (or canalised rivers) which run through the town. The mud has assumed very strange shapes and it glistens in the sun. The general impression of the town is that it is, in the best sense, a peripheral place, far from the major centres of economic growth and change and beyond commuting distance from what planners used to call the 'coffin' of industrial England. Traffic is relatively sparce, calm and polite. There are a lot of bicycles. There are terraced houses on offer at £12,000 and detached bungalows at £25,000. In some part of England, average prices have *risen* more than that in the last year.

Walking out of Boston, along a small, drainside road, the town seems to fade into the fen rather than to end. The houses get smaller and the gardens bigger and the vast fields (if you can call something which stretches to the horizon a 'field') lap up between them: a pattern of dwelling which seems unaffected by development control. For a time, I walk between the bare soil and the dense vegetation which surrounds a drain. There is a path clearly marked by a signpost and on the map, but no sign of anything that could be called a footpath. I am uncomfortably half-way between long grass and soft earth. Of the latter there are uncountable acres, a fine brown tilth unblemished by weeds or stones. A rich land: add seeds, water in dry spells. Inform bank manager.

I head north-east on narrow metalled roads. There is a road called Willoughby Hill, which is entirely flat, and one called Boston Long Hedges which has no long hedges. This may be some of the best land in the country (or, for that matter, the world), but it would win no prizes for prettiness. It is utterly flat, broken up only by the lines of pylons, telephone wires and drains. The farmhouses are all modern brick with extensive functional outbuildings. There are no villages, the only settlement being a kind of hamlet, a desultory row of brick houses along the lane where you can watch the vegetables grow.

The crops are impressive, though. Cauliflowers stretching to the horizon. They are being harvested, two-thirds of them thrown away as imperfect and the good ones stacked on tractor trailers. There are bluish lakes of cabbage, sprouts and leeks and mountains of potatoes. Turnips and beets with yellowing leaves are being harvested. There are also small patches of marrows, suffering badly from leaf mould.

There is no traffic at all on these roads, except for tractors, grinding past me with their trailers full of vegetables, their drivers waving polite greetings. There are few animate things; some seagulls in a field and a vole scurrying into a ditch. In five miles I meet only one person, a lady of about sixty in a headscarf and boots hoeing lines of seedlings of some kind of brassica which stretch for many acres. 'Hello,' she says, enthusiastically, pleased to see someone. 'That's a big garden you've got there,' I reply, for something to say. 'It'll take a bit of knocking off,' she says, though I can't see any weeds.

The road is pleasant enough to walk on, just like a metalled path slightly above the countryside. All along it there stretches a trail of cauliflower 'florets' as they are called in the cookery books. From time to time I pick one up and eat it; they are fresh and succulent. I have a recurring desire to be an animal grazing in a field and this goes some way to gratifying it.

Following the trail, I am able to reach Old Leake in time for a late lunch. The village has a huge church, with a tower very broad in relation to its height, but most of the houses are plain and modern. The White Hart is also a very plain pub, but it affords me an adequate lunch of ham and cheese sandwiches and two pints of Bateman's bitter from mearby Wainfleet. In my opinion, Bateman's bitter is very good indeed and I am not surprised to read that it has won prizes at this year's Cambridge and Tyneside beer festivals, making the brewery's established slogan, 'Good Honest Beer', seem rather modest.

The landlady is a stand-in, I heard her telling the workmen who were playing darts. She comes down to let the landlord and his family go on holiday. When the workmen leave there are only three of us left in the pub: she, I and an old man. She goes to sit with the old man. 'I 'ope you're still 'ere when I next come, luv, I really do,' she tells him. He doesn't seem too disturbed by the implication of this remark. She seems terribly disappointed when I leave and wishes me a good journey.

But I have set myself a considerable athletic standard by the time I leave: four hours' walking at not much less than four miles an hour in order to catch the last train, the 7.10, back to Boston. For a time I walk by the main road and then cut down a long, desolate lane to the coast in order to walk on the dyke which separates the marshes from the drained fen. A notice on a gate on the dyke says 'BEWARE OF BOMBS AND BULLS'. This is an RAF range and also used for grazing bullocks. The prospect from the dyke is very big, but it can be described quite briefly. On the right, brown marshes with some boats used as targets by the RAF, a sliver of blue water (the Boston Deeps) and the distant Norfolk coast. On the left, vast flat fields, one of which is being processed by four tractors, which plough, turn, harrow and seed in succession. The horizon on one side is bounded by the long, very low, ridge of the Lincolnshire wolds and on the other by a hazy glimpse of Norfolk. A landscape which is classical, perhaps, in its scope and simplicity of form. It is in no way romantic; it has no mysteries, nor hidden depths. Here one is not *in* the countryside, but merely *on* it. If it has a charm, it is that of being emotionally undemanding, of encouraging the broad view and the clear mind.

No bombs explode, though there are signs of excavation for various unexploded objects. The nervous curiosity of the bullocks along the dyke is harmless enough. The real problem is a creek which threatens to make me walk two miles to gain ten feet. I've dealt with this situation before: I throw the rucksack across, put my heart in my mouth and jump, effecting a slightly uncertain landing in the damp grass on the other side.

Even so, the 7.10 seems an unlikely prospect, especially as I can't find a bridge across the Steeping River at Gibraltar. But there are two yachtsmen on the other side and when I ask them about the bridge they arrange to give me a lift, first in their boat and then in their car. What splendid chaps, that mess about in boats.

And so to Skegness, a place which made its name with one of those advertising campaigns that makes a virtue out of a weakness. The North Sea Coast is cold, Skegness is *bracing*. Out of season, on an autumn evening, it seems more refined than I expected, leafy and laid-back, with a wealth of solid inter-war building. Over the sea, a full moon is being partially eclipsed by the charcoal shadow of the earth. The 7.10 is actually the 7.18 and I am pleased to say that, when it rattles off across the fen, I am on it.

36 Return to London

(October 1986)

A jay squawks and flies up into a sweet chestnut. Several deer, fifty yards away, watch me with only mild wariness, starlings perched on their backs. Leaves fall from clumps of trees like slow, dancing rain. I pick some of the sweet chestnuts, but, as usual in England, they are pale and skinny.

I had intended to retrace exactly my route across London seven and a half years ago. But curiosity stirred an impulse to come here, to Richmond Park, to see what it looked like. I recall the same impulse in 1979, but I was then put off by the distance between Richmond station and Richmond Park. The park has a quality of fostered antiquity: on a misty morning like this it stretches to the horizon and, apart from being worn in places and having too many paths, its ferns and oak groves and rolling grassland fulfil an image of an ancient British countryside.

Curiosity satisfied, I leave the park by way of East Sheen Cemetery, which is very large. At first the cemetery is just a convenient way to walk towards Kew, but I find myself lingering, as so often in graveyards. Norman McLeod (Nim) Hall, died 1972 aged 46: 'A courageous captain in the field of English rugby union'. Piotr Pawel Dudzinski, air force colonel, born Lvov 1889, died London 1974: 'Ziemi Slaskiej'. In a cemetery, on an eerily still autumn day like this, death should seem so natural. Yet, at another level, the thing is incomprehensible and terrifying. I find myself thinking about the two men, Dudzinksi and Hall; they lived more interesting lives than mine and I have strong images of them both. Dudzinski's grave has fresh flowers on it, but Hall's doesn't; this confirms my belief that the Poles would be more likely to honour the dead than the English. In any case, these thoughts of death are most unhealthy. Walk on.

Richmond is prosperous and very leafy. It has grand sports grounds in the Old Deer Park: the rugby fields of Richmond and London Welsh, beautifully smooth hockey and cricket pitches. Many of them are being watered in this rainless autumn. I keep being bombarded by conkers, so I pick some of them up and put them in my bag for my sons.

The entry fee to Kew Gardens is now 25p. I point out to the man on the gate that it was 1p last time I came. 'You should come more often,' he replies. Even at 2,400% inflation, it is well worth the price. Autumn did not entirely suit Richmond Park; it looked brown and worn. But it suits Kew like a tastefully chosen cosmetic: there is every shade of brown, red and yellow leaf (and the odd green one as well), the sharp–sweet smell of quince and that wonderfully silly pagoda towering over the trees. A squirrel (grey, of course) crouches on his hind legs in front of me, as if begging. I have never been approached as boldly as this by a squirrel. But I've probably never had conkers in my bag before. I give him one and he puts it in his mouth and runs over to a bush with it. A second one is taken to a bush in the opposite direction. How did he know I had them?

With something of a shock I notice that the bench I am sitting on is a memorial to Richard A. McNealy, 1946-1981. I was born in 1946. The landscape seems to be issuing me with death threats. Why this unhealthy obsession? It is autumn and I am a few days off my fortieth birthday. But perhaps the main reason is that the seven and a half years since I last walked this way seem to have taken no time at all. At that rate, I'll be dead soon, however long I live. For the moment, I have a strong desire to get away from this part of London which seems to contain nothing but trees and get to somewhere which has some people.

Barnes seems more chic than ever: a model Georgian town with its pond and neat little shops. The Barnes Wine Shop has wine from all over the world and many books and magazines about wine. It was started two years ago by a young ex-policeman and most people in Barnes now wonder how they got by without it. You may wonder how I know all this? I can read it on an enlarged *Times* 'review' of the sort that many restaurants and shops now have in their windows.

On the west side of Barnes Common a man helps me to find my way to Wandsworth. On the east side, I am required to help an elderly Australian in a hire car, who wants to find the Fulham Road and insists on turning the map round so that it is pointing the same way as reality. The east side of the common is slightly poorer, but not much. There is an estate agent's called Warren's; the average price of the 'properties' shown in their window is *in excess of a quarter of a million pounds.* By Putney Bridge, on a busy pavement, is a metal plaque which claims that the road is 'not designated as a road and is not a public right of way'. How very odd. I suppose I could use it as an example of the distinction between formal and customary rights. There is also an oddity outside a house in Wandsworth: a single parking meter, showing an excess; the house looks no different from any other.

I take lunch – plaice and chips, £1.95 – in a pub called the Queen Adelaide. Everybody there seems absurdly cheerful, slapping each other on the back and roaring with laughter, saying, 'Look ah'er yersel, me ould son', when they leave. Outside, the sun has broken through and the mist and cloud have disappeared almost instantly. It is going to be a beautiful autumn afternoon.

Slowly and subtly, moving east, the territory becomes poorer. The green bits are more strewn with litter, barer and less rustic. From the middle of Wandsworth, there are black faces in every crowd. The houses are not quite as fully used or as thoroughly renovated. This must be interpreted relatively, though. By the standards of other places, or of itself in 1979, London seems rich and its houses well cared for. Everybody knows that money is moving east and that 'yuppies' are everywhere.

The word is in very common currency. When I first came across it in America it related generally to certain young middle-class attitudes: hedonism, high expectations, champagne brunches and certain labels on clothes. But in London it seems to have taken on a more specific meaning related to the house market. Yuppies are people trying to get on to the London housing ladder, trying to spot areas on the up and end in a place of high status. The average price of houses in London has risen by twenty-five per cent in a year and is now over £100,000. By traditional standards of how much money a person should borrow in relation to his income, this is a ridiculous situation: the people simply can't afford the houses. But traditional standards don't apply in a panic-stricken and speculative market. Last night, I had dinner with a couple who live in Hong Kong who were divided and desperate on the question of how to get into the London property market. The arithmetical problem facing them is stark: on the assumption that they will, eventually, live in an average sort of house in London, they could have saved £25,000 in the last year and still be no better off.

Yuppies are very recognisable. There is a shopping street which shows evidence of poverty – a junk shop, some old people with poor clothes, many black people – and among them move smart women of about thirty with babies in pushchairs. Yuppies are a good thing: their speculative buying breaks up social and racial ghettos, brings money to streets and shops which need it. They bring organisation: tens of thousands of London houses now sport 'Neighbourhood Crime Watch' (Rob Somewhere Else) stickers. Above all, yuppies are winning.

People keep asking me the way. A middle-class blonde girl has to get to Wimbledon, which is miles away, in three minutes. A drunken Irish lorry driver wants Teddington. A cockney van driver, with the sort of accent an orang-utan might have if it spoke English, wants to get to Maidstone. A German van driver, who doesn't speak English but, unlike the others, does have a rudimentary sense of direction, wants Lansdowne Road, W2. There are fifteen Lansdowne Roads in London, none of which is in W2. Why do they all ask me? I come from Colne. But I do my best and this is reciprocated. Every time I pull out my *A to Z*, there is somebody there (usually young and male), saying, 'Where yer lookin' for, mate?' Are Londoners more friendly and communicative than they used to be? Or am I a more sympathetic figure?

Clapham Common has developed many artificial cricket wickets, but dogs have a tendency to regard these as toilets. I wander round Brixton for a while, around Brailsford Road and Railton Road. It is grotty by the standards of south-west London, but prosperous by many other standards. There are a couple of derelict houses and a few in poor condition, but much larger numbers in good condition. Some strange wording on the wall links hatred of South Africa with hatred of Juventus Football Club. A great deal of work is taking place on the houses, with black and white workmen in equal numbers. For every self-stereotyping young black man cooling it round the streets in dreadlocks or a floppy hat, there are two black schoolboys in neat blazers. I watch as one of these boys commits a small crime, stealing the tennis ball off the ball joint of a car's tow bar. But then he realises it has no use as a tennis ball and puts it back.

Everywhere there is evidence of fairly complete racial integration on a superficial level. Black and white schoolgirls talking about their spots together. Black and white boys slouching home together. Black and white housewives chatting. Black boys with white girls. Whatever is wrong with 'race relations', it isn't mutual distaste on the part of the majority.

A narrow, rather sinister alley leads one down into Herne Hill. Now begins a long trip through south-east London, following a route slightly to the south of my original walk: Dulwich, Peckham, Brockley, Ladywell, Lee, Lewisham. This is the clay belt, beyond the tube trains. Endless brick houses, solidly built, late Victorian and Edwardian. It is neither grand nor scruffy, but always at least in sight of respectability. As a caricature, one could say that this is 'poor white' territory: cars which are old, but clean, posters for the British National Party. At one point, it is strangely rural, because there is a valley with a wooded hill to the south and a hill terraced with allotments to the north. Then suddenly, in Lee, the houses are built after 1918 and the cars are pretty well new. I have reached the suburbs.

I trudge it out to the brand new railway station at Eltham, on the south side of Shooter's hill. I am cream crackered (as they say in London), but I've walked further at both ends than I did the first time, perhaps a total of six miles further. This pleases me.

This next morning is mistier and the featureless contours of Blackheath make it very difficult to know which way to walk. But then my companion looms out of the mist, muttering something about, 'I'll kill that bloody girl, so I will.'

I hadn't meant to have a companion at all, but I could hardly have chosen a better one. She's about twenty-two years old with dark blonde hair and blue eyes. She is extremely pretty and comes from Dublin. She works in the publicity department for the Borough of Greenwich and she is supposed to be attending a course in Greenwich on problem-awareness (roughly), but her lift never showed at Blackheath Station. She'll walk with me, she says, even though it means getting her feet wet on the grass.

Three years ago she came for a holiday to stay with her sister for three days. But her sister was breaking up with her husband, so she stayed to look after her. She had and she hadn't got a job in Ireland at the time (very Irish, that) and then she was offered a job in England. She prefers England, but she misses her family (she's the sixth of nine children) and her mother misses her. 'You'd tink with noine she'd not care, wouldn't you? But it's not true.'

I like her enormously. I can easily imagine that in other circumstances I could have fallen in love with her, persuaded her to marry me and we could have spent the rest of our lives together. But I get that feeling about approximately eleven per cent of the (young) women I ever meet and in the real circumstances we part at Greenwich, offering hearty good wishes to each other, she to the course and me to the tunnel.

The tunnel still smells of damp and urine, exactly as it did before. But on the other side, back in the Isle of Dogs, the whole atmosphere has changed. I remember it as one of the quietest places I've ever been, but now diggers and drills and generators grind and roar and bang. A little old man is watching a digger clear a site of about four acres. 'What are they building? I ask.

'Ahziz . . . ahziz everywhere. This island's fillin up wiv ahziz.'

'Do you like it? . . . the changes, I mean.'

'It's orl roight. Down't myke now diff'rence to me. Course, they're orl stryngers, cammin' in.'

(Who did he expect?)

He points me in the direction of some of the new houses along by the river. They are in a modernised vernacular style, built in brick but with steep roofs and a lot of brightly coloured metal. There are little overgrown patios and courtyards planted with trees.

I had expected to see that some houses had been built on the Isle of Dogs: everybody knows that has happened. But I had no idea of the scale. There are not just thousands of brick houses and flats in a, more or less, traditional style. There is also a new overhead railway snaking across the island. The *A to Z* is useless because new pink-brick roads have appeared everywhere. There are gleaming office buildings in reflecting bronze glass, metallic silver factories and new concrete quays on the docks. Rows of new street lights and saplings have appeared. It is by far the greatest development, taken as a whole, I have ever seen, its only rival being Central Milton Keynes. The comparison is a relevant one, because all this is done by a Development Corporation, the London Docklands DC, a system of combining ownership and control with a lot of money which was proven in the new towns.

At Waterside and South Plaza a huge palace in reflecting glass is rising above the water. There are elegant brick houses below it and what appear to be dhows in the distance. If you want to be a part of this development you have to ring a firm of agents called Healey and Baker. Curiously, I have had dealings with Healey and Baker and remember their chaps as having had very sharp suits, though the development in question, I now realise, was miniscule by their standards. In fact, they are having some sort of conference in the houses which are, as yet, unoccupied: lots of chaps in sharp suits, the wine and the snacks laid out in a room near the water's edge. The sun is shining and it is hot for October. Two cormorants fly over (or are they shags?).

At the north of the island, where they are renovating the warehouses of the Millwall Dock, a young man approaches me, clipboard in hand:

'Excuse me. I'm an 'A' level geography student and we're doing a survey of local residents to find out what they think of all the new development here. I wonder if. . .'

I explain to him that I am not a local resident, but I do want to know what he's found out. He is unequivocal about his researches so far: 'They like it.' He likes it, too; having seen some of the unreformed docks, he is entirely in favour.

I think on the whole 'they' probably do like it, but it isn't as simple as that. There exists a sharply divided class structure on the Isle of Dogs. You can tell the 'stryngers' from the 'local community' at a glance. The former are yuppy and the latter are a very poor, traditional, inward-looking, working class. In their territory, in parts of Cubitt Town, I felt hostility to me and my camera, expressed in glances and muttered remarks, as nowhere else.

But I don't really care whether they like it. I like it. The place was dead before, an unused resource. London needs a truly modern place, like La Defense in Paris; the water should be used for people to live on. The 'local community' was doomed, anyway, by the nature of urban change and nothing I have heard about it makes it sound remotely attractive. So they should build something new, and if it takes development corporations and enterprise zones and the boys in suits from Healey and Baker to override the 'local community' and the Borough of Tower Hamlets, then good for them. But what am I ranting about? He said they like it.

After this, the rest of the East End seems dirty and boring and unchanged. Poplar and Limehouse are covered in an immense amount of litter. I find it quite baffling how much litter there is, given that modern technology (i.e. big vacuum cleaners) has gone a long way to solve this problem elsewhere. It's as if somebody has chosen *not* to clean it all up as a kind of collective version of the adolescent who chooses not to wash as a protest. I do find a pleasant way of walking northwards, though, on the Canalway created by the late GLC. There's a certain amount of lethargic fishing going on and quite a lot of inter-racial canoodling, Asian boys kissing black girls, and black boys kissing blondes. It is the Asians who will get in the most trouble, if caught.

By this means I reach Bethnal Green. I like Bethnal Green. It has many Georgian houses, though some of them are in poor condition; it has an interesting 'Museum of Childhood'. I have a pint of beer in a pub which says it has food, but doesn't, and then a doner kebab in one of the many takeaways, before going on to Hackney which also has many Georgian houses, generally in better condition. Dalston, though, is the nearest thing to being a full-blown, traditional slum that I have seen in London. There are shops boarded up, houses falling down and black men mooching about. I suspect a lot of people think Brixton is like that, but it isn't. There is a betting shop and a 'dumplin' takeaway. I can't see any white people.

Stoke Newington is very cosmopolitan even by London standards. There are Greeks, Turks and Bengalis. There are many orthodox Jews with black coats and hats and ringlets of hair cascading round their faces. There is a handsome black couple with a beautiful child; the man's dreadlocks must be two feet long. There are middle-class white girls with punky hairstyles talking about how you cook tofu. In a greengrocers I count eleven different vegetables of which I don't know the names, but which I am willing to try.

I make my way over to the Lea for a bit of peace and quiet. The houses are posher on the hill overlooking the valley, with its reservoirs and parks and playing fields. After a mile or two I make my way into Tottenham, past two gypsy encampments of extreme photogenic scruffiness and across the High Road to Broadwater Road.

A change of destination. I am not going to finish in Epping Forest this time, but drinking tea in the home of two former students, Malcolm and Christine Bell. To be properly accurate, Malcolm was a student of mine, but I knew Chris well socially. A year ago there was a horrific riot in the Broadwater Farm Estate in which PC Keith Blakelock, a forty-year-old father of three, was hacked and bludgeoned to death by a howling mob. The Bells' house was hit by a petrol bomb which bounced back into the garden and one also went under their car, but went out.

Mal is away, making a television programme about agricultural land going out of production. Chris greets me in a white dress on her way back from a 'do' at the school. She is chairperson (as they say) of the governors of the school built for the estate. The kettle is soon on and I ask Chris about the riot.

There were two, she says. The trouble on the estate began at seven o'clock in the evening. But after it had been on the news at nine o'clock, all sorts of people started arriving in Broadwater Road, on the other side of police lines. It was like a Spurs' match, Chris says. Their 'disturbances' peaked between eleven o'clock and midnight. They crouched in the house with sticks and buckets of water at the ready until they had the relief of seeing a regiment of police re-establish control.

The area is about fifty per cent West Indian, she says. The rest of the people are very mixed: Greek and Turkish Cypriot, Asians, some English who've been around for fifty years and odds and sods. They get on very well with their neighbours, especially the West Indians, whose children are well-behaved. The school is a good one and works well. After the riot, some non-black parents took their children away, but enrolment is already back up to more than it was originally. It is only when they reach adolescence, and usually after leaving school, that the blacks pose problems. Eight double-glazed windows were just broken by stones at the school but it wasn't the blacks who did it. It was the 'travellers' whose children are forced to attend the school; they are genuinely difficult people

They have never been burgled. Once some black youths charged their door down when they were out, but a black neighbour shouted at them and waved his camera, telling them he'd got pictures of them all, so they all ran away. But when Chris came home with her two daughters she found the door open and decided not to enter. She rang the police and sat in the garden until they searched the house, feeling a bit of a fool when they found nothing.

Left to themselves, they could solve the problems here, Chris says; nearly everybody has a will to get on with each other. But there are dangers. West Indian youths seem to rebel against everything once they break out. Some of the black politicians are dangerously naïve, with a paranoia bordering on racism; you have to be firm with them without stimulating their fears. She has no time for the police. She was relieved to see them restore order and she liked the policeman who lived upstairs for a week, trying to catch a heroin dealer across the road. But, generally, they seem to be barmy. They go around knocking people's doors down and arresting people on charges they can't make stick. She and her husband work for a neighbourhood law centre, arranging solicitors for people who are generally poor and young. Sometimes the police are very sympathetic, but more often they tell lies, or hang the phone up or are just yobbishly unco-operative.

Mal rings up in the middle of making his television programme. Chris laughs and reports that I'm interviewing her. Mal shouts down the phone that Tottenham is the best place to bring up children in the late twentieth century; so there you are: that's his 'quote'. Certainly, his daughters see happy and well-behaved.

I must go. I have a train to catch and Chris offers to run me to Seven Sisters tube station. I came to talk about the problems of Tottenham, but I'm as interested in her as in her surroundings. She runs me through the estate telling me about cockroaches and damp problems and where she would spend money. I've known her since she was eighteen. She was always a charming girl, though rather vacuous, even childlike, the sort of girl who would leap into the arms of the nearest man on principle if she saw a spider. Perhaps she would have stayed like that if they had remained in the Cotswolds, where they lived for a couple of years. But now she seems fit, shrewd and tough and far cleverer that I ever remember her; some people thrive on problems.

Well, what of it all? Is there anything to say *in general?* I know London better now, but I still feel a complete outsider. The way they bustle about, treating each other as mere obstacles, the sharp little remarks they make, the inconveniences of commuting and dirt and expense they will put up with in order to pursue their ambitions, all combine to make me feel very slow and calm and alien. This is true regardless of class: Cockneys and 'Sloane Rangers' seem similar in these respects and the gap between capital and country as wide as it ever was.

Now I've seen London again, after Glasgow, Liverpool, Manchester *et al.*, I have a simple, visual observation to make about the condition and future of the city. The immensely complex process of urban change, with all its dimensions of race, class and politics, all the interactions of the financial and land markets, can be reduced to a simple observation: the money is there. In London, it is clear that there is money to fill the space and behind that is something more real than money, confidence. Much of London is going 'up'. This is not so clear in other cities where the issue is in doubt and there is nothing which can be done to transfer more than a little of London's cachet and attraction to those other places. Of course, London's condition brings its own problems: relative poverty, homelessness and lack of space, the sheer stress of thwarted ambition, are probably worse here than elsewhere. But the balance of problems is different from that in other cities.

I try to compare walking across London now with what it might have been like in 1936, 1886 or 1386, extrapolating from the historical record to compare with the direct experience. Everything suggests that people now are richer, healthier, more informed and more free. My mind goes back to two women of my own age in the pub in Wandsworth, chatting about their jobs, their children, their trips to Crete and Cornwall. It would be odd to believe that they do not, in any tangible or measurable sense, get more out of life than their ancestors.

And yet there is a threatening insecurity nagging from every wall. Even the black man to whom I am now showing my underground ticket is reading a pamphlet, the title page of which asks, 'What is wrong with our society?' Unilateralists threaten the apocalypse. Dieticians send people rushing for fibre and trembling at the sight of butter. Environmentalists frighten us with pollution, which has been worse, taken as a whole, in every age when compared with this one. Feminists rail against the wickedness of a male society, Socialists and Christians against the emptiness and cruelty of materialism.

So what is wrong with 'our' society? Correct answers, on the traditional postcard, please, might include: 'Not a lot', 'Depends what you compare it with and how you define its boundaries' and 'It's full of ill-informed Socialists, ranting Christians, nostalgic reactionaries and other self-fulfilling purveyors of doom. Stuffed with ignorance and bad philosophy.'

But isn't everywhere?